MADCAP MAY

MISTRESS OF MYTH, MEN & HOPE

Yours faithfully

May L. John

MADCAP MAY

MISTRESS OF MYTH, MEN & HOPE

RICHARD KURIN

SMITHSONIAN BOOKS
WASHINGTON, D.C.

This book may be purchased for educational, business, or sales promotional use. For information, please write:

Special Markets Department
Smithsonian Books
P. O. Box 37012, MRC 513
Washington, DC 20013

Published by Smithsonian Books
Director: Carolyn Gleason
Production Editor: Christina Wiginton
Edited by Owen Andrews
Designed by Kate McConnell

Library of Congress Cataloging-in-Publication Data

Kurin, Richard, 1950-
    Madcap May : mistress of myth, men, and hope / Richard Kurin.
        p.   cm.
    Includes bibliographical references and index.
    ISBN 978-1-58834-326-0
1. Yohe, May, 1869–1938. 2. Singers—United States—Biography. 3. Women singers—United States—Biography. 4. Actors—United States—Biography. I. Title.
    ML420.Y64K87 2012
    973.91092—dc23
    [B]   2012006210

Manufactured in the USA
16 15 14 13 12   5 4 3 2 1

Excerpts from *Hope Diamond: The Legendary History of a Cursed Gem* by Richard Kurin courtesy of HarperCollins and Smithsonian Books.

For permission to reproduce illustrations appearing in this book, please correspond directly with the owners of the works, as seen on p. 263. Smithsonian Books does not retain reproduction rights for these images individually, or maintain a file of addresses for sources.

For Allyn, who is so not May

Sketch of May Yohe, 1895.

CONTENTS

PREFACE

MAY YOHE (1866–1938) was *the* drama queen of her time, a woman who lived an amazingly tumultuous life in the period spanning the Gay Nineties, the Roaring Twenties, and the Great Depression. With her outsized personality, roller-coaster career, and endlessly complicated love life, she was the Elizabeth Taylor, Lady Di, Britney Spears, and Tina Fey of her era, all rolled into one. Yet today, her truly fabulous story is unknown, her name, pronounced "yo-e" (rhymes with "snowy"), unrecognized.

May Yohe, a popular entertainer from humble American origins, married and then abandoned a wealthy English lord who owned the fabled Hope diamond—one of the most valuable objects in the world and now exhibited at the Smithsonian Institution in Washington, D.C. Nicknamed "Madcap May," Yohe was a favorite of the tabloid press. She was a romantic who had numerous lovers and at least three husbands. The tabloids claimed she had twelve, including the playboy son of the mayor of New York. May separated from him, not once, but twice. Her next husband was a South African war hero and invalid whom she later shot.

May Yohe was a sweet-voiced, foul-mouthed showgirl who crossed paths with many famous people, including Ethel Barrymore, Boris Karloff, Oscar Hammerstein, Teddy Roosevelt, Consuelo Vanderbilt, and Edward, Prince of Wales. George Bernard Shaw, the Nobel laureate and playwright, praised her for her lively presence and performance and then rebuked her soon after for going stale. In later years she faced several maternity claims and a lawsuit, which she won. She was hospitalized in an insane asylum and escaped. She ran a rubber plantation in Singapore, a hotel in New Hampshire, and a chicken farm in Los Angeles. When all else failed, she washed floors in a Seattle shipyard and, during the Depression, sought a job as a government clerk. Shortly before her death, she fought successfully to regain her lost U.S. citizenship.

How was May Yohe able to charm her way to international fame, live an improbably complicated and adventurous life, and find the strength to persevere in light of the losses she suffered—in wealth, citizenship, love, and sanity?

This book, assembled from her writings and historical interviews, archival records, newspaper stories, scrapbooks, photographs, playbills, theatrical reviews, souvenirs, and silent film, tells her heretofore lost story.

That story is one of a particular kind of feminism. Yohe was pretty, but not beautiful. She had an alluring, almost innocent sexuality that she used ably, willingly, and often to attract admirers and lovers. Yet she had her greatest success on the stage playing young male roles. Her ability to radiate sensuality as both *faux* male and *femme fatale* set her apart.

So did her quick wit and verbal prowess. May could regale a dinner party with humorous anecdotes, but also curse like a Marine among men. Her one-line retorts were widely quoted. "What did she think about the bonds of matrimony?" asked a reporter. "Never paid me a dividend," she snapped.

May shared with contemporary suffragettes and intellectuals a deep-seated faith in the natural, God-given ability of women to succeed. She was a so-called "new woman" of her time—an exemplar of femininity, applauded by some, scorned by others. But unlike pioneers of women's rights such as Elizabeth Cady Stanton and Susan B. Anthony, May was more concerned with her own success than the success of women in general. In a man's world, she fought for a woman's right—her own—to live freely. She conquered skeptical audiences to gain stardom and fought British nobility to gain legitimacy. Her public persona often appeared selfish, even narcissistic, yet time after time she defied expectations, doing charity work for London's poor and Ireland's farm workers, ministering to war wounded as a nurse, and defending chorus girls from moral attack. She repeatedly challenged authority figures who stood in her way or sought to do her wrong—the courts, the critics, the government, the British peerage. She also surmounted her ambivalence about the curse of the Hope diamond—a legend she herself helped invent.

May Yohe's resolve to win her battles and continually pick herself up from divorce, deceit, fraud, poverty, and disenfranchisement stemmed from a strong, almost uncanny adherence to her own self-made, ever-changing image. May saw herself not as a victim, but rather as a protagonist who had the power to fight, fend off wrongs, and gain her just rewards.

Her strength of character was built upon her upbringing as a Moravian, a member of a religious sect that emphasized female spirituality, musical virtuosity, sexual frankness, and a worldwide ecumenical outlook. Though May was by no means religious, these values, in a secular (some would say profane) form, became part of her personality. What is more, May was literally born at the inn in Bethlehem. While this was not the Bethlehem of biblical repute, but a small, bustling town in Pennsylvania, May made much of the eponymy. It gave her license to construe her own life story as myth, legend, and fairy tale. She had the uncanny ability to tell and sell stories with herself as the central character. Her stage roles—as a modern-day Cinderella, as possessor of a magic gem, as discovered starlet, as rags-to-riches heroine, as lady slave working to support her down-and-out household—all crossed over into her real life. Her character themes—possessing miraculous power, pursuing true love, fighting injustice, weathering curses, and finding redemption—captured the spirit of her times, and also the imagination of friends, fans, the press, and the general public.

Besides being a good tale of a fascinating and overlooked historical figure, *Madcap May* provides a cultural study of how an exceptional "new woman" emerged from a communal religious sect and how a small-town girl made the world her global stage during the formative period of modern American and British society. It demonstrates how a woman possessed of an indomitable spirit took control of her life and fought against entrenched institutions founded upon class, gender, and social and occupational privilege—and did so with incredible panache.

As a cultural anthropologist, I never imagined I would write such an account, but having conducted preliminary research about May a few years ago for my book *Hope Diamond: The Legendary History of a Cursed Gem*, I was struck by the sheer improbability of her larger-than-life story. Overcome with a sense of admiration for her fortitude and perseverance, I just had to write this book.

Richard Kurin
Smithsonian Institution
Washington, D.C.

I just wanted to be different.[1]
- *May Yohe*

CHAPTER ONE

Bethlehem's Daughter

MAY YOHE ALMOST ALWAYS LIED. She was born in Bethlehem, Pennsylvania, in 1866 but often said it was 1869. She claimed she was a "true American," but "no Yankee."[2] May proudly boasted, more than once, that her mother was an American Indian, specifically a "blue blooded" member of the "brave" Narragansett tribe.[3] That fact, May said with absolutely no modesty, "sort of connects one with the creation of the world."[4] These claims typify May's habit of myth-making and overstatement, for there is no evidence that she was descended from American Indians or that she ever acted upon any Native American beliefs.

At other times, May claimed to be a distant descendant of William Penn, founder of the Pennsylvania colony. When it suited her or her audience, she asserted a Parisian birth. May pronounced her last name "Yo-ey"—"without any accent anywhere,"[5] she'd tell reporters, simultaneously acknowledging and obfuscating her Germanic ancestry. Indeed, when she said she was Pennsylvania Dutch, newspapers erroneously reported that her father was from Holland. May smiled and winked at that.

❖ ❖ ❖

May was born to William and Elizabeth Yohe in Bethlehem's Eagle Hotel. The hotel was owned by her grandparents, Caleb and Mary Yohe, though May sometimes referred to Caleb as her uncle. May spent her early years in Bethlehem, and the community had an enormous influence on her.

Bethlehem, about sixty miles north of Philadelphia, was founded in 1741 by a small band of Moravian settlers who had migrated from Georgia in a quest to convert Indians to Christianity. Moravians were industrious, ingenious, and community minded. They esteemed education highly, kept music at the center of their lives, and accorded women a high degree of independence and respect—values that would help shape May's character. As May wrote, "I was brought up very strictly in the austere faith of the Moravian Church."[6] Though she may have been more mischievous than austere, and while she may not have been steeped in Moravian theological notions, May picked up many of the community's values, particularly with regard to a girl's horizons.

The Moravians were an early reformist sect that predated Martin Luther. Founded in the mid-fifteenth century, they were inspired by John Hus (1369–1415), an early Church reformer who was burned at the stake as a heretic. The sect was centered in Bohemia and Moravia, in what is now the Czech Republic. Persecuted in their homeland in the 1500s and 1600s, they reinvigorated their faith by developing a strong missionary purpose in the 1700s under the leadership of Count Nicholas von Zinzendorf (1700–1760), a Lutheran Saxon, on whose estate they settled. After originating in central Europe, the Moravians spawned communities in Denmark, Ireland, England, the West Indies, North America, and even East Africa.

Count Zinzendorf visited Pennsylvania and gave Bethlehem its name on Christmas Eve 1741. The settlement would in ensuing years become the American capital for the Moravians, attracting a diversity of followers not only from Europe's Germanic region but from countries such as Great Britain and Denmark. Moravian missionaries also brought former African-American slaves and Native Americans into their fold. Other Moravian settlements included Nazareth and Lititz in Pennsylvania and several towns near

Salem in North Carolina, a region known as Wachovia and named after Zinzendorf's ancestral lands.

The German-speaking Moravian settlers in Bethlehem quickly exploited the ample surrounding forests and wildlife, cleared farmland, and established cottage industries on the Monocacy Creek of the Lehigh River. They used water wheels to power a mill, an iron foundry, a pottery workshop, a tannery, and a system for pumping water uphill to their village through wooden pipes—an invention that impressed such visitors as Benjamin Franklin and John Adams.

Guided by Zinzendorf's philosophy and funding, the Moravians practiced a form of communalism called the "General Economy." For the first generation, until Zinzendorf's death in 1760, the Moravians were organized into "choirs." These were groups of people of a common age and gender who lived together in a common house, sharing work and joining in worship. There were choir houses for boys, girls, married men, married women, and widows. In the early days of Bethlehem, it was the choir, rather than the nuclear family, that animated local society.

Education mattered deeply to Moravians, who saw it as a path to salvation. An early Moravian bishop, John Amos Comenius (1592–1670), a widely respected and influential Czech educator who had once been considered for the presidency of Harvard, was a strong advocate of universal education—a much more contentious proposition then than it is today. In Comenius' view, science, rationality, and innovation were means of using God-given abilities to flourish as a human being. He believed in educating not only white men from privileged backgrounds, the norm at that time, but women and men in every social stratum and from every race and condition.

Though he never visited America, Comenius's views strongly shaped the American Moravian community, where literacy approached one hundred percent and where schools were established for women, for African Americans, and for learning American Indian languages.

Music was also central to Moravian life. Music and singing were regarded as part of the liturgy, a vehicle for communing with the divine. Moravian choirs sang sacred songs in church, serenaded the sick and elderly, and entertained the community. All Moravians were also expected to be proficient on at least one instrument—often the piano, organ, violin, or trombone.

The community's orientation toward women was especially significant to Moravians, their neighbors, and eventually May Yohe. In early Bethlehem's General Economy, people of opposite sexes lived in segregated quarters. Women's roles were clearly defined and encoded in dress, as indicated in the mid-eighteenth century paintings of John Valentine Haidt (1700–1780).[7] Haidt's portraits of women in the community depict them modestly, with long dresses and nary a hair protruding from their *schneppelhaube*, white linen head caps. Colored ribbons indicated their sexual status. Young girls tied their caps with red neck ribbons, eligible maidens with pink ones, wives with blue, and widows with white.

Despite such conventional representations, Moravian women, even in the eighteenth century, enjoyed a greater degree of equality with men than most of their contemporaries. Although boys and girls attended separate schools or classes, Bethlehem was noted for its girls' schools, most notably the Female Seminary, known as the "Fem Sem."

Both men and women were encouraged to pursue an advanced education. Women could own land and businesses, go to college, be ordained to direct communal religious rites, and lead the beloved choirs in song and prayer.

The special role of women among Moravians is related to their theological beliefs about the Christian Trinity. In American colonial times, these beliefs led to civic confrontation and even physical conflict with Protestants of other denominations. Moravian theology suggests that the Holy Spirit is female and that Jesus has a divine feminine aspect. Bethlehem's early folk art echoed these ideas, depicting the crucified Jesus' bleeding side-wound as a life-giving, vagina-like spiritual womb.

Moravian women could thus identify personally and intimately with Jesus and the Holy Spirit and, by calling upon their divinity, be secure in their roles as preachers, leaders, and teachers. Moravians' spiritual elevation of women challenged the more patriarchal orientation of other Protestant sects in the region, such as Lutherans, Methodists, and Dutch Reformed, who regarded some of the Moravian teachings as blasphemous.

Similarly, the Moravians were not shy about teaching their children about sex and depicting sex organs. Moravians strongly approved of legitimate sexual relations between a husband and

Young Moravian Girl, *c. 1755–60.*

wife, not only for the purposes of procreation, but in their own right as a God-given pleasure. Sex was not shameful or devilish, or associated with one's lower nature, but worthy of celebration.

The communal treatment of sexuality was unavoidable in the married choir house. There, men and women lived segregated by gender. With the full awareness of other house occupants, married couples scheduled and coordinated when they would copulate in the "marital chamber." As other communities became aware of these Moravian practices and beliefs, they characterized them as shameful, promiscuous, and sinful.

By the 1760s, Bethlehem's Moravians began to change some of these ideas and practices. They abandoned the mandatory General Economy, and the community's several hundred members started living as families in nucleated households with private property. Some of the communal choirs continued on a voluntary basis.

Bethlehem's industry served it well during the American Revolutionary War. Its workshops made guns for Washington's army, even though its inhabitants did not fight—not because of pacifism, but rather out of respect to England for recognizing the Moravian Church. Bethlehem hosted what was then a state-of-the-art hospital whose physicians and nurses treated American war wounded, including the Marquis de Lafayette. During the war, the town's premier hotel, the Sun Inn, hosted a "who's who" of the time.

After the Revolutionary War, because these distinguished generals and leaders had visited the progressive town and learned about the quality of education offered at the Moravian Seminary and College for Women, "Fem Sem" opened its doors to non-Moravians at their urging. One of those visitors, George Washington, enrolled his niece, Eleanor Lee, in the school, and wrote the school rector in 1796 to seek admission for others. The student body of the 1780s and 1790s included daughters of prominent New York Dutch families, German families from Pennsylvania, and French families from the South. When families brought their daughters to "Fem Sem," they stayed at the Sun Inn.

Increasingly after the war, Bethlehem opened up to new, non-Moravian migrants. In the late 1820s, investors built the Lehigh Canal to transport anthracite coal, mined in the region and known as "black diamond," from the hinterland to Philadelphia and beyond. Along with coal, lumber and other natural resources brought economic prosperity to the region—and transformed it. The canal lowered water levels in the Monocacy Creek, ending Bethlehem's early cottage industries. The building of the railroads accelerated the scale of industrial development, making the exploitation of forests and coal mines even more profitable and attracting many new laborers. Several hundred non-Moravian immigrants from a variety of European countries moved into the area.

With the growth of industry and the continued success of "Fem Sem" in Bethlehem, the Moravian community needed another inn. In 1822, they built the Eagle Hotel on the site where Count Zinzendorf and the first Moravians, along with their animals, had huddled in a modest log-cabin style shelter and founded the original Bethlehem settlement. At first, the community hired managers to run the hotel. In 1843, it was sold to Caleb Yohe and his wife Mary Straub, a non-Moravian couple who had run a smaller inn in the region.

In 1845, the previously independent Moravian community of Bethlehem became a civilly administered borough of the state of Pennsylvania, with a population of more than one thousand. In the 1850s, iron ore was discovered in the nearby Saucon Valley, leading to the formation of the Saucon Iron Company. As the enterprise grew, building furnaces to smelt the ore, many more laborers came to Bethlehem, and the town's population reached five thousand in the 1860s. The company, renamed the Bethlehem Iron Company in 1861, eventually became the giant and world-famous Bethlehem Steel Company.

The Eagle Hotel was one of the centers of the community. By the time of the Civil War it had a reputation as one of the finest and largest hostelries in Pennsylvania. It sat in a prominent position in Bethlehem, welcoming travelers and summer tourists who enjoyed the picturesque local landscaped gardens and parks, including nearby Calypso Island. It would, over the course of the ensuing decades, host its share of wealthy and famous Americans such as the Waldorfs, the Astors, and Mark Twain, not to mention scores of ordinary honeymooners and vacationers.

Caleb and Mary Yohe were active and respected members of the community. While they did not themselves formally become Moravians, they brought their children up in the Moravian Church after moving to Bethlehem. They lived at the inn with their five children: Anna (the eldest), George, William, Charles, and Samuel. A sixth child, Edward, died in infancy. Anna enrolled in the Female Seminary and Samuel attended Nazareth Hall, the Moravian boys' boarding school. Edward was buried in the Moravian cemetery, God's Acre.

Conscious of the Biblical echo in their roles as proprietors of the inn at Bethlehem, the Yohes were wonderful hosts. The children pitched in, carrying out hotel chores. The Eagle hosted church and town functions, including elections. It was extremely well kept, and according to travelers' accounts, guests enjoyed the home-cooked meals. The hotel's brook trout, caught in nearby tributaries of the Lehigh River, was a specialty. But the Lehigh

The Eagle Hotel, c. 1874.

River also became a source of tragedy for the Yohes when their son Charles drowned in a terrible accident at the age of seven.

Among the hotel's special features were its *putzes*. A putz is a large-scale model or miniature replica of a series of vignettes, typically of a religious nature, such as the Nativity scene and other events in the life of Jesus. Moravians had a tradition of making putzes for Christmas, and the putzes in the Eagle Hotel were especially renowned in the region. Caleb's son William, who would later become May's father, had an artistic bent and a particular talent for constructing the Christmas displays.

In 1861, William, known as "Bill," was twenty-one years old. He was of average stature, with dark eyes, a swarthy complexion, and wavy black hair. His mouth was small, his nose almost Grecian. He was not a particularly good student, but he had a fine voice for Moravian hymn singing and serenading.

With the onset of the Civil War in April 1861, Bill enlisted as a 3rd corporal in Company A of the 1st Regiment of the Pennsylvania Volunteers. The regiment was organized in Harrisburg, the state capital, in response to President Lincoln's call to arms. Bill was issued a musket and twelve rounds of ball cartridge, a muslin haversack, and hard tack and bacon. Only weeks later did he get a uniform. His company trained briefly, and was then assigned to guard roads and rail lines in Harper's Ferry, Frederick, and other sites in Maryland and Pennsylvania in order to prevent incursions by Confederate troops. The company didn't see any combat. By July 1861 the regiment was dissolved, and its men mustered out of service.

In November, Bill joined the 112th Regiment, a heavy artillery unit, for a three-year enlistment as a private. His unit, Battery G, served at Fort Delaware and then in 1862 was sent to Washington, D.C., to help defend the Union's capital against Confederate incursions. Yohe's unit was under the command of General Abner Doubleday, who had led Union forces at Fort Sumter. Yohe's job was to help build fortifications and protective earthworks on the north side of the District of Columbia. He was promoted to sergeant.

In December, Bill Yohe was back in Pennsylvania, in Harrisburg, at Camp Curtin, the largest Civil War military training facility in the Union. There he met twenty-year-old Elizabeth Batcheller. At five feet and three inches, "Lizzie," as she was called, was six inches shorter than Bill. Thin, with a high forehead, grey eyes, long face, and pointed chin, she provided a marked physical contrast to Bill. They were married on Christmas Day, December 25, 1863.

Lizzie's family was from Massachusetts. Her mother died young. Lizzie had been raised by a mean stepmother who had then handed her over to an aunt. According to family history, Lizzie began making her own way in the world at the age of twelve, living for some time in Canada. How she survived is not clear. Bill brought Lizzie back to Bethlehem, where she took up residence in the Eagle.

In June 1864 Yohe's unit joined with the Army of the Potomac and laid siege to Richmond and Petersburg. Bill had been reduced in rank to a private, presumably for some kind of infraction. His artillery battery pounded Confederate positions for months with mortar fire from thirty miles of trenches surrounding Petersburg. As the Confederates fought doggedly to stave off defeat, Bill Yohe's 1,800-man unit experienced heavy losses of more than 200 lives.

The siege wore on through the year. In November 1864 Yohe completed his three-year contractual enlistment. He was discharged and returned home to Bethlehem, his family, and Lizzie.

A few months later, on March 9, 1865, Bill rejoined the Union army, enlisting with the 95th Regiment of the Pennsylvania Volunteers. Bill's unit was sent back to Petersburg, where the ten-month siege ended with the Confederate retreat to the west on April 2. Yohe's unit joined other Union troops at Robert E. Lee's surrender to Ulysses S. Grant at Appomattox Courthouse on April 8, and then marched into Richmond, the defeated Confederate capital. On June 8, with the Civil War over, Yohe's regiment participated in the Corps Review, marching down Pennsylvania Avenue in the Nation's capital.

In mid-July of 1865, Bill returned to civilian life in Bethlehem, settling in with Lizzie at the Eagle Hotel. Nine months later, on April 6, 1866, Lizzie gave birth to a dark-haired daughter with beautiful blazing eyes, and dark skin like her father. Bill and Lizzie named her Mary Augusta Yohe.

In 1867, the girl was baptized in the Moravian Church in a ceremony at the Eagle Hotel together with her cousin, John T. Parke, who was the son of her paternal aunt, Anna Yohe, and her uncle, John P. Parke. Her "sponsor" and godfather was a Bethlehem resident, Richard Goundie, who had been Bill's captain in the army. May would later take the initials of her first, middle and last names to form her own nickname, "May." She would also remain close to the Parkes, her nearest relatives, for much of her life.

The end of the Civil War was good for business at the Eagle Hotel. Bethlehem hosted a railway station, Moravian College, the newly established Lehigh University, and other institutions. The Bethlehem Iron Works was growing quickly, with furnaces and foundries to produce the iron needed for the nation's expansion in the post-war Reconstruction period.

Caleb Yohe was busy enlarging the hotel; an 1868 newspaper article reports him constructing a 450-square-foot addition to an already sprawling building. To beautify the town, Caleb also planted hundreds of trees along the street, on the river bank, and on Calypso Island. Bill increasingly specialized in putz-making. Though putzes were normally exhibited only during the Christmas season, Bill's work was so artistic and popular that his putzes stayed up year-round. Caleb and Bill even constructed a special room at the hotel for the putzes, described by a guest of the time as follows:

Behind the bar of the Eagle tavern, at Bethlehem, in the common room, there has been a large aperture made in the wall of the house, ten feet long, by four feet high, opening

May Yohe, age two.

into a room built outside of the house, about ten feet square, covered over with a glass roof, as in hot-houses. In this room, William W. Yohe, son of mine ancient host, Caleb, erects each fall a putz; some miniature winter scene. In the spring he replaces this by a summer view, sometimes imaginary, oft times real. On one occasion he made a view of a town in Western Virginia, the scene of one of the earliest battles of the late Rebellion, which a Union refugee at once recognized as the home he had just fled from. Mr. Yohe is quite celebrated in Bethlehem as a putz builder of much good taste.[8]

Aside from working in the hotel, making and repairing its putzes, Bill could not find satisfying work. Lizzie sewed bonnets, hats and other clothing for girls at "Fem Sem." She, like Bill, had a fine singing voice and sang with the choirs, even though she was not Moravian. She also developed a reputation as a free spirit.

Things did not go well between Bill and Lizzie. In 1869 they tried setting up a household in Philadelphia, a two-hour train ride from Bethlehem, likely relying on help from Bill's sister Anna and her husband John Parke, a conductor for the North Pennsylvania Railroad and city resident. The move did not help matters; Bill and Lizzie separated and divorced in 1871.

After the divorce, young May lived with Lizzie on Chestnut Street, as her mother set up a milliner and dressmaking shop. She would often visit with her father and grandparents in Bethlehem, going back and forth with the Parkes.

❖ ❖ ❖

May was aware of her childhood in a divided household. Rather than blame her parents for the failed marriage, she claimed that they "did not belong" in Bethlehem with "the thought, the gossip, the habits, the vision of the small town."[9]

Though later in life she scarcely remembered her father, May formed good, strong memories of her grandparents and pleasant recollections of life at the Eagle Hotel. Decades later, Bethlehem's old-timers recollected hearing a nursemaid's shrill voice calling out "May!" to get her out from behind the boxes, barrels, and trunks at the hotel.[10] As a child in Bethlehem, May was able to develop some of her natural talent for singing by joining in with the community choirs, observing the wonderful *Lieberkranz* singing groups, and performing for guests at the hotel. Visitors remembered the young girl singing and dancing in the lobby.

Between Lizzie's own outlook and the "Fem Sem" training of Anna Parke, May did not think being a girl put her at any disadvantage. She called herself a "tomboy" and played ball and climbed trees, mostly with boys. She developed a self-confidence that was to serve her well, and also sometimes spur her to take risks.

Recalling her earliest memories, she wrote, "I've always been a devil."

> *My earliest recollection is of picking a bank. It was my own bank, but I had all the delicious thrill of a real robbery. My relatives had given me half-dollars, quarters and dimes until I had quite a little sum. My mother had told me to keep this money in my toy bank and I would buy Christmas presents for my family and friends with the money.*
>
> *But in the meantime, I had got into bad company. I had a little friend named Rachel who taught me how to open the unopenable bank with a hat pin. I would pry and pry into the bank, get a handful of money at a time, and I would take Rachel and myself to the theater and buy candy and ice cream.*

At last, the week before Christmas came and my mother said, "Now we will open the bank." When she had opened the little iron house in a legitimate way, she found there just thirty-five cents. She got a confession from me.[11]

In school, whether in Bethlehem or Philadelphia, May benefited from the Moravians' emphasis on education. She spoke German and English, and appreciated the tutelage that awakened her "soul to the beauties of music and art."[12]

❖ ❖ ❖

In 1872 May's father Bill married Rebecca Lewis. He ran for and was elected chief engineer of the Bethlehem Fire Department. He asked for the community to help him "do the right thing" in bringing the department up to a proper standard, and the *Bethlehem Daily Times* endorsed that view. Bill conducted drills in German, and he and Rebecca lived at the fire station. Lizzie continued to live and work as a seamstress in Philadelphia.

In 1874, Caleb and Mary Yohe sold the Eagle for a whopping $30,000 to George Myers. Myers closed the Eagle temporarily to have its exterior remodeled by architect Stephen Decatur Button in his popular Cape May style. Bill continued to make and repair the putzes at the Eagle for the new owner and went to work as a detective. In November of that year he had to deal with the harrowing case of a delusional mother who drowned her infant in the Lehigh River.

The next year, Bill was approached about creating a huge putz for the floral section of the Centennial Exhibition of the United States, to be held in Philadelphia in 1876. The proposed putz, which was expected to be a big draw for visitors to the exposition, was to be 60 feet wide by 50 feet deep and would depict the scenery of Pennsylvania with its hills, valleys, forests, and grasslands. The scene would include flowing water, mosses, ferns, flowers, and plants, as well as rustic bridges, farm scenes, mills, vehicles, an iron furnace, the railroad, and other features. Hoping for more stable work, Bill also applied, without success, for a long-term fabricator position with the Centennial Exhibition.

Yohe continued his detective work, gaining notice for his observational skills in solving crimes, but failing to find regular

MAY YOHE'S FAMILY

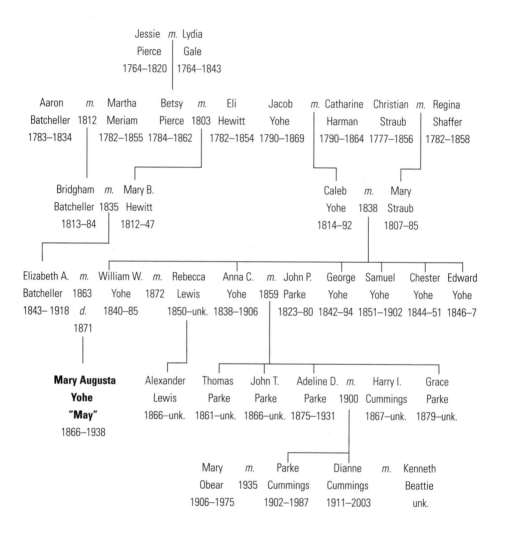

Jessie *m.* Lydia
Pierce │ Gale
1764–1820 │ 1764–1843

Aaron *m.* Martha Betsy *m.* Eli Jacob *m.* Catharine Christian *m.* Regina
Batcheller 1812 Meriam Pierce 1803 Hewitt Yohe Harman Straub Shaffer
1783–1834 1782–1855 1784–1862 1782–1854 1790–1869 1790–1864 1777–1856 1782–1858

Bridgham *m.* Mary B. Caleb *m.* Mary
Batcheller 1835 Hewitt Yohe 1838 Straub
1813–84 1812–47 1814–92 1807–85

Elizabeth A. *m.* William W. *m.* Rebecca Anna C. *m.* John P. George Samuel Chester Edward
Batcheller 1863 Yohe 1872 Lewis Yohe 1859 Parke Yohe Yohe Yohe Yohe
1843– 1918 *d.* 1840–85 1850–unk. 1838–1906 │ 1823–80 1842–94 1851–1902 1844–51 1846–7
1871

Mary Augusta Alexander Thomas John T. Adeline D. *m.* Harry I. Grace
Yohe Lewis Parke Parke Parke 1900 Cummings Parke
"May" 1866–unk. 1861–unk. 1866–unk. 1875–1931 │ 1867–unk. 1879–unk.
1866–1938

Mary *m.* Parke Dianne *m.* Kenneth
Obear 1935 Cummings Cummings Beattie
1906–1975 1902–1987 1911–2003 unk.

❖ ❖ ❖

employment. Using his parent's proceeds from the hotel sale, Bill bought a two-and-a-half-story brick house at Hillsdale Garden in Bethlehem to house Caleb, Mary, and his family.

Because the country was in the midst of an economic depression, good jobs were hard to find. Bill opened a restaurant, the Hillside Garden. It specialized in wine, beer, cigars, private rooms for social occasions, and lunch for respectable ladies and gentlemen. The town's Coronet Band furnished the music on opening day as customers enjoyed beer and lunch. But success eluded Bill. Later that year he pulled out of the restaurant business to become a detective for the New Jersey Central Railroad. Failing at that, too, he became a private detective with a friend in Easton, Pennsylvania. In 1878, he applied for a passport, purportedly to go to Brazil, but never went.

Bill Yohe's best moment came perhaps one day in the winter of 1880. As a detective, he was called to Santee Mills, a few miles north of Bethlehem, in the early hours of a brisk and snowy morning. More than a hundred local folks had gathered at a farmhouse, where neighbors had found the bodies of Jacob and Annie Geogle, brutally axed to death. It was clear the murderer was a boarder, Joseph Snyder, who had unsuccessfully attempted to rape the Geogles' teenage daughter. She had escaped, and now Snyder was missing. Yohe cleverly discerned his hiding place in a pile of straw, handcuffed and questioned him, and held him for arrest. The incensed crowd called for vengeance, assaulted Yohe, and moved to lynch the suspect. Yohe valiantly tried to turn back the crowd and prevent the lynching, putting himself at risk, and even entangling the rope—all to no avail. Snyder was hanged by the mob. Newspapers, though, described Yohe as a hero.[13]

Such heroics in Yohe's life, as in the course of his Civil War service, were often followed by failings. In 1882, veering from the law, he was arrested twice for forgery. He wrote a fraudulent check for $200 and tried to cash it at the First National Bank of Bethlehem. Two weeks later, he tried to cash two checks of $200 and $225 at the town's Lehigh Valley National Bank. As a newspaper report pointed out, this "act of a wayward son falls with crushing effect upon his aged parents."[14]

It turned out that Bill had forged other checks—about $3,000 in all. Given their prominence in the community, the elder Yohes were embarrassed and paid off their son's debts, though additional claims emerged afterward that were paid by a public sale of Bill's personal effects. Bill left Bethlehem and headed west to Montana and Colorado, fully out of May's life, and never to be seen again by the family.

❖ ❖ ❖

After the sale of the Eagle, the eight-year-old May increasingly spent time at her mother's in Philadelphia. Lizzie may have chaffed at the constraints and embarrassment she had faced in Bethlehem's tight-knit community as a divorcee, leaving a mark upon May's own perceptions. Indeed, May's mythologizing of Lizzie's Native American background may have been a way of asserting that her mother (and, by extension, May herself) retained their freedom and independence from the small-town mindset. In any case, May saw her mother and herself as cast-offs from Bethlehem.

In Philadelphia, Lizzie was becoming a successful dressmaker and costumer. Lizzie was a superb artisan, and "her originality brought to her the theatrical stars of the period," according to May.[15] Philadelphia's Arch Street Theatre opened in 1879, and costumes were needed for performances. May remembers Mrs. John Drew, Georgia Drew Barrymore, Victoria Creese, Clara Louise Kellogg, and Marie Van Zandt as prominent women who ordered dresses from Lizzie.

According to May, these actresses "fired my childish imagination and fanned that desire for the footlights which later led me to the heights—and to the depths...I was happiest when purloining some fantastic costume and portraying some imaginary character."[16]

Decades later, May recounted an episode where her childish imagination got her into trouble. She and a friend wanted to play-act for a neighborhood picnic. Having no costumes, they searched the house and found out-of-the-way boxes containing what appeared to be two old and forlorn gowns. May and her friend cut up the gowns to compose their costumes and proudly went off to the picnic to "create a sensation." That's exactly what they did, as a prominent lady recognized the garments as composed of family heirlooms she had left with Lizzie for repair. "We had ruined them beyond redemption,"[17] May wrote.

May was no less wild or imaginative in Bethlehem. With other children, she would explore the river bank near the Eagle, and

May Yohe, age 13.

Calypso Island, the local resort in the Lehigh River. Once, riding a horse in a Wild West children's circus, she was thrown "head over heels into a hedge" and rescued by a "gypsy" who brought her back home "more dead than alive," and also insisted on telling her fortune—accurately, May swore.[18]

May was self-admittedly "ungoverned in some of these impulses"[19] of fantasy, but enjoyed play-acting and taking roles in school plays.

Though May could have continued her education in Philadelphia or Bethlehem, another option beckoned. Most likely because of Aunt Anna's "Fem Sem" influence, May was sent to Europe for schooling. May knew German well enough, and Anna knew of a girl's school in Dresden run by educators influenced by Comenius' Moravian pedagogical theory. Caleb and Mary Yohe probably provided the funds for travel, room, board, and tuition from the ample proceeds from the sale of the Eagle.

Years later, May offered several alternative versions of how she came to be educated in Europe. In one, Lizzie's theatrical friends were so impressed by the teen's talent that they pooled money and used their contacts to send her to a private school in Germany. In another, more legendary account, May delivered such a rousing performance to an audience of poor Pennsylvania miners that they were inspired on the spot to take up a collection in order to send her to school.

Whatever the case, off to Dresden May went—"I was sent away like a bride in a C.O.D. package," she later wrote. "A big yellow trunk contained six of everything she needed, in accordance with the school regulations." May later said she was ten years old when she left, but in fact, she left in 1879, when she was thirteen, and her mother took her to the pier in New York, handing her over to the ship's captain "with a tear and a kiss."[20] Sometimes May reported that she spent four years at the school in Dresden, and at other times she said she spent one or two years there. Then she went on to what she called "finishing school" in Paris for a year, though sometimes she said it was for a longer period.

At Madame Florence Leonharbie's school in Dresden, May's classmates included daughters of the wealthy and prominent, including several Americans such as Louise Corbin from Long Island and the Patton sisters of Washington, D.C. Some of the English girls gave May a hard time, teasing her that only "bad people went from England [to settle] America." May argued and fought back. "It made me real proud to be American," May later recalled.[21]

May studied dance, improved her German, and learned French. She claimed that the eminent Dresden pianist, composer, and conductor Hans von Bulow taught her music. Sometimes May reported that she'd received voice training at the school, and at other times she'd vociferously deny it, taking pride in her untamed and natural talent. One event, a devilish episode that foreshadowed her future career, stood out for May as emblematic of her experience.

The school girls were to dress up for a *tableaux vivant*, a popular form of late nineteenth-century Victorian entertainment in which costumed participants formed themselves into a posed "picture." May conspired with another American teenager to go on stage dressed in tights. This, she thought, would scandalize and surprise the staid German parents of the other girls—but wouldn't get her or her friend in trouble, because their parents wouldn't be

May Yohe as a teenager in Dresden.

in the audience. May and her friend crafted risqué bodices and made tights by stitching together pieces of several pairs of silk stockings with red petticoats. They covered up with raincoats off stage, and when the time came to make their appearance, shed their cover in full view of the audience. As May recalled,

> *In later years I played many parts which called for scant costumes, but in all my professional life I could never have*

been persuaded to appear in such a costume as that one. I can realize now why, when we came from behind the scenes there was a quick gasp from the audience and then a minute of dense, pregnant silence.

Then there was a shout from the German officers [who were present].

The shout grew into a hilarious guffaw and a great din of pounding canes.

I looked down into the audience and saw the faces of dignified, adipose mothers and fathers blanched white. But I didn't care. The approbation of the officers and the young men students from the nearby university was elixir to me.

My chum and I whirled into our dance, kicking and jumping merrily, although not without a terrible fear on my part that the improvised tights would give way where we had sewn them onto the trunks, or perhaps the knitted junction above our knees unravel.

To say that our dance was a success is putting it mildly— it was a sensation.

The other girls hugged and kissed us rapturously when we danced off the stage. But there was no such greeting from our teachers and school authorities. We were almost expelled. Still, I meant no harm. I didn't understand the heinousness of my offense—I just wanted to be different.[22]

This adventure pretty much summed up May's approach to life and provides an almost paradigmatic model for future episodes, whether in the theater, her marriage, or other matters. She took risks. She was creative. She adored attention and appreciation. She wanted, almost needed, to stand out. And her attendance at a Paris finishing school—she sometimes reported it as the Convent of the Sacré Cœur, and other times as Madam Bronier's school on Rue de Passy—did not suppress a thing.

❖ ❖ ❖

As May was finishing up her term in Paris in 1885, her grandmother and namesake, Mary Yohe, a stalwart of the community, died after a long illness. If this loss was not enough, days later the family got word from a Denver newspaperman who was originally

May Yohe in Paris, age nineteen.

from Bethlehem that William Yohe had died. Apparently Bill had been in contact with a group of Moravians and former Bethlehem residents who had gone West. These acquaintances were now the mourners in his funeral service.

May had lived in Europe without her family—but they were always present in her mind as being "back home." Now, she was on her way back to America and to a family bereft of her friendly grandmother and of a father she idealized, though hardly knew. May, who often feared abandonment and longed for social acceptance and close ties of affection, was now headed back to an uncertain home.

Reporter: *Do you know, Miss Yohe, that yours is the sort of voice that goes right to the heart?*

May: *Is it? Well, perhaps that is because it comes straight from it—at least from the chest, which is somewhere in the same neighborhood.*[1]

CHAPTER TWO

Footlights Goddess

MAY'S DARING TURN BEFORE AN AUDIENCE in Dresden thrilled her. Performing on stage, being the center of attention, playing out fantasies, and assuming somewhat whimsical, risqué roles had a visceral appeal for her. Later, in Paris, she attended theater performances and met actors and actresses, further strengthening her attraction to the stage. Aspiring to a life in theater, she sailed home across the Atlantic to Philadelphia. While at sea, she had her first romance at the age of nineteen, becoming "engaged"—as she euphemistically called it—to the ship's second officer, a handsome young Frenchman.

❖ ❖ ❖

In Philadelphia, May moved in with her mother Lizzie on Chestnut Street, a bustling neighborhood full of music halls, bars, and whorehouses. Lizzie was sewing theatrical costumes and running a small boarding house; a dentist, a dry-goods salesman, and one of her sewing assistants lived with the family. Lizzie gave May her unconditional love and support. Her father was dead, his long-standing absence now final. May made him out to be a hero, a brave and gallant soldier, an officer in the Civil War. "My father was a soldier, a man of courage and of the spirit of adventure," she later wrote.[2]

May also depended upon the tutelage and love of her aunt, Anna, who lived about a mile away. Anna and her children, Tom, John, Adeline, and Grace, had also been "abandoned" when Anna's husband, John Parke, died while May was in Dresden. The widowed Anna and divorced and widowed Lizzie both had families to care for alone, and they depended upon each other in the big city. In previous years, Caleb and Mary Yohe had provided a lifeline of financial and spiritual aid from Bethlehem for both. Now, with Mary gone, Anna was taking care of the elderly Caleb, who spent much of his time at a farm that Anna and John had purchased years earlier in Yardville, near Trenton, New Jersey.

Anna and Lizzie continued to instill in May the belief that a woman can survive and even flourish without depending upon a man. May was coming to grips with her sexuality, her dreams of romance, and her aspirations for a career in theater. She had heard her mother's tales of how she had been abandoned as a young girl by her parents and raised by a wicked stepmother, and how she had had to make her own way in the world with no family support or stable home. From Anna, the Bethlehem "Fem-Sem" graduate, May heard about Moravian ideals of womanhood. These were progressive ideas about a woman's God-given abilities and potential, about the divine feminine and the importance of music—and even about secular singing as a vehicle of spiritual grace. They resonated well with what May had learned in Europe.

May helped her mother sew costumes and run the boarding house. Though she dreamed of a "life of excitement," she wrote that she found instead "only routine without revelry."[3] That may only be partially true. May no doubt visited Anna and grandfather Caleb in Yardville, where there was a famous old roadhouse and inn (which, years later, hosted the likes of Annie Oakley and Buffalo Bill when they were on tour). Legend has it that May visited the roadhouse and met lovers there.[4]

In Philadelphia, May received her first invitation to perform (as an amateur) for the congregation in "little old" St. Andrews Church. She was "frightened half to death," and it seemed as if she was being "stared at by thousands of people." But her stage fright passed, and her performance was a resounding success. "I created a sensation I will never forget," she wrote.[5]

May joined a burlesque chorus and had her professional stage debut at Philadelphia's Temple Theatre on February 8, 1886. It was a role in an American-Japanese comic opera called *The Little Tycoon.* May played Dolly Dimple and sang the lead contralto part. She had a distinctive voice, later described as sounding like a foghorn. As she said whenever she was asked about it, "I possessed a *soprano* voice, but on my way home to America, from Dresden it broke . . . just like a boy's voice."[6]

By August 1886, May was working for the McCaull Opera Comique Company. John McCaull, a Scottish-born lawyer and former Confederate colonel, had defended John Ford, of Ford's Theatre in Washington, from a suit brought by Gilbert and Sullivan producer Richard D'Oyly Carte. Moving from the bar to the stage, McCaull operated a touring company and a network of theaters and came to be regarded as the father of American comic opera. He gave May her first professional opportunity, a bit part as Esther in *Josephine Sold by Her Sisters* at the Wallack's Theatre in New York. While Wallack's was on Broadway, it was at Thirteenth Street near Union Square, not in the Broadway theater district of today. The production starred McCaull mainstay De Wolf Hopper, an actor, singer, and comedian who was six feet and five inches tall and who went on to star in some three dozen musicals. Hopper later popularized the poem *Casey at the Bat* and performed it thousands of times.

May again performed with Hopper in McCaull's production of *Lorraine,* a three-act musical farce about Louis XIV at the same theater, renamed the Star, in February 1887. May had a small part, and the play was a flop, closing within two weeks.

As May tells it, she got her big break from Mrs. John Drew, née Louisa Lane. Mrs. Drew had been born in London to a family of actors; her father died when she was seven, and her mother took her to the United States, where she became an acclaimed actress. She was married three times and went by the name of her last husband. When May met her, Mrs. Drew was the well-respected manager of the Arch Street Theatre in Philadelphia. She was also helping to raise her grandchildren, Lionel, Ethel, and John Barrymore, who later become major stars of stage and screen.

May Yohe at the beginning of her acting career, c. 1888.

Mrs. Drew was a customer of May's mother Lizzie, commissioning gowns and stage costumes from her. According to May, Mrs. Drew came to the house to pick up some gowns. While Lizzie was engaged with another patron, May got up the courage to tell Mrs. Drew of her desire to perform and then sang a popular song, accompanying herself on the piano. Mrs. Drew advised May to learn a more dramatic, interpretive piece and then come to her place for an audition. May wrote:

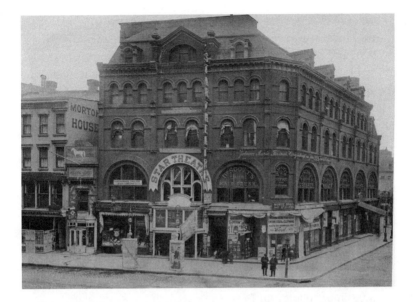

Star Theatre (formerly Wallack's Theatre) at Broadway and Thirteenth Street, New York City.

> *I was quick at study and very impatient. I soon had a new piece by heart, and Mrs. Drew gave me another hearing, this time in her own hotel suite. When I had finished, she said, 'quite nice child.' Then putting her hand on my shoulder she remarked, 'If you work hard I don't see why you shouldn't win on the stage; but remember it is work, work, work.*[7]

Louisa Drew encouraged May to pursue her dream of a career in the theater. She even wrote letters to two leading New York impresarios, Albert M. Palmer and Augustin Daly, recommending May for an audition. Both Palmer and Daly worked with Louisa's son, John Drew Jr., and her son-in-law, Maurice Barrymore.

Palmer, who ran the Madison Square Theatre, responded. He had a fine sense of artistry and a soft spot for young, untested talent—traits unconnected to his own route to show business. He had earned a law degree at New York University and worked as a librarian and as an accountant for New York City before grappling with the business end of the theater as a bookkeeper. He developed great skill in theater management, and when the Union Square

Theatre was in danger of going under, he turned the vaudeville into a playhouse with a serious acting company, earning critical acclaim and financial success. By the time he met May, Palmer was at the height of his career. Often interviewed by the newspapers as the theater industry's de facto spokesman, he was producing new works by American authors and had recently helped found the Actor's Fund of America.

May wrote of her audition for Palmer:

> *My gracious! I'll never as long as I live forget my first trial. I had to recite to Mr. Palmer in his theater. The place was empty except that mother and Mr. Palmer were in the gallery. The theater was cold and dreary, for it was a winter evening; everything looked dim and miserable. There was no scenery, no audience, no music, no lights; the theater smelt very badly of stale cigars. I felt wretched; my heart was in my boots and I was sick.*[8]

May performed, and her despair turned into perhaps the happiest moment of her life. "Mr. Palmer, from the chill, dark gallery, listened to my voice and responded—'not so bad little girl, not so bad.' He promised me my first engagement as an actress." For May it opened up a new world, a "fairy land in which only the chosen may enter."[9]

Mythic though it might have appeared to May, Palmer signed her for nine dollars per week. "It was a pitiful chance," wrote May, but a chance nonetheless for recognition and a career. "That counted. It bred confidence."[10]

❖ ❖ ❖

May's entry to the theater and onto the stage of broader popular culture came at an opportune moment, on the cusp of the "Naughty Nineties." While her early performances earned her modest accolades, May's celebrity and notoriety grew from both her strong performances and her backstage and offstage escapades, elopements, and engagements—which helped animate a new era in American social life.

The "Naughty Nineties," a decade later more commonly called the "Gay Nineties," was characterized by people like May who defined the period as one of increasing personal freedom and social license, particularly for women. The decade saw a gradual loosening of some of the social strictures of the Victorian era, both in Britain, where it was rooted, and in the United States.

The era took its name and moral atmosphere from Queen Victoria, who had been Great Britain's monarch since 1837. Throughout her long reign, she espoused values and policies that encouraged the development of a middle class aligned with the positive aspects of industrialization and urbanization. Middle-class social values congealed around the sanctity of the home, family, proper etiquette, and public decorum and opposed the perceived moral ills of the rapidly growing British cities, beset with problems such as broken families, child labor, and prostitution.

Victorian attitudes—favoring frugality, propriety, the social hierarchy, and the repression of sexuality—had become increasingly prevalent in American social life by the mid-nineteenth century. In the 1860s, Victorian attitudes began to affect public entertainment in American cities, which heretofore had largely been raucous men-only evenings of song and dance as an excuse for smoking, drinking, and whoring. A new group of entrepreneurs, such as Chicago's lead impresario J. H. McVicker, promoted "a better class of entertainment in keeping with the artistic tastes of the public." Over the next decades, a more serious, family-friendly theater emerged, typified by clean, genteel surroundings for mixed-sex audiences and a new innovation, the matinee, which aimed to attract women and children.

But even as Victorian middle-class ideals reached dominance in public life in the 1870s and 1880s, they were already being challenged by the behavior of a new class of wealthy Americans living in what Mark Twain called the "Gilded Age." A certain immorality characterized the "robber barons"—Rockefeller, Vanderbilt, Carnegie, Morgan, and Flagler—as they gained unimagined wealth. Entrepreneurial license came with boundary-breaking excesses of individual desire and its fulfillment in houses, fashion, food, romance, and, later, philanthropy. These excesses contrasted with Victorian mores and drove the narrative tension in many real-life stories and fictional tales in the era's popular literature and entertainment.

The late 1880s and the 1890s found expressions of personal freedom and independence spreading to a broader group of people:

the urban, educated, Anglo-Saxon middle class, including women as well as men. May Yohe and her ilk offered an alternative to Victorian stuffiness precisely when many parts of the United States, particularly New York, Boston, and Chicago, were rapidly changing. Northern cities were growing larger and more cosmopolitan, awash in new wealth from trade and the Industrial Revolution. The movement for women to gain the right to vote was stirring. Popular entertainment and entertainers offered up a new American rebellion from Victorian English cultural norms.

American entertainment provided a potpourri of staged performances; by the late 1880s some four hundred theater companies were touring across the United States. In a big city like Boston, you could see the comedy *Dandy-Dick*, hear the National Opera perform Wagner, or attend a concert of the First Regiment Drum, Fife and Bugle Corps. You might also sit for a lecture on Spiritualism or instead stomp your feet at a banjo concert. The World Museum, with its menagerie and aquarium, offered skits, comedians, magicians, clowns, and wild animals! At the time, theatricals flush with costumed and musical spectacle, with casts of hundreds and special effects, were all the rage. Burlesque, popular opera, musical comedy, and the variety show dominated the scene.

The American stage at that moment provided a wonderful setting for May's own freedom-loving, boundary-breaking proclivities. May's infatuation with her own talent was soon to be tested before audiences, well-wishers, and critics in the theaters of New York, Chicago, Boston, and even London.

❖ ❖ ❖

May's first big billing was in *The Arabian Nights: Aladdin's Wonderful Lamp* at the newly opened Chicago Opera House in the summer of 1887. David Henderson, a Scottish-born newspaper man who worked closely with McCaull, built the Opera House and was responsible for its theatrical productions.

The Arabian Nights was regarded as "a spectacular burlesque." Like other such productions of the genre, it was short on plot but full of pageantry, with great costumed marches involving as many as 180 actors in one scene. It included the ominous "crypt of crimson crystal" as a prop, a vapor curtain used for tricks and special effects, and featured ballets, topical songs, a grand chorus, and an intriguing dolls' quadrille, with actors and actresses magically "wound up" to dance. May, playing Princess Balroubadora, was the featured singer in a "charming" balcony serenade. She totally enthralled some of the reviewers:

> *In the center of them all is Yohe, lustrous of eye, dusky of tress and modest of mien . . . A girl of slight lithe build and a grace of carriage . . . She has great solemn black eyes, with a sparkle of mischief in them . . . She has the misfortune of being pretty. Not kittenishly aggressively pretty, but slyly, seductively, amiably pretty, with the prettiness of a Lillian Russell or Marie Junson, without the corporeal liberality of the one or the perverse come-and-be-sacrificed whimsicality of the other. . . She doesn't walk; she glides. She doesn't dance; she floats. And when she sings—well, she sings . . .*
>
> *There is a hush, and then Yohe takes two steps forward and sings . . . Every note is true as steel and has the ring of a bugle call in it . . . It is the very deepest sort of a contralto— rich, mellow and resonant.*[11]

The Arabian Nights fit well with a growing and popular interest in the East. Orientalism, as a theme in fashion, design, literature, philosophy, spiritualism and even drama, was on the rise. With Aladdin's lamp and its ability to conjure up the supernatural, *The Arabian Nights* highlighted the magic of the Orient. May's appearances in this and other Orientalist dramas would later provide a repertoire of ideas and characters for her own tale-telling.

The play had a popular and critically acclaimed thirteen-week run in Chicago, and May's performance was especially noted and lauded. However, she became ill during the run and had to be replaced. Nevertheless, May had done such a good job with her singing role that the theatrically powerful Henderson became her manager and agreed to include her in the touring version of the show produced by his Imperial Burlesque Company. May rejoined the cast in New York for the fall and in Boston and at Philadelphia's Chestnut Street Opera House for the winter.

One promoter opined that the play was "equal in brilliancy and novel effects to anything New York has seen."[12] The show did well in New York and Boston, attracting audiences every night and for three weekly matinees. Some 27,000 people a week came on foot, in horse carts, and by train, and paid from twenty cents for general admission to seventy-five cents for a box seat to see the show.

In New York, May's rich singing performance drew special praise—so much so that when she later, on tour, suffered fits of fainting, the *New York Times* applauded her heroic resolve.

> *Bravery of spirit and genius are inseparable in the accomplishment of great results, whether upon the so-called mimic-stage or upon the field of battle. This young heroine has been so much worn down by many daily rehearsals and nightly performances, that at last the arduous labor overcame the powers of her mortal frame, but not of her daring and aspiring soul.*[13]

Apparently, May fainted ten different times—each time she came into the wings during the performance. Yet, despite Henderson's urging, she was determined to return to the stage each time. "No amount of argument could keep her off the stage." An assistant would administer "restoratives" every time May lost consciousness, including at the end of the show, when the audience applauded "long and loud, while the little songstress lay in the wings insensible of it all."[14]

The "heroic" May next performed in *Natural Gas*, a social satire in the form of a musical comedy that opened in Chicago in 1888. Crowds packed in to see the touted actress. The plot followed an Irish scrubwoman who inherits land rich in natural gas, becomes wealthy, and puts on airs to mimic ladies of fashion and standing—another theme that would resonate with May later in her life. May was grateful to her mother Lizzie for making her "exquisite" gown and attending the premiere. "It was to my mother that I sang that first night, driving away my nervousness and fright."[15]

The play was popular, but the *Chicago Daily Tribune* reviewer summed up the performance as "a flat extravaganza [by] a clever and hardworking company." He noted that "there are a number of pretty girls in the cast who add much to the entertainment by their singing and dancing. Among them is Miss May Yohe who displays to advantage her rich contralto voice in a number of selections."[16] May, recalling that opening night decades later, wrote that she

Chestnut Street Opera House Theatre in Philadelphia, 1874

became "overnight a celebrity."[17] Despite the overstatement, May became more well-known and Henderson increased her salary to $200 per week—a hefty amount at the time, equivalent to about $4,700 a week today.

The *New York Times* recognized her ability and called Yohe "the maiden for the money."

> *May Yohe at once arrested the attention of the audience with her rich, rare contralto voice and high-toned diction. This young girl has the organ, the bearing and the spirit of which grand singers are composed.*[18]

May went on to get her first major role in *The Crystal Slipper*, a musical take-off on the Cinderella story, featuring, among others, the very popular entertainer Eddie Foy. Opening at the Chicago Opera House in June 1888, May was greeted by an overflow crowd with wild applause and flowers. A review in the *Chicago Current* noted that:

> *The Crystal Slipper, or Prince Prettiwitz and Little Cinder-*
> *ella proved the greatest theatrical success ever known in the*
> *city. At every performance crowds were turned away un-*
> *able to obtain admission. The scenic splendors of the piece,*
> *the beauty of the large ballets, and . . . the great chorus are*
> *important factors in this success. Robert E. Graham, Eddie*
> *Foy . . . and May Yohe may be credited with having scored*
> *emphatic hits.*[19]

May was on the road to celebrity, followed by dozens of male fans, or "mashers" as they were called at the time. May played the title role of Prince Polydore von Prettiwittz. It was the first of several male roles she would play.

Yohe took to the part, perhaps partially because of her self-proclaimed tomboy youth, but also because of her somewhat androgynous demeanor. She was an attractive woman who drew many a male gaze. Her stature was slight and willowy and her features delicate. A reviewer called her "angelic," another "vestal."[20] As a fellow troupe member recalled, "In those days, when plumpness was the vogue with stage femininity, May was almost painfully thin. In spite of it she was a vibrant personality, with dark hair and flashing eyes."[21] She had a complexion in which "lilies and roses seem striving for supremacy" as one reporter described her.[22] Made up as a man, she was also alluring in a boyish, cute, adolescent way.

The play was a tremendous success, with a run of 855 performances. May's fame and public presence grew—and so did the trouble she spawned.

❖ ❖ ❖

On the Fourth of July, 1888, the *Chicago Daily, New York Times,* and *Washington Post* all reported that the previous day, after an afternoon of drinking too much wine at the races, May had boarded a Chicago train bound for New York with a companion by the name of E. B. Shaw. Yohe was a "no show" for her *Crystal Slipper* performances, and was reported to have eloped with the good-looking, rich, and reputedly restless and wild "Elbie" Shaw.

The act seemed impetuous and scandalous, all the more so because Shaw was married to the daughter of a prominent and influential businessman. Shaw's father was in the bakery business and was also part-owner of the Chicago Opera House.

One news report had May getting on the train at the Lake Shore station with Shaw to say goodbye, and then inadvertently getting stuck on board as it sped off toward points eastward. Shaw and other travelers had a good chuckle at her expense, and May herself joined in with her fabled silvery sweet laugh. But she faced a dilemma. She would surely miss her *Crystal Slipper* performance that night. She could get off at Elkhart, Indiana and be marooned there overnight, or could stay on the train until arriving in Toledo the next morning, where she could catch a train back to Chicago. May chose to stay on board. By some accounts, she spent an intimate night with Shaw, but left him the next morning in disgust after discovering that he was married.

Likely tipped off by a masher, a reporter visited May's Chicago rental flat and confronted her mother on her whereabouts. Lizzie denied that May was away. She claimed instead that she was in the apartment, quite ill and unable to receive visitors. She admitted that May had attended the races with Shaw and had drunk wine, but had eaten nothing, was overcome by the heat, and, as a result, had taken sick.

The next day, appearing in front of reporters after her stage appearance, at which she was said to have successfully "faced a large and silent audience with a swagger," May held to that same story.[23]

A week later, Elbie Shaw's wife Jessie filed for divorce, citing her husband's repeated adulterous affairs, including "improper and immoral relations" with May Yohe.[24] Several months later that divorce was granted. The ruling was based upon the testimony of the train conductor, who swore that May was indeed on the train and that she'd spent the night in the sleeping car with Shaw.

Interestingly, that was not the end of the story. A year later, Shaw reconciled with his wife and they were remarried. A *Chicago Tribune* reporter called May Yohe a "footlights goddess" and noted that her "tinsel and paint" "were not the most desirable adjuncts to a happy life."[25]

May Yohe, c. 1880s.

Soon after the Shaw episode, May was confronted with an un-settling claim. Alexander Lewis, a U.S. Marine stationed in Boston, had written a letter to the legendary producer J. H. McVicker in Chicago claiming to be Yohe's step-brother.

Lewis wrote that he hadn't seen May since she had gone to Europe eight years before. Given the publicity surrounding May's episode with Shaw, McVicker was reluctant to bring the letter to May, questioning its veracity. Nonetheless, McVicker, worried it might be truthful, brought the matter to her attention. According to McVicker's account, May told him "I never heard of his [Lewis'] existence. Nevertheless, if he is my brother bring him to me. If he is my step-brother bring him to me. Bring him to me in any case. I will not deny him. Recent events have shown me the futility of denying anything or anybody."[26]

There is no record of any meeting or subsequent communication between May and Alexander Lewis, but Lewis' claim may have been real. He could well have been the son of Rebecca Lewis, the woman May's father, William, had wed in 1872. Perhaps May had either never known about him, or knew about him and brushed the fact aside. Since Alexander Lewis enrolled in the Marines in 1887, he was probably born before that marriage, and was either William's illegitimate son or, more likely, given his self-described status as May's "step-brother," Rebecca's son by a former marriage. Alexander was a ne'er-do-well as a Marine, imprisoned in the "brig" numerous times during his military service. In any case, Lewis' attempt to reach out to May would not be the last time someone sought to establish kinship with her.

Another backstage matter also emerged later in the summer of 1888. The co-star of *The Crystal Slipper*, Ida Mulle, who played Cinderella, complained that May was being unfairly favored in the production. "Although to the spectators each night the Prince and Cinderella seemed to be the most devoted of lovers, they were really at swords' points behind the scenes," the press reported.[27] Mulle claimed Yohe had had some of Cinderalla's lines cut and that she suffered in duets because May did not have the singing range to support her part. Though a few concessions were made by the stage manager, May largely prevailed and the enmity continued.

All of this riled David Henderson, her manager. Despite his position and stature, he could neither control nor guarantee May's behavior. Henderson dropped her. John Russell became May's manager. He noted that he might not be able to get May good roles since they required her showing up for performances. Russell quipped that while she might be on stage in the evening, he "never knew where she would be by daylight the next morning."[28]

On cue, just as May's stage life was on the rise over the next year with her 1889 tours of *The Crystal Slipper* and *Natural Gas*, new reports about her love life surfaced in the press. May was rumored to have secretly married Jack Mason, an actor in the Boston Museum Company, and often touted as the handsomest man in America. May put aside the report, saying she'd never marry an actor—not "one of those jays!" "If I ever marry I shall want to make a splurge. Give me a nice little dude; soft blonde mustache, patent leather boots, plenty of boodle."[29] A follow-up article in the *Boston Daily Globe* supposedly based upon an interview with May contradicted this denial.

May told the reporter she had indeed been married to Jack Mason and that they had set up a household. Then, much to her chagrin, Mason cheated on her. May reacted by pawning some of her jewelry, packing her things, and insisting he take her to the train station. She wanted to make a show of leaving him. May was seated on the train by an open window, speaking to Jack, who was standing on the platform. May continued,

> *All this time I had been acting . . . I wanted to give Jack a good scare . . . I expected every moment to hear him say, "you little goose, quit your foolishness; come home and I'll be a good boy." If he had said it I believe I would have jumped right through the window into his arms. He would have said it too, I know he would, but just then a couple of girls came along. They threw sheep's eyes at him, and one said to her companion: "Oh, Mame! that's Jack Mason. Doesn't he look sweet!" The cars began to move. He drew himself up to his full height, raised his derby and made me a most formal bow.*
>
> *I, what did I do? Why, I fell back in my chair and broke out into tears, the most miserable girl in America. I had a good cry and then I felt relieved. My pride began to assert itself and I said, "I will never go back to him unless he comes after me."*[30]

Mason wasn't the only one supposed to have married May. May barnstormed in the West, traveling with fellow show people, drinking, and learning to play poker and to gamble. She liked the risk, she said. She also "loved" Western men, those beyond the Rocky Mountains, for their chivalry and understated, though strong, sense of justice. "I wonder why God ever makes any other kind!" she opined.[31] Apparently, she loved them a lot. A report

May Yohe, 1890.

from San Francisco claimed that May had taken up with and married Thomas H. Williams, a wealthy young sportsman known as the "Duke of Union Island." Williams, the scion of a powerful political family, was so incensed at the *Evening Post* account of this affair that he battered the skull of the newspaper's editor.

May Yohe performing in The City Directory, *1891.*

Perhaps to gain some control over the libidinous and free-spirited May, Lizzie took her across the Pacific Ocean to Australia in 1890. In Australia, May starred in a production of *Josephine Sold by Her Sisters*, appeared in other plays in Melbourne and Sydney, and earned notice from the public and the press as "a bright, sparkling, pretty, piquant, little brunette" with a "wonderful contralto voice."[32] The Sydney papers reported that May, dressed in "Eastern costume, sang in a very pleasing manner" and that she "was loudly applauded."[33]

Returning to the United States, May performed in a number of productions in 1891: *The City Directory, U and I, Hoss & Hoss,* and various testimonials and variety shows. Though she was not accorded the same reverential status as the leading actresses of the day such as Sarah Bernhardt and Lillian Russell, May thought herself a rising star. She was a strong performer who was popular with audiences and generated high billing and good reviews. She was sought after for stage roles, toured Boston, New York, Philadelphia, Washington, D.C., Chicago, Los Angeles, and San Francisco, and had a following for both her onstage career and offstage antics. In the spring of 1892, she went to England, hoping to find a manager to arrange theatrical appearances, but was unsuccessful.

Rumors of other supposed affairs and marriages cropped up again, some quite absurd. One news story alleged that May had married one of Massachusetts' U.S. senators—highly unlikely given the status and visibility of both Senator Henry Davis, who was 76, and Senator George Hoar, who was 66. The *New York Times* and other newspapers exuberantly sang May's praises, touting her good looks, her jewelry, and her talents, while at the same time acknowledging her exuberant, romantic escapades, both truthful and alleged. Her refreshing eccentricity earned her a nickname: "Madcap May," a timely moniker she herself only rarely used, but no doubt deeply enjoyed.[34]

Goodness Maysie, you've
caught a Lord!
—*Lizzie Batcheller Yohe*[1]

CHAPTER THREE

Nobly Courted

"NO VISION OF DIAMONDS OR OF DUKES troubled my early days," wrote May.[2] Such would have been unfathomable, even as May courted stardom in her young career, had she not chanced to meet Francis Hope at a dinner party at the famed Delmonico's restaurant in New York City in November 1892. The meeting cast her in the role of a real-life Cinderella and eventually sparked the growth of one of the greatest urban legends of our times.

May always claimed that when she first met him, she did not know that Francis was a wealthy English lord, in line to inherit one of the most prestigious dukedoms in Queen Victoria's British Empire. To her, he was a well-spoken, British-accented, kind and attentive dinner companion who politely offered to accompany her to the Horse Show at Madison Square Garden. May was charmed by this "Mr. Hope." He was poised, polite, and entertaining. Instead of "talking down" to the actress, he impressed May by treating her as an intellectual equal as they discussed politics, world affairs, art, and society.

May's narcissistic desire to be the center of attention was apparent in her account of their first evening together. At Madison Square Garden, May enjoyed Francis' discussion of the horses and the rapt attention he paid her. As she wrote,

> *I began to notice lorgnettes from all over the seat tiers turned in my direction. In the boxes near me, the splendidly coiffed heads of wealthy society women, matrons of families known throughout the world for their leadership of fashion, were turned upon me with stares that were frank and curious. And here and there I caught bows of friendly recognition to my escort. I thought, of course, these society women, whom I knew only by sight, were just interested in a close-up view of the famous May Yohe, the new star in the theatrical firmament. I was greatly excited about their interest, and talked and laughed about it with my companion.*[3]

Francis, politely deflecting the true cause of the audience's stares, told her, "You are so very beautiful Miss Yohe, I can quite well understand anyone's wanting to get a good look at you."[4]

Francis courted May in the ensuing days. He met her mother Lizzie, who was impressed by him. May toured New York City by day with Francis, and in the evening dined with him and his friends. Again, as May tells it, Francis conspired with those friends not to reveal his true identity.

Later that week, May announced to him her plans to return to London with her mother to consider contracts from theatrical managers to appear in new stage productions. Francis, obviously smitten, asked May and Lizzie to be his guests while in London and offered to show them around the city.

As May later construed it, this 1892 trip across the Atlantic played out like a theatrical love story in which she starred as the beloved princess. Francis met May and Lizzie upon their arrival. The "beaming" Francis held May's hand for a "long time" and insisted she stay at the Savoy, London's most expensive hotel—and first modern luxury accommodation.

The Savoy was a treat for May. The hotel had opened just a few years before in 1889. Owned by impresario Richard D'Oyly Carte, it was built on the Strand in Central London with the profits from his productions of Gilbert and Sullivan operas. The Savoy was opulent in every way for the time, with electric lights, elevators (or "ascending rooms" as they were called), speaking tubes between rooms, and even private bathrooms in the more exclusive suites. Arthur Sullivan was on the board of directors, and the hotel was managed by Cesar Ritz, who would later found the Ritz Hotel and define swanky style.

May recounted her first Savoy dinner with Francis:

> *That night when we were ushered into the dining room we found that one whole end of the big room had been roped off with silver ropes, and that behind it was a table set for three—decorated so lavishly I almost gasped. London knew I had arrived, and before dinner was well under way the word got out that May Yohe was at dinner in the Savoy dining room. Soon there was a regular parade of London Johnnies, sticks, silk hats, evening clothes and Inverness capes, marching along the silver ropes in one endless procession.*
>
> *I was almost hypnotized by the novelty of it when the parade began. I didn't know what it meant until Mr. Hope explained that the London Johnnie was an established institution, and that this was its customary reception to a new idol. It meant, he said, that I was already enthroned in the heart of London.*[5]

Francis no doubt orchestrated the display, feeding May's ego and desire for public attention. The next day they discussed what May claims were "hundreds of offers" from London theater managers and producers to have her appear in their shows. Francis offered to help May and Lizzie sort through the proposals and advance her career.

Then, in conversation with May, Francis' offer went further. As May recounted, Francis confided, "You know, Miss May, I am hoping awfully that you are going to let me have a lot to do with your affairs—perhaps have the same interest in them that you have."[6]

May's reaction was dramatic. "It took my breath away," wrote May. "I looked at him quickly. He was just smiling, a strange, whimsical sort of smile, but there was a very earnest light shining in his eyes."[7]

May took this as Francis' signal of a forthcoming marriage proposal. May politely responded in a rare, demure way, "That will be very nice, Mr. Hope." As May reports, Francis "took my hand, gave it a little squeeze and said in a matter-of-fact way, just as if he were making a casual arrangement for tea or something like that, 'Then it is all settled. I'm terribly glad.'"[8]

According to May, she learned of Francis' real identity the next day. Still at the Savoy that afternoon, Francis was meeting with May and Lizzie in their suite, discussing possible managers and theatrical offers, when there was a knock at the door. Lizzie opened the door to find Francis' valet, who said, "May I ask his lordship whether he will wear his tuxedo or his evening clothes?"

"Ask 'his lordship'? Lordship who?" responded May's perplexed mother.

"Lord Francis, Madame," responded the valet.

As May recalled,

Mother turned toward us breathless. I had heard and was stunned. Then my heart gave one big jump. I thought I was dreaming. I looked at our guest. He [Francis] was looking at me with a sort of quizzical expression and smiling humorously . . . "You'd have to find it out some day, anyway. Will you care any the less for me now that you know if you keep me you will have to some day be the Duchess of Newcastle?"[9]

May was overcome. Lizzie gasped, "Your Lordship." They broke out in a flabbergasted, polite laugh.[10] Francis, whose full name was Lord Henry Francis Hope Pelham-Clinton-Hope, responded graciously, "No, just Francis to you both," as he took May's hand.[11]

Later, as Lord Francis left their suite, May knew she was in for an interesting time, like some fairy tale princess, when her mother turned to her and said, "Goodness Maysie, you've caught a lord!"[12]

Lord Francis Hope—one of the
best men that ever lived.
—*May Yohe*[1]

CHAPTER FOUR

Hopeful

P OSSESSED OF A KEEN SENSE of aristocratic entitlement, Lord Francis was a tall, handsome, debonair young man of twenty-six when he met May. He was the second son of the deceased sixth duke of Newcastle; his mother was Henrietta Adéle Hope. His elder brother, Henry Pelham Archibald, the seventh duke, was childless and sickly, and thus Francis was regarded as likely to be the next duke. But it was as a descendent of the prominent Hope family that Lord Francis literally made his name.

❖ ❖ ❖

The Hopes earned their wealth in the 1700s and secured land, art, public office, and aristocratic titles in the 1800s. Originally Scots, they had become a transnational family of merchant bankers headquartered for several generations in Amsterdam and then in England starting in 1762. They provided major loans to national governments, including Russia, Sweden, Spain, and Portugal. The Hopes were important trading partners with the United States during the Revolutionary War. When Napoleon decided to sell his

Lord Francis Hope.

American holdings for 80 million francs in 1803, Hope & Company and Baring of London made the loan to the United States to finance the Louisiana Purchase.

In their mercantile heyday, the Hopes were in the vanguard of a newly evolving European society. They were more disciplined and rational, more engaged in trade, finance, and generating wealth, than they were in enhancing aristocratic privilege. As the American and French Revolutions demonstrated, monarchies were dying institutions; healthy nations would be defined by economic growth and productive social investments, not by the preservation of excessive, consumption-oriented aristocratic lifestyles. Indeed, Lord Francis' great-great uncle, Boston-born Henry Hope, who was eminently successful and a friend of Thomas Jefferson, John Adams, and Benjamin Franklin, declined the offer by Russia's ruler Catherine the Great to bestow upon him an aristocratic title. Possessions and power were being passed from the nobility to the newly rich and powerful merchant class, and the Hopes were foremost among them.

Unfortunately for the Hopes, they fell victim to the very system they had initially begun to displace. Enormous wealth and mercantile power, built up by talented, entrepreneurial ancestors, was frittered away by descendants who were more interested in

Thomas Hope in Oriental dress, c. 1798.

the attainment of high social rank and its correlated conspicuous consumption than in displacing the aristocracy. By the nineteenth century, the Hopes sought to become aristocrats. Two items characterized this quest: the acquisition of a title, or peerage; and the acquisition and display of an extraordinarily conspicuous diamond.

Lord Francis' great-grandfather was Thomas Hope (1769–1831). Thomas and his younger brothers, Henry Philip Hope and

Adrian Elias Hope, were beneficiaries rather than producers of mercantile success. When Hope & Company sold out to Baring in 1813 it left millions for the brothers' pursuits. They were among the richest families in Great Britain.

Thomas Hope was an eminent author, expert in decorative arts and design, and collector of Flemish and Dutch paintings, passions he shared with George, the Prince of Wales and eldest son of King George III. Thomas also shared with the Prince a fascination with things Oriental and was drawn into a number of decorative projects for George's transformation of his mansion at Brighton into a "pleasure palace." The writer Lord Byron called Thomas Hope the "house furnisher withal."[2] Thomas adorned his own London townhouse with artistic treasures to be enjoyed by his wife Louisa and his three sons.

While Thomas was a scholar and aesthete, his wife Louisa was ambitious and aspired to an aristocratic title. When the Prince of Wales became King George IV in 1820, Louisa became a "woman of the bedchamber," or lady-in-waiting, and her son "a lord of the bedchamber," purely honorary titles with no formal powers or privileges.

The Hopes developed a relationship with the King's right-hand man, Sir Arthur Wellesley, the first duke of Wellington, the hero who defeated Napoleon at Waterloo. Louisa instigated a scheme to offer the duke a huge £10,000 bribe (about $1 million today) if he would help them obtain a baronetcy, thus making them aristocrats. Wellington was outraged but did not want to expose the famed and crown-friendly Thomas Hope.

By 1828, Wellington had become a close family friend. While Louisa still harbored aristocratic ambitions, her connections to Wellington and the King did not get her nearer to a peerage.

These connections, however, did get the family closer to a marvelous, exceptional diamond. Thomas' brother, Henry Philip Hope, lived modestly, never married, and built up one of Europe's most fabulous collections of precious gems, including hundreds of diamonds. The collection was valued at the time at about £150,000, or the equivalent of about $15 million today.

In 1830, George IV died. Wellington was the executor of his estate. George had bankrupted the crown with years of extravagant purchases and his successor and brother, King William IV, was eager to sell off George's property to relieve royal debts and avoid

Henry Philip Hope.

provoking public outrage over his brother's extravagance. One of George's prized possessions was a large forty-four-carat rare blue diamond.

The blue diamond had a long, if somewhat purposefully obscured history. It was originally a 112-carat rough cut gemstone acquired in India in 1653 by French diamond merchant Jean Baptist Tavernier. In 1668, Tavernier sold it at Versailles to Louis XIV,

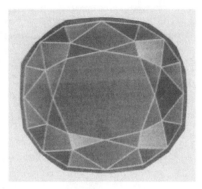

Sketch of the Hope diamond.

who had it recut into an exquisite sixty-seven-carat heart-shaped gemstone, the second most valuable in the French crown jewels. It was placed in an ensemble of other gems, a decoration signifying membership in the knighthood of the Golden Fleece, and worn in that form by Louis XV and Louis XVI as well. The stunning and valuable blue diamond was then stolen from the royal treasury in Paris in September 1792 amidst the tumult of the French Revolution and "disappeared." Napoleon tried to find it in his effort to restore the great crown jewels and France's national pride.

The blue diamond resurfaced in its forty-four-carat cut-down form in 1812, and came into George's possession by 1823. It was then called the "George IV Diamond," and the King had it set into his own version of the Golden Fleece, a knightly decoration, presumably to insult Napoleon.

When George died, Wellington sought a discrete buyer for the diamond, and knowing the Hopes and Henry Philip's collection, consummated the sale—reportedly for the bargain price of £18,000, though no records have been found to confirm that.

The blue diamond was first formally recorded in Henry Philip Hope's catalogue *Collection of Pearls and Precious Stones* in 1839, and was modestly designated as "No 1." The catalogue noted that the diamond is mounted on a "medallion, with a border *en arabesque* of small rose diamonds, surrounded by 20 brilliants of equal size, shape, and cutting, and of the finest water, and averaging four grains each."[3]

Thomas Hope died in 1831 leaving £180,000, an incredible art collection, the London home on Duchess Street, and a mansion and estate at Deepdene in Surrey to his wife and three sons. When

King George IV of England, c. 1820.

his brothers died childless—Adrian Elias in 1834, and Henry Philip in 1839—Thomas' sons inherited another £1 million, more property, more art, and the gem collection.

Thus the three surviving Hope children, Henry Thomas, Adrian, and Alexander Hope were fabulously wealthy. Henry Philip had written a letter to his three nephews, to be delivered posthumously, advising them "to cherish and cultivate a fraternal regard and affectionate feelings for each other, and not to dishon-

Sketch of the Hope diamond set in a medallion, c. 1839.

our or disparage the memory of your parents and uncles by un-worthy differences among yourselves."[4]

What ensued was exactly the opposite, with years of frater-nal argument, vitriol, and lawsuits especially over control of the immensely valuable gem collection for which no clear bequest existed. Given that two of the brothers, Henry Thomas and Al-exander, were members of Parliament and that the Hopes were in-volved in high society, the dispute was well known, even to Queen Victoria, who had assumed the throne in 1837. Benjamin Disraeli, a member of Parliament and later Prime Minister, knew the Hopes personally. He commented,

> *The three brothers Hope, though the wealth of the whole family had become concentrated in them, were always at war. There were some famous jewels, which had belonged to their uncle Philip Hope, which were a fruitful subject of litigation. There was a blue diamond that all the brothers wanted. They hated each other.[5]*

Henry Thomas Hope.

After a decade of dispute, the brothers finally settled. Henry Thomas Hope received the blue diamond and seven other important gems, Adrian inherited property, and Alexander came into possession of the huge Hope pearl and some 700 other gems and precious stones. Their mother, Louisa, who had remarried in 1832, retained much of her money.

When Louisa died in 1851, Henry Thomas married his long-time French mistress Anne Adéle Bichat who had, some ten years

LORD FRANCIS HOPE'S FAMILY

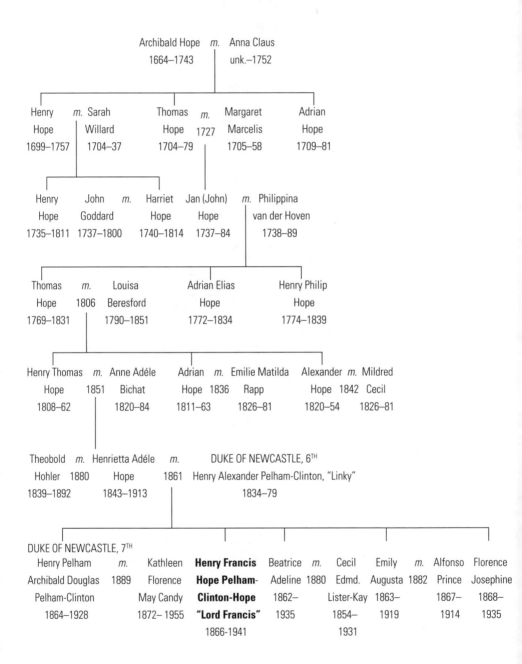

Archibald Hope *m.* Anna Claus
1664–1743   unk.–1752

Henry   *m.* Sarah   Thomas   *m.*   Margaret   Adrian
Hope   Willard   Hope   1727   Marcelis   Hope
1699–1757   1704–37   1704–79   1705–58   1709–81

Henry   John   *m.*   Harriet   Jan (John)   *m.*   Philippina
Hope   Goddard   Hope   Hope   van der Hoven
1735–1811   1737–1800   1740–1814   1737–84   1738–89

Thomas   *m.*   Louisa   Adrian Elias   Henry Philip
Hope   1806   Beresford   Hope   Hope
1769–1831   1790–1851   1772–1834   1774–1839

Henry Thomas   *m.*   Anne Adéle   Adrian   *m.*   Emilie Matilda   Alexander   *m.*   Mildred
Hope   1851   Bichat   Hope   1836   Rapp   Hope   1842   Cecil
1808–62   1820–84   1811–63   1826–81   1820–54   1826–81

Theobold   *m.*   Henrietta Adéle   *m.*   DUKE OF NEWCASTLE, 6TH
Hohler   1880   Hope   1861   Henry Alexander Pelham-Clinton, "Linky"
1839–1892   1843–1913   1834–79

DUKE OF NEWCASTLE, 7TH
Henry Pelham   *m.*   Kathleen   **Henry Francis**   Beatrice   *m.*   Cecil   Emily   *m.*   Alfonso   Florence
Archibald Douglas   1889   Florence   **Hope Pelham-**   Adeline   1880   Edmd.   Augusta   1882   Prince   Josephine
Pelham-Clinton   May Candy   **Clinton-Hope**   1862–   Lister-Kay   1863–   1867–   1868–
1864–1928   1872– 1955   **"Lord Francis"**   1935   1854–   1919   1914   1935
                            1866-1941   1931

before, given birth to an illegitimate daughter, Henrietta. They moved into the London home he built at 116 Piccadilly.

Henry Thomas wanted to show off his blue diamond. His opportunity came with London's Great Exhibition of 1851 in an innovative, newly constructed structure, the Crystal Palace. The Great Exhibition was a benchmark for the Victorian era, displaying all sorts of machinery, weapons, models, scientific equipment, craftwork, and treasures to six million British and foreign visitors. It defined the genre of nineteenth century world expositions. Among the featured items was the Koh-i-Nur diamond, recently acquired by the British East India Company and presented to Queen Victoria. Next to it was a diamond of "177 grains tinged with blue and known as Mr. Hope's." This was the first naming of the "Hope diamond," and on July 12, at the exposition, Hope had the honor of placing the gem into the hand of Queen Victoria for inspection.

Henry Thomas Hope was a conservative politician and a patron of the arts. His inheritance provided him with wealth, and the Hope diamond became its symbol. Owning such a diamond, as well as a fine London house, the inherited art collection, and a castle in Ireland, provided the trappings of aristocracy—without the title. A position in Parliament was respected, but, having married his former mistress, a French woman with no standing, late in life and having fathered a child out of wedlock, the status-conscious Henry Thomas felt somewhat deficient in Victorian society. The legitimization he sought could still only be achieved through genuine aristocratic status—just what his mother Louisa sought.

To achieve that aim, in 1861 Henry Thomas Hope helped engineer the marriage of his daughter Henrietta to Henry Pelham Alexander, the earl of Lincoln and son of the duke of Newcastle. Though the Pelham family had been a distinguished one, counting among its immediate ancestors Prime Ministers of England, it was, like the Hope family, having problems. Henry Thomas had to bribe the prospective groom—"Linky," as he was known to friends—into the marriage. Though only twenty-seven years old, Linky had accumulated a mountain of debt—some £230,000 (about $24 million today) from horse racing alone. Linky was a deceitful, spendthrift drunkard; Queen Victoria called him "worthless." He even extorted extra money out of Henry Thomas just before the wedding.

Linky's immediate family was also beset by disorder. His parents were divorced, his estranged father a dour character, his mother half-mad, his sister an opium addict, and his brother a transvestite. Given Linky's behavior, the Hope fortune could very well be squandered and the diamond, so ardently contested, lost.

When Henry Thomas Hope died in 1862 his widow, Anne Adéle Hope, inherited the estate at Deepdene, a collection of fine paintings, the castle at Blayney in Ireland, the London house on Piccadilly, and the Hope diamond.

When she finalized her will in 1876, she had two concerns—the Hope fortune and the family name. Normally, Adéle would have left the Hope family wealth to her daughter, Henrietta. But Henrietta's husband Linky, now the sixth duke of Newcastle, was living at the edge of bankruptcy. Adéle knew how hard her husband had fought for the family treasures and how little regard he had for Linky, despite the aristocratic title he conveyed to the family.

Adéle thus decided to skip a generation and leave the Hope treasures to Henrietta's children—her grandchildren—hoping they would be more capable than Linky of maintaining the family's legacy. She also decided to make them heirs not outright, but "tenants for life." This was a particular legal status. It meant that the Hope estates and heirlooms could not be easily sold off. They would be available for the use of the heir during his or her lifetime, but then had to be passed on, either to the descendants, or back to a sibling and his or her descendants. This, she thought, would assure continuity of the Hope treasures.

Adéle had labored long and hard for the legitimacy of her daughter and acceptance into the Hope family. With no son there was no one to carry the Hope name forward. Henrietta had five children: Beatrice, Archibald, Francis, Emily, and Florence. Archibald, the eldest male, would succeed his father as duke of Newcastle. So Adéle chose Francis, then only ten years old, as her primary heir, with the stipulation that he change his name to Hope upon reaching legal adulthood.

In 1879, Linky died. Henrietta remarried the next year, taking Thomas Theobald Hohler, a singer, as her husband. Given these circumstances, Adéle was dissuaded from changing her will. In 1884, Adéle died. To inherit, Francis had to wait three years, until he was twenty-one. On April 7, 1887, he became Lord Henry Francis Hope Pelham-Clinton-Hope ("Lord Francis"), and inherited the Hope home, castle, estate, art collection, and famous blue diamond.

The Hope diamond had been gathering fame as one of the

Henrietta Adéle Hope, duchess of Newcastle under Lyne.

largest and rarest of diamonds. Speculation about its origins had
increased since the 1851 London exposition. The prominent Victorian gemologist, Edwin Streeter wrote about the ill-luck that had
pursued diamond dealers like Tavernier, who first brought the blue
diamond back from India. His scholarly account was heavily influenced by a fictional detective story, *The Moonstone*, penned in 1868
by Wilkie Collins, a friend of Charles Dickens. That story featured
a yellow diamond—"the Moonstone"—which originally formed
the eye of a Hindu idol in an Indian temple. It was purloined from
the treasury of an Indian ruler by a thieving English soldier who
then incurred the curse of the god. Smuggled to the English countryside, the Moonstone was at the center of theft, kidnapping, and

murder. The god's curse followed the English possessors of the diamond until the Moonstone was rightfully returned to India and set into the eye of the idol from which it originally came. Collins based his story on tales of the Orloff diamond and an incident described in Tavernier's travelogue. *The Moonstone* was, in part, a moral commentary on colonialism, as symbolized by the British acquisition of the fabulous Koh-i-Nur diamond for Queen Victoria—literally, the "jewel in the crown."

Understandably, with more large named diamonds from India coming into public view, and Orientalist stories of "cursed diamonds" becoming something of a fashion, newspapers and other popular accounts often conflated the diamonds and their stories. A *New York World* article in 1888 reported that

> *The Hope Diamond [is] the property of an English gentleman of that name, who brought it from India. Its history is surrounded with wild traditions of the East, and more than once it has been stained with blood, lost and recovered, bought and sold, stolen and yielded as ransom. It has gleamed in the gem encrusted turbans of the great Maharajas, hung on the breasts of odalisques, and is said once to have formed the single eye of a great idol.*[6]

Concocted stories like this had no historical basis whatsoever, yet contributed to the renown of the diamond, and, not insignificantly, to its worth.

❖ ❖ ❖

Now, in London, as unlikely as it seemed given his wealth, privilege, and entitlement, Lord Francis was courting May Yohe, a talented girl of humble origins from America. Lord Francis could not possibly have imagined where his infatuation with May would take him.

For her part, May was on the threshold of unimaginable fame and fortune. She was to embark on an amazing personal and professional journey, traversing distances far greater than her voyage across the Atlantic.

*Pit and gallery joined the wildest
demonstration ever given in a London
theater, when men threw pocketbooks
and women their jewels at my feet!*
—*May Yohe*[1]

CHAPTER FIVE

My Honey

MAY'S STAGE CAREER TOOK OFF IN LONDON. As one astute commentator noted about her, "with the witchery of her voice, her *beauté du diable* and her *chic* little figure, she comes triply armed to conquer."[2] Her success benefited from Lord Francis' help, but was sealed when May entertained and charmed English audiences with a superb performance on January 19, 1893, for the opening at the Lyric Theatre of a comic opera, *The Magic Opal.*

The Lyric, newly opened in 1888, was a handsome 1,300-seat theater in London's West End. Comic opera was flourishing as entertainment. Also known as "light opera," it replaced a form of bawdier burlesque, translated French operettas, and more improvisational comedic theater. It was perfected by the partnership of W. S. Gilbert and Arthur Sullivan, whose polished, well-staged story-telling resonated with Victorian audiences entertained by the clever, if transparent farces, parodies, and commentaries of *H. M. S. Pinafore* (1878), *Pirates of Penzance* (1879), and *The Mikado* (1885).

The Magic Opal was crafted by the Spanish composer Isaac Albéniz based upon a text by the English librettist Arthur Law and produced at the direction of Horace Sedger, the manager of the

Lyric Theatre, London, 1889.

Lyric Theatre. The year before, Sedger had worked with W. S. Gilbert to produce *The Mountebanks* at the Lyric.

The Magic Opal is set in Greece, though its music is decidedly Iberian and Andalusian. A love story, it provided fodder for May's later myth-making. In the convoluted plot, a brigand chief, Trabucos, is in love with Lolika, the daughter of Aristippus, a wealthy merchant. Lolika, though, is in love with Alzaga, son of the town's pompous mayor, Carambollas. The rebel and the mayor's son compete for Lolika's affection. She disdains the rebel Trabucos, who has Alzaga kidnapped and sent away to the mountains. Trabucos then plots to gain Lolika's affection by stealing back a magic opal ring previously stolen from him. The opal ring, in the mayor's private collection, has the power to make the wearer fall in love with a person of the opposite sex when they touch—though no one save Trabucos knows of that power. As townspeople gather for the wedding, the mayor gives the magic ring to his daughter as a present. Trabucos' sister Martina (played by May), is disguised as a peddler

Newspaper illustration of a scene from The Magic Opal *at the Lyric Theatre, 1893.*

in the crowd. She steals the ring from Lolika's hand, substituting a counterfeit. The mayor touches Martina, falls hopelessly in love with her, and proposes marriage to this seeming vagabond, to the shock of the crowd. The two-act play continues as characters inadvertently fall in and out of love with each other as the ring is worn by different women.

May sang a duet with Trabucos, played by Wallace Brownlow, and also performed a solo, in which she lamented the hardships of the peddler's itinerant life. Overall, the play was well received, so much so that Sedger, within weeks, put together a second company that performed it in Glasgow, Edinburgh, Manchester, Brighton, Leeds, Liverpool, and Newcastle.

Reviews of May's performance were particularly noteworthy. One critic noted May's excellent contralto song sung "with a remarkably powerful though, at present, somewhat rough voice." Another found that "the four notes of her voice—deep and gruff as that of a basso—fairly astonished critics and audience alike. But it was novel, and Miss Yohe is graceful and pretty and so she and her voice were at once accepted as awfully fetching."[3]

Newspaper illustrations of The Magic Opal, *1893.*

The impression May made on the audience and even those on the theater staff was memorable. "The Call Boy," an anonymous commentator on the London theatrical scene recalled:

The lady is the olive-complexioned, hazel-eyed, neat-fig-ured, uncommon-voiced beauty who, in the character of a gipsy, stole away my heart on the first night of The Magic Opal at the Lyric on Thursday, January 19th, 1893; at which time, at which house, and in which piece, Miss May Yohé made her bow to an admiring British Public.[4]

The great playwright, critic, and future Nobel prize-winning author George Bernard Shaw also reviewed the play. His praise of May's performance was all the more impressive given his trenchant critique of the opera itself and the other leads.

The only success of the first night was made by a Miss May Yohe, who, though she spoke the American language, actually had not ordered her florist to deliver half his stock to her across the footlights. She is personally attractive; her face, figure, and movements are lively and expressive and her voice is extraordinarily telling: it sounds like deep contralto; but the low notes beneath the stave, which are powerful in a normally trained contralto, are weak; and she has practically no high notes. But the middle of her voice, which she uses apparently by forcing her chest register, is penetrating and effective.[5]

Shaw pegged Yohe's distinctive, trademark voice. Another called it a "steam calliope contralto."[6] When one inquirer asked who trained her "extraordinary voice," May responded, "Its owner." A follow-up question asked, "Do you know Miss Yohe that yours is the sort of voice that goes right to the heart?" "Is it?" she said, "Well perhaps that is because it comes straight from it, or at least, from the chest, which is somewhere in the same neighbourhood."[7]

Throughout her career, Yohe was said to have a limited vocal range with a small number of notes. Indeed, the notes in her repertoire became a metaphor for various accomplishments and setbacks on and off stage. When she added a romantic conquest, commentators would write that she added a note; when beset with a financial downturn, critics would say she lost one.

The rich tone and foghorn quality of her voice, coupled with her delicate stature, placed her in a wonderfully ambiguous, alluring position. The contralto is the deepest female singing voice in the classical theater. Parts could be sung by females or by male *castrati*, male singers in Italian opera who were castrated before their larynxes matured. Contraltos may play female parts, but more often female villains or "trouser roles"—adolescent or feminine

Newspaper caricature of May Yohe in
The Magic Opal, *1893.*

males. As *cognoscenti* say, contraltos play "witches, bitches, or britches." May's voice was intriguing because it seemed to cross and conflate gender lines, creating a dramatic tension between her and the audience. If her voice came from her heart, was it male or female? How was its sexuality heard by her listeners? And what did it then say about their sexuality?

T. H. L., a theater critic, contemplated the question and captured the sensual effect of May's performance upon the audience:

> *That voice of hers has often puzzled me. Why does it fix you in your seat, rivet your whole attention, and somehow stir your heartstrings as they have rarely been touched before? The jeunesse dorée in the stalls actually sprang to life under its quickening vibration, while the gallery boys went mad over it.*[8]

Though accolades for May's performance were considerable, praise was not universal. An artist for one of London's illustrated weeklies made fun of May, depicting her as an awkward amateur and reflecting what seemed to be some anti-American sentiment.

Despite the good reviews and requests from other theaters for the touring show, *The Magic Opal* had a disappointing run of only forty-four shows before closing at the Lyric on February 27, 1893. Theater finances, rather than quality, proved its undoing. The production expenses for the show were inordinately large, and high ticket prices kept audiences below the size needed to break even. This was a problem not uncommon for theaters of the time; indeed newspapers often published commentary about how music hall entertainment was drawing off audiences and revenue from the theater. The *Sunday Chronicle* parodied Horace Sedger's problem:

> *Dear O-pal, costly O-pal,*
> *Dear O-pal, costly O-pal.*
> *Making for Sedger,*
> *A hole in the ledger;*
> *Give us one better than dear Opal.*[9]

Sedger responded by asking Albéniz to revise the play, which he did by April. Characters and some numbers were eliminated; the plot was simplified. Interestingly enough, the title was changed to *The Magic Ring*. This was a concession to a popular belief that opals were cursed—something that may have dissuaded audiences from attending the show, or at least accepting its story line. That belief had originated as a superstition invented by Hungarian and Slovak mine owners in an effort to keep Australian opals off of the European market in the early nineteenth century. Sir Walter Scott based his 1829 novel *Anne of Geierstein* on that superstition, and it became part of popular culture thereafter.

May appeared neither in the touring company nor in the retitled production. Instead, she starred as the lead in *Mam'zelle Nitouche*, which opened at the competing Trafalgar Square Theatre on May 6, 1893, and ran through the summer. Called a "vaudeville opérette," this is really an operetta within an operetta. First produced in Paris a decade earlier, it was written by Henri Meilhac and Albert Milaud.

The story is set in nineteenth-century France, where a mischievous and playful young convent girl, Denise de Flavigny,

May Yohe as Denise in Mam'zelle Nitouche, *1893.*

discovers that Célestin, the organist and music teacher, secretly composes operettas for his lover Corinne. Denise gets Célestin to take her to a performance in town. A quarrel between the two lovers forces Denise to take the stage under the name of Mam'zelle Nitouche. Denise proves adept, starring in the performance, and then falls in love with a young soldier named Fernand.

The role of Denise was a joyful (if somewhat narcissistic) one for May. It recalled her playful innocence at the Dresden girls'

Newspaper illustration showing May Yohe in Mam'zelle Nitouche, *1896*

school and affirmed her confidence in her own talent. Her performance again charmed London theater aficionados. "She possesses many of the qualifications required for a successful impersonation of Nitouche," wrote the *Times'* theater critic.

> She has a pleasing vivacity, a pretty voice, and no little espiéglerie. At times her gestures are somewhat brusque; but, on the whole, her performance has the merit of refinement. Miss Yohe's success on Saturday was unequivocal, repeated encores manifesting the appreciation of the audience.[10]

Another critic wrote,

> This very vivacious actress [May Yohe] at once leapt into favour in the part. Her tireless spirits, her rich fresh voice, the feverish energy of her electrical style at once challenged

attention, compelled amusement and extorted admiration.
Unmitigated silliness is the characteristic of the piece—a
jumble of exaggerated conventualism flanked by distorted
Bohemianism—but the actress is equal to gracing the petty
and obscuring the inane . . . Miss May Yohe is an important
acquisition to the London stage, and for bringing her thus
prominently forward the clumsy stupidities of 'Nitouche'
must be excused.[11]

By September 1893, May was again on stage at the Lyric Theatre playing the title role in *Little Christopher Columbus*, a burlesque opera with a poor, convoluted plot, where the action, song,
and spectacle move from Cadiz, Spain to Chicago's Columbian
Exposition.

May plays the young Christopher, a Spanish lad serving as a
cabin boy on an American vessel who jumps ship to be with his
sweetheart Guinevere during the celebration in Cadiz of Columbus'
400th anniversary of the discovery of America. Guinevere is the
daughter of Silas Black, the millionaire "Bacon King of Chicago,"
who would rather have his daughter marry a duke than fall in
love with this young Columbus. After being arrested and extra-
dited, and swapping clothes and identities with Pepita, a dancing
girl, Columbus and Guinevere end up on the Midway in Chicago,
where it is revealed that Columbus is, after all, the long-lost son
of the duke of Veragua. All ends well with a number of senseless
diversions, choruses, costumes, and dances.

May's return to the Lyric was no doubt aided by Lord Francis,
who had become a part-owner of the theater. Whether by virtue
of Lord Francis' fiscal clout or May's track record as a rising star
among London audiences, she strongly asserted her will on the
production.

Eva Moore, who played the dancing girl Pepita in the opera,
recalled in her memoir that May continually denigrated the performance of other actresses in order to be the center of attention:

May Yohe played "Christopher," and played it very well too;
I impersonated her, in the action of the play. We had to
change clothes, for reasons which were part of the plot. She
was not an easy person to work with, and she certainly—at
that time, at all events—did not like me.[12]

May Yohe in Little Christopher Columbus,
1893.

The account rings true. May squabbled with the musical director, complaining about her songs, the staging, and the roles of other
actresses. As reported at the time, "At the Lyric Theatre, it was soon
apparent that Miss Yohe was absolute queen."[13] The music director
was forced to resign. He sued, asserting in his court testimony that
the conflict revolved around the refusal of May Yohe "to be bound
by the ordinary rules of the establishment."[14]

It was a re-occurring theme; May wasn't one for rules or
boundaries. As one of her fellow actors said, she was "intensely
jealous of anybody getting applause beside herself" and "repeatedly threatened to leave the company."[15] Sir Henry James Wood, an
honored conductor of the period, called May the "most extraordinary *prima donna* I have ever met."[16] As reported in the newspapers, Ivan Caryll took the music director's place and rewrote "all
the songs to Miss Yohe's peculiar compass and by degrees cut out
everybody else's songs until she was able to shine alone."[17]

Music sheet cover showing May Yohe in Little Christopher Columbus, *c. 1893.*

May's recounting of *Columbus'* opening night made her out to be the toast of London. Among her musical numbers was "Oh Honey, My Honey," known in the day as a "coon song." Performances of "Negro Pickaninny" bands depicting somewhat exotic scenes of Southern life were becoming exceedingly popular on Broadway at the time and would later flourish on Tin Pan Alley and with singers like Lillian Russell. May took full advantage of her opportunity with this genre piece imported from her own country across the Atlantic. These songs, racist by today's standards, used the purportedly natural sensuality of African Americans to express the romantic feelings of middle-class whites repressed by Victorian morality.

Dressed in her *faux* plantation costume, May belted out what was to become her theme song in a deep-throated, sultry way.

Oh, honey, my honey, 'tis a dark and stilly night
And only the stars can see,
Won't you wander through the grove by the pale starlight
And whisper a word to me?
Where the shadows all lie deep
Oh, so quietly we'll creep
Not a little bird shall hear us in its nest upon the tree
Oh, honey, my honey, while the other darkies play,
While the merry banjo's ringing
And the darkie girls are singing,
Come and listen to the music far away!
Oh, come, my love, come with me
Oh, come, my love, come with me,
You shall nestle to my breast
And we'll dream awhile and rest
While we listen to the music far away
Oh, honey, my honey, if the night would only last,
And never the daylight come,
In a love-dream we would live while our hearts beat fast
And only our lips were dumb.
All alone, my dusky queen
We would live and love unseen,
'Mid the singing of the woodbirds and the insects'
drowsy hum,

Oh, honey, my honey, while the other darkies play . . .[18]

The effect on the audience was stunning. May wrote that when she sang the number,

> *Pit and gallery joined the wildest demonstration ever given in a London theater, when men threw pocketbooks and women their jewels at my feet and down from the gallery came that rare tribute, the show of programs which is the final approval.*[19]

George Bernard Shaw, who criticized May's overall acting performance as lacking in comic genius and a bit too vulgar, nonetheless was again fascinated by the extraordinary register of her voice as well as the spirit in which she rendered her song, "which took her completely out of her forced role of burlesque actress, and gave her an opportunity of appealing to the audience on the imaginative and sentimental side."[20]

Ironies abounded in May's performance and perhaps captured some of the underlying tensions of the Victorian era. Here were audiences, proud of the British Empire, applauding an American. Here were patrons, aspiring to English middle-class respectability and propriety, hooting for May singing a song born of presumably backward, plantation slavery. Here was May lauded for her beauty, yet saluted and celebrated for playing a young boy.

May's physical features mirrored the intrigue about her voice. Her skin color was described as "striking," being of a "rich and radiant darkness that has something weird about it."[21] It was often attributed to her supposed descent from an American Indian mother. Her raven hair, big black eyes "that flash at one a volley of rays,"[22] and small form made her appear both powerful and delicate. Her "shapely limbs," "go and glow," "serene depth of confidence," and "brilliant bravado" animated her graceful movement.[23] She was called a "wild child of lavish nature," a "pert Pocahontas of lyric art," "contemporary society queen," and "enslaver of men."[24] In some cases May felt she had to tone down her femininity in "goody goody London."[25]

Indeed, a thread of Victorian morality opposed to more risqué theatrical displays ran through the press—as one aristocratic

Enameled cigarette case featuring May Yohe in Little Christopher Columbus.

Lady argued, "This letting women make public merchandise of the beauty of their bodies is the gravest insult and dishonor put upon women in our time."[26] Not that May really minded. Yet, May said "boy's parts" such her role in *Little Christopher Columbus* were what she liked best and what really captivated Lord Francis—and no doubt others. Cute, vulnerable, and seducible as a boy, brashly feminine as a woman, May was incredibly appealing to her largely male audiences.

Not everyone was convinced. There were critical laments about the show marking "the lowest attainable level of theatrical enterprise," and accusing it of "unrelieved vacuity."[27] Overall, though, *Little Christopher Columbus* turned out to be a huge hit

Player's Cigarettes.

MAY YOHÉ in "Little Christopher Columbus."

May Yohe depicted on a cigarette card.

with an eventual run of 421 performances. It generated a cottage industry of products—cigarette cases, souvenir plates, and other paraphernalia graced by May's image.

May became a kind of "pin-up" girl for men at Cambridge and Oxford; a verse published in *Granta* captured some of the adulation:

> *There's a Trinity man whom I know. He*
> *Had photographs all in a row. He*
> *Had one of Mama,*
> *And one of Papa,*
> *And about 25 of May Yohe.*[28]

While May delighted men, she also intrigued some women who were entranced by her slim-necked, deep-voiced sensuality, as this 1895 poem by one "Sister Olive" shows:

You butterfly!
You singing bird!
You dainty sweet,
Sweet woman with the dancing feet!
At sight of you, I know not why,
All tenderest little thoughts are stirred
In my soul's depths—when you flash by.
I love you at each swift heart-beat,
Yet sit and never say a word—
So many "loves" thrill thus unheard.
O! little throat,
So slim and white!
Dear voice as deep,
Restful, and wonderful as sleep—
Our whole souls ache at each full note,
Fall faint with rapture, swoon to flight,
And follow where your love-songs float!
And learn to laugh and long and weep,
In slumberous calm shut safe from blight,
Strange, dreamful singing, brief delight;
Good-night, good-night![29]

May was a public figure who dramatically exposed tensions in British society over matters of nationality, sexuality and respectability. She was a humble American, yet a refreshingly London presence, a woman who flaunted her sensuality, yet did so by playing males. May was viewed as a boisterous character in a profession that placed her at the edge of social respectability, and her romance with Lord Francis was aimed at the heart of a staid and insecure aristocracy. These tensions increasingly came to the fore, played out both publicly and privately in May's battles with the Newcastle clan.

What's a poor girl to do?
I'm sure I can't help it—could you?
To be young and pretty
Seems almost a pity
But it has its advantages too!
—May Yohe[1]

CHAPTER SIX

Aristocratic Artist

WITH MAY ON STAGE AND IN THE SPOTLIGHT, the London press was awash with notices about Lord Francis and May. If Lord Francis married May, one day she would likely be the duchess of Newcastle. The fact that she was a theatrical performer, an "ex-chorus girl," who might enter the highest level of the British aristocracy was news—and scandalous to more conservative members of society. This contrasted with the American press, which gushed: "still another triumph is included in this capture of a British lord by an American girl...which must naturally thrill our American pride of nationality."[2]

In August 1893, rumors began to circulate that the couple had been married. The source of the rumor was May herself, "whose evidence might be thought conclusive were it not for the fact that it is not the first time she has claimed to have entered into the bonds of matrimony and found it difficult to support that claim," wrote one astute reporter.[3]

Thus began the battle between May and the Pelham-Clinton-Hope family of Newcastle in the newspapers. Francis' family and friends strenuously denied the rumor of marriage, declaring it to be "nonsense." They did not deny Lord Francis' interest in May—a friend of the couple even reported to the press that May and Lord Francis were "intimate friends."[4] No one doubted it.

The Newcastle clan acknowledged that Lord Francis was helping May with her stage career. In fact they chided him for having "squandered" large amounts of money to "advance her fortunes." Lord Francis was going broke, and helping May was one reason for his "unfortunate pecuniary situation," they said.[5] Lord Francis had not only invested in the Lyric Theatre, he had also bought a major share in the *Morning,* a London newspaper, to tout May and promote her career. He produced posters featuring her image that hung in many of the shops and advertised her performances.

The issue of English aristocrats marrying wealthy Americans was amply discussed in the British press and in high society. A number of high-profile lords had taken American wives, presumably for good reason. These were high-society "Newport [Rhode Island] brides," Americans with good family connections and with money who could help sustain impoverished noble family trees. Such was the case not only in England, but also on the Continent.

The British were quite conscious of the American duchess of Manchester, the American countess of Essex, the American baronesses of Abinger, Vernon, and Playfair, and the American marchioness of Anglesea. To those British-American unions would soon be added the marriage of Consuelo Vanderbilt to the duke of Marlborough for a settlement to the groom of about $3 million (or about $75 million in today's currency). While these matches occasioned press stories, gossip, and serious commentary, they were understandable.

Less understandable in England were the dalliances of the nobility, particularly the fondness of profligate ne'er-do-well aristocrats for showgirls. There were a number of them. The "weak" Lord Dunlo met his bride Belle Bilton at a late-night dance club and married her the next day, whereupon she became the countess of Clancarty. The marquis of Allesbury, who had mortgaged his family estate and been involved in several swindling schemes, married Dolly Tester of the music hall stage, making her the marchioness. The disowned Viscount Hinton, who sold off most of his inherited possessions, married ballet dancer Lydia Ann Sheppey. And there were many more. These cases were regarded as examples of the

May Yohe, 1893.

May Yohe, 1893.

emotional foolishness of degenerate dandies, a sign of amorality, instead of the pragmatism of a financially weakened nobility.

One friendly newspaper account distanced May from the realm of these foolish affairs:

> *Lord Francis Hope's marriage to May Yohe cannot be considered to possess the same features as the mesalliances of*

*the others mentioned. In the first place, May is an actress of
the legitimate stage, a young woman of many accomplishments . . . She knows more in a minute than her husband,
who is a particularly boyish young fellow of twenty-five, will
in all his life.*[6]

Another story praised May's competitive edge. "Miss Yohe, an
American exponent of leg opera, has beaten her English stage sisters at their own game."[7]

The Newcastle family fired back. They hired an investigator
to examine and discredit May's past. A newspaper article revealed
one of their findings, her rumored marriage to Jack Mason: "At one
period in her checkered career she possessed a *bona fide* husband
from whom she has never been legally separated."[8]

One of Lord Francis' relatives publicly declared that he "was
sure that foolish as the boy [Francis] had been, he had not committed that crowning act of folly!"[9] Francis' mother, Henrietta Adéle
Hope, the dowager duchess of Newcastle, was dead set against the
marriage. The attractive Henrietta had been born out of wedlock,
had been purposefully wedded to gain a title, and had, of her own
volition, married a singer, Theobold Hohler, soon after the death
of her husband, the duke nicknamed "Linky." These were all char-
acteristics that may have otherwise allowed her to identify with
May's struggle for legitimacy. However, Hohler died in 1892, and
Henrietta, influenced by a charismatic priest, had an epiphany of
sorts. She converted to Roman Catholicism and increasingly became devoted to the Church, to simple, almost monastic living,
and to community service. She was put off by May's madcap reputation for loose morals.

To dissuade Francis from the folly of marriage, his family offered
him between £200,000 and £300,000, more than $1 million dollars
then, and now worth about $30 million, "on the sole condition that
he breaks off absolutely forever this connection to May."[10]

The family was clearly worried about their reputation and the
drain on Hope's fortune. A commentator noted:

*Unlike most wealthy Englishmen of his age, Hope is a quiet
young man, who goes in for business . . . Yet young Hope will
find his income is none too large if he continues to support
May Yohe, a theater and a newspaper.*[11]

Sketch of Dowager Duchess Henrietta Hope, c. 1894.

May was up against the full force of the Hopes and the Pelhams of Newcastle. What the Hopes had fought for so hard for three generations—aristocratic status—May Yohe was now taking for a song; respectability, so long sought by Henry Thomas, Adéle, and Henrietta, would suffer from associations with the tawdry music hall. May's standing did not fit at all with Henry Thomas' "Young England" vision of the nation, which he had defined as a politician with a young Benjamin Disraeli. That movement, now somewhat anachronistic but coloring the family's ideology, had called for conservative social values, a strong monarchy, high church religion, and a responsible and charitable aristocracy. May's music hall cavorting was anathema to the conservative Hopes.

The Pelhams of Newcastle, too, were conservative, despite the dysfunctions that characterized the family. The duke, Archibald, no doubt influenced by his mother, was the President of the English Church Union, a leader of the High Church Party, and a member of the London School Board. He sought a more moral, religious England. Furthermore, he and the Newcastle family were still enmeshed in complicated financial dealings that threatened their estate and standing. The treasure, already squandered by his father Linky, and saved by the Hopes, could now lost all over again merely to promote the career of the American interloper.

May's lifestyle simply did not fit the ideals professed by these Victorian aristocrats. Though she never said it herself, May was a dramatic example of the "new woman" of the 1890s, a breed heralded in English and American progressive writing of the time. Contrary

May Yohe, 1894.

to the more conservative Victorian ideal of woman as mother and as nurturing, passive angel of the home, the "new woman" worked outside of the home and was independent, assertive, and sensual. Many writers and commentators associated her with modernity itself, a new egalitarianism of the sexes, consistent with the drive by suffragists and suffragettes to gain the vote and the same rights as men. The "new woman" had several variants; the "wild woman" was one. She would be zestful, youthful, humorous, audacious, even shocking, and not shy about her own gratification, sexual and otherwise. Overall, she would not only be willing to cross the boundaries of convention, but would also possess an uncontrollable desire to do so. May, as an attractive, outspoken "new woman," and Lord Francis, as an undisciplined, degenerate Victorian dandy, would make for a dynamic, voracious, almost destructive pair.

Speculation about the couple accompanied the run of *Little Christopher Columbus* with its play on ducal marriage. One headline called May the "Comic Opera Duchess."[12] Another wondered whether May would be properly received by Queen Victoria at court. Some saw the theater and May's association with it as a threat to English civilization. The discordance of May at court provoked all sorts of commentary, some quite iconoclastic, reflecting what many recognized as the contradictions and hypocrisy of Victorian respectability beset by a rampant, scandalous aristocracy. Yet May seemed to rise above the clamor by virtue of her talent and force of personality. She performed a burlesque opera for the duke of Edinburgh and the Prince of Wales at a dinner hosted by Arthur Sullivan—and the royals were reportedly "delighted." When he heard about the possible marriage, Lord Carnarvon, a young and risqué English peer (later the sponsor of the excavations of the tomb of the Pharaoh Tutankhamen) who knew May from her backstage parties, captured the irony, "Well, we are honored, indeed: her ladyship's adjectives would even make a marine blush."[13]

In 1894, the *Washington Post* reported that the couple had been married. By March, the Windsor *Peerage*, a publication on the British aristocracy, announced that May and Lord Francis had been married. May immediately issued a denial.

Years later, May revealed what happened. That March, Lord Francis took May to his shooting box outside of London over a weekend. Francis asked May to marry him "in a peculiar way"— with a five-month "probationary" marriage. As May explained,

If at the end of the five months I still loved him we would be married formally. If by that time I had found him wanting and had grown tired of him, or found someone I liked better, I could leave and forget him.[14]

May also asked Francis, "Will you be bound by the same privilege—that if you are disappointed with me you will withdraw on your part?"[15] Francis agreed, and so the two later announced their engagement to a small group of friends and told them also that they would begin to live together.

May rented a lovely cottage in Maresfield Gardens, Hampstead, just outside of London at the time. Here, as May says, "Lord Francis came to be husband and suitor at the same time."[16]

A few weeks later, on her birthday, May recalled a behatted Francis coming into her boudoir one night as she was preparing for bed. May suspected a surprise, and when she lifted the hat, she found a case containing a string of gorgeous, pear-shaped, perfectly matched pearls. He told her they cost $350,000. The pearl necklace became, in May's words, "Aladdin's Lamp," as Francis soon "showered" her with rare and expensive gems from every corner of the globe. For May, her time with Francis was like "a lover's dream."

During this "probation" period Lord Francis was as careful in his attentions to me as if he were indeed, just a suitor for my hand. He was with me constantly, and took me everywhere. His kisses never lost their warmth. We never spoke of our being together as a "trial."[17]

While May and Francis were certainly lovers there was a familial aspect to their relationship. To some extent, Francis was like a father to May—the attentive, nurturing, provider she never enjoyed as a child. He looked after her needs and took care of her. Francis showered May with gifts, money and affection. On the other hand, May was like a mother to Francis, taking care of him, guiding him in matters of relationships, and playing the diva figure to his proud delight.

In August, an exhausted May took time off from *Columbus* to go yachting and prepare for her next role. By October 1894, May was starring in a new, well-received operetta, *The Lady Slavey*. The story line uncannily presaged her future. May plays Phyllis, who must go

May Yohe in Lady Slavey.

to work as a domestic "slave" to keep her bankrupt father from his creditors. In it she sings "What Is a Poor Girl to Do?" a catchy song by Jack Watson that immediately became a popular hit:

> *Was there any poor girl so run after?*
> *I can't imagine why it should be so;*
> *It's enough to make me split my sides with laughter,*
> *When I think of how my "mashers" come and go;*
> *Ev'ry time that I'm sent out to do the shopping*
> *Half a dozen I am almost sure to meet,*
> *One by one they slyly up to me come hopping,*
> *They await me at the corner of each street! Well,*
> *What's a poor girl to do?*
> *I'm sure I can't help it—could you?*
> *To be young and pretty*
> *Seems almost a pity,*
> *But has its advantages too![18]*

May Yohe as Lady Slavey.

It is hard to understand how Lord Francis' precarious situation —amply reported on by the English press—did not cross May's mind as she sang this song and performed in the play. In June, the English papers and even the *New York Times* reported that Lord Francis had filed a statement of bankruptcy with reported assets of £104,042 and liabilities of £405,277. Yet May wore her precious jewelry, gifts of Lord Francis and other admirers—gifts worth "a King's ransom." She would drive up to the theater in the "neatest of broughams with a coachman in livery and accompanied by her maid" and dine regularly at the Savoy.[19]

Lord Francis Hope and May Yohe as a young couple.

On November 27, 1894, Francis arranged for a brief, quiet ceremony at the Hampstead Registry Office for him and May to be
formally married. A few close friends accompanied them. As May
wrote with the dreamy, fairy-tale exuberance of the Cinderella-like
characters she played,

> *If there was any change in Lord Francis after that noon
> time, it was only that now he had become in sight of all the*

The duke of Newcastle's Clumber Castle, Nottingham, c. 1900.

world my really true husband. And for me—well, now I was
Lady May, on the way to becoming one of the proudest and
richest duchesses in the British Empire, the mistress of half
a score of wonderful castles and palaces—the Maysie of "Oh
Honey, My Honey" transformed into a peeress of the realm
and a prospective Her Grace!

Now I, the poor dressmaker's daughter, was in line for
the strawberry crown of a duchess, for my husband was heir
to the duke of Newcastle, one of the most conservative and
wealthiest dukes in the empire.

As the prospective Duchess of Newcastle, I was in line
to be mistress of famous Clumber Castle . . . filled with
old masters, wonderful furniture and art treasures of immense value . . . It contains ten beautiful old cabinets from
the Doge's Palace at Venice. On its walls hang Van Dyck's
"Rinaldo and Armida" . . . and a number of family portraits
by Sir Thomas Lawrence. Clumber is packed from garret to
cellar with art treasures, the Sevres and Dresden porcelain
being unrivalled. . .

The estate consists of 35,600 acres of land . . . The present Duke has built a splendid private chapel on his estate in
Gothic style. This is almost a cathedral in size . . . The Duke

has an income of $600,000 a year, largely due to coal mines on his property . . .

Lord Francis has inherited from his mother the great Deepdene Castle and estate . . . like Clumber, it contains many rare paintings and works of art. The Hope diamond also came to Lord Francis from his mother, who, as the daughter of a wealthy banker, Thomas Hope, brought a large fortune to the Newcastle family. The country residence of Lord Francis is Castle Blayney, in County Monaghan, Ireland.

All these became mine when I became Lady Hope.[20]

*I was envied by the richest and noblest of a great nation.
I was received in the most select circles. I was the rage
of London in the music halls and to me came not only
the highest salary ever paid an actress but the homage
of gifts. . . . I had a husband who, seemingly, adored
me. Yet almost from that first hour the course of fortune
changed until I was forced down through all the humili-
ations that can come to a proud woman.*
—May Yohe, recalling the period after her marriage[1]

CHAPTER SEVEN

Destitute Duchess

L ORD FRANCIS' FINANCIAL SITUATION was more dire
than it appeared to May and was captured in newspaper commentary:

> *Lord Francis Hope was married the other day to May Yohe,
> the young actress, and this week he has been spending part
> of his honeymoon in Froway, the unromantic precincts of
> bankruptcy courts. The proceedings showed that he badly
> needed someone to look after him, and he ought to be thank-
> ful that he has now got a clever young woman as his wife,
> who will be able to keep him out of the hands of money-
> lenders if any one can.*[2]

The situation led George Bernard Shaw to cleverly remark,
"He's Hope, and it's a cinch he has faith, seeing that he married
Yohe and she hasn't got a dollar in the world; so I guess it's a case
of Faith, Hope, and Charity"—referring to the three key Catholic
virtues.[3]

Lord Francis' checks at the Lyric Theatre were bouncing. He
couldn't pay for the *Morning*, his London newspaper. He tried

to sell a number of his family's paintings, but was stopped by his siblings, who claimed in court that if the sale went through, "the money would just be frittered away."[4] Lord Francis' debts at the bankruptcy proceedings were found to amount to more than £650,000, the equivalent of more than $3 million at the time and roughly $81 million today.

Hope argued that his financial troubles were largely caused by payments of succession duties, payments for the liabilities of family members, and interest paid to lenders. This was true, but much of his debt was also incurred by extravagant overspending, speculation in the theater business, and huge gambling losses.

The bankruptcy settlement was harsh. All of the income due Lord Francis from his estate was to go into a sinking fund, controlled by trustees, to pay off his debts. He was left with £2,000 annually to provide for himself and his wife. For many in England, this was a substantial amount, but it was totally inadequate to cover the couple's extravagant lifestyle. Among those expenses were the home in Hampstead, a yacht, several servants, and, of course, May's pets—a wheezy bulldog and a baby tiger. Seemingly oblivious to it all, the couple continued to sail in the Cowes regatta, race horses at Langtry, and dine at the Savoy.

❖ ❖ ❖

Meanwhile, May continued her role in *The Lady Slavey*. Reviews were mixed. Critic Henry Hibbert noted that May "gambols very agreeably through the part of the neat-ankled Phyllis. There is a crudity in her acting which is undeniably piquant; and her clarion voice—to my ear its timbre seems precisely that of a cornet-à-piston—is certainly unique, though its beauty may be open to question."[5]

Nonetheless, May was a celebrity. Her songs were sung and performed around London. Other actresses tried to imitate her contralto voice. Her stage costumes—especially those of *Little Christopher Columbus*—were inspiring fashion. A gold mine in South Africa was named after her. So too was a carnation: reddish-pink, sweetly fragrant, handsome in form, strong and vigorous in growth. This was somewhat ironic, as May couldn't stand to have flowers near her when she sang, claiming their perfume "utterly destroyed" her voice.

May Yohe, 1895.

With *Lady Slavey* winding down in January 1895, May was
ready to be introduced to London society as the prospective duchess of Newcastle. May claimed this happened at a dinner hosted by
Lord Alfred de Rothschild, scion of the famously wealthy Jewish
banking family, former head of the Bank of England, patron of the
arts, and close friend of the Prince of Wales. May wrote:

It was my first society recognition, and my presence caused a great sensation . . . I wore, for the first time, the great diamond . . . The Prince of Wales was to be a guest, but he arrived late. When he came in there already was a tacit agreement among the others that they would snub poor little May Yohe. The Countess de Mannin walked by me with her nose upraised, looking me over quite superciliously. The Duchess of Edinburgh . . . walked up to me, looked at me and walked away as stiff as you please.

But when the Prince came in what did he do but walk straight up to me. When I curtseyed he said: "So glad, Lady May, to see you here. Now I know we won't be dull. I don't know where they have put me but I hope they have put you beside me" . . . There was a scurrying about to see that I was placed beside him. Then it was funny how the Countess de Mannin and the Duchess of Coburgh-Gotha fawned upon me . . . be assured I snubbed them good and plenty.[6]

The dinner lasted until five o'clock the next morning, whereupon the Prince escorted her to the door. May wrote, "I was very happy when I went home that morning with the Hope diamond blazing about my neck." "After that I was as popular as Lady Francis Hope in society as I was as May Yohe on the stage."[7]

There is no corroboration that this dinner actually took place. There are, however, ample press accounts about the Prince of Wales attending May's performances; he came to *Little Christopher Columbus* at least twice. The prince had an eye for alluring young actresses, having had affairs with both Lillie Langtry and Sarah Bernhardt. He attended some of May's friendly backstage gatherings, and they appeared together in public several times. Once, May greeted the prince, "Shake, old cock of the walk—how do you do?"[8] The brazen familiarity shocked reporters, but lent some credence to May's account.

If the dinner led to May's acceptance in the upper realms of British aristocracy, there was a glaring exception—Lord Francis' own family, the Pelhams of Newcastle. Things were still cold between May and Lord Francis' brother, the reigning duke, her mother-in-law Henrietta Hope, and other relatives.

May's recounting of the dinner, written almost twenty-five years later, places the Hope diamond around her neck. That is almost surely a fiction, and raises doubt that the dinner ever happened. According to court documents filed by Lord Francis in late 1898, the Hope diamond had never been removed from a vault at Parr's Bank in Cavendish Square, where it had been deposited since 1894. Newspaper stories noted the prohibitive cost of insuring the Hope diamond and the measures required for its security. Lord Francis himself, decades later, declared to the press that May never wore the Hope diamond.

May could have been lying about wearing the gem. It would not by any means be her last fictional or apocryphal tale about the Hope diamond. More charitably however, she could have been exaggerating. Lying and exaggerating were both mainstays in her repertoire. The couple had a replica made of the Hope diamond, and May could have been wearing that costume jewelry diamond to the dinner—if it indeed occurred.

❖ ❖ ❖

Even as May sought acceptance into British high society, she nonetheless flaunted the fact that she was American. She relished her role as an "outsider." It evoked her devilish, roguish nature. Her brazen attitude stood in marked contrast to the American women sent by their extremely wealthy, status-aspiring, Gilded Age parents to marry failing British aristocrats and play their wedded roles dutifully and quietly. Not so for May. First, she married Lord Francis without a million-dollar dowry. She earned her position with her own wiles, not family wealth. "I am a real American," she'd always tell the press. "I am settled down in London for good—but I'm a real American for all that."[9] As if to exaggerate the point, she would often say she was "a real native American . . . I am not a Yankee—because my mother is an American Indian."[10] She even had that written in her theatrical biographies.

May was long planning to bring her stardom back to the United States. She envisioned a U.S. tour of *Little Christopher Columbus* even as she prepared for her next London stage role in *Dandy Dick Whittington*, where she was again playing the male lead. That production generated great interest from her admirers, with considerable competition for the good seats—and she was greeted with "a most enthusiastic reception" according to the *Times*.[11] But her performance generated some harsh reviews. One pointed to her theatrical extravagance.

May Yohe as Dandy Dick Whittington.

> *Then there is May Yohe, who, whenever she is not on the stage, must evidently be in the hands of her dresser, so many are the costumes in which she successively appears. As a London apprentice in brown velvet knickerbockers, as a sailor, as a midshipman, and as a jockey. And of course she sings a plantation song with lots of 'honey' in it.*[12]

Another provided a stronger, broader, more troubling indictment:

> *The star of May Yohe does not seem to be glittering so effulgently as of yore. Last season, she was the most discussed woman in London; her photographs were in the shop windows along Regent Street and the Strand; a life-size transparency of her swung from the wall of the Lyric Theatre.*
> *But now the novelty of the fact that she is Lady Hope is no more, and those strange few tones which emanate from her throat and remind one of the bullfrog when he is doing*

*his best, do not suggest at present to London Theatre-goers
the victorious song of the siren.*

*Possibly in a short time, when the old Duchess of Newcas-
tle is dead and Miss Yohe has succeeded to that title, she will
once more magnetize them. But at present, the burlesque,
Dandy Dick Whittington, in which she is appearing at the
Avenue is not attracting as many people as the management
could wish.*[13]

Income from the theater was not enough to right Lord Francis'
debt. In bankruptcy, his trustees came up with a plan to sell a portion of his lands at the Deepdene estate in Surrey. This wonderful
property with a beautiful mansion was being rented by Victoria
Cross awardee Lord William Beresford and his twice-widowed
American wife, Lillian Hammersley, née Price, the former duchess
of Marlborough. They agreed to the sale by the assurance company
holding Lord Francis' debt. Thomas Hope's lovely estate would
now be sold off in lots.

The trustees also wanted to sell the Hope diamond, even
though it was a family heirloom. According to the newspapers, they
hoped to get about £24,000 or approximately $13 million in today's
dollars for what one story described as a "rather ugly blue stone
about the size of a hen's egg"—not quite how May described the
blazing gem she said she'd worn at Rothschild's princely dinner.[14]

As the newspapers had it, Lord Francis had now "tumbled
into the deep abyss." [15] When Miss Yohe married him she pictured
herself living in his many fine houses, surrounded by luxurious
pleasures which would be her due as the wife of a noble lord. Now,
Lord Francis' creditors had put a stranglehold upon him. "May's
victory," declared one article, "has been an empty one."[16]

The assurance company sought to liquidate Lord Francis' assets to pay off his debts. By December 1895, while the diamond was
still unsold and resting in the Parr's Bank vault, the bankruptcy
was discharged. Now the couple had a fresh start. May took it upon
herself to earn income to support the couple, a fact bandied about
in the press. "Work for Lady Hope" blared the headline:

*May Yohe has seen all of this grandeur slip rapidly out of
her hands, and now she is preparing to go back to her old
work of wearing boys' clothes and singing topical songs in*

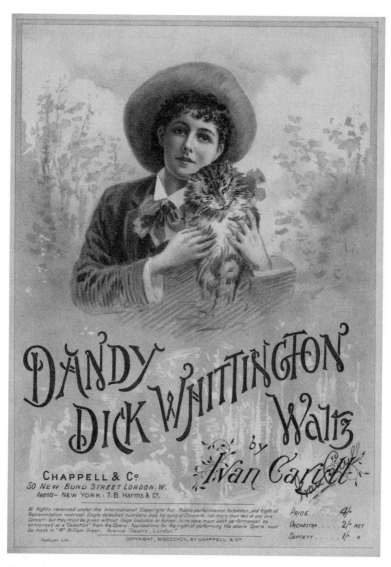

Music sheet cover depicting May Yohe in Dandy Dick Whittington.

The Hopes' Deepdene estate, Dorking, Surrey, England, c. 1891.

> *the concert halls of London. She is credited with being the*
> *best boy impersonator in London to-day and aside from her*
> *title, can command a good salary through real merit.*[17]

By the spring of the next year, May revived the previously successful *Mam'zelle Nitouche* at the Court Theatre in order to bring in income badly needed by the couple. She initially took on the lead role. It turned out to be a critical disaster. Wrote Hibbert of the production, "The comic opera has degenerated into a rough-and-tumble absurdity, with musical interludes of a music-hall type, in which Miss May Yohe . . . abandoned herself to a series of gambols which highly amused the audience, but stood in no definable relation to musical or histrionic art."[18]

Alan Dale, an American reviewer, was even more critical,

> *I went impelled by curiosity. I left amazed that critical*
> *London could possibly tolerate such a singularly second-*
> *class entertainment.*
>
> *Miss Yohe's voice has sunk into a husky whisper and the*
> *three notes she used to disport herself are now lamentably*
> *pallid and feeble . . . I confess I was totally unable to discover*
> *any excuse for Lady Hope's popularity.*[19]

The review by George Bernard Shaw, a one-time fan of May's, was even more devastating:

Miss May Yohe might, I think, have given us something fresher at the Court Theatre than a revival of Mam'zelle Nitouche. I take it that Miss Yohe is not now living by her profession . . .

Miss May Yohe is too clever—too much the expert professional—to be dismissed as a stage-struck fashionable amateur; but, on the other hand, there is nothing either in "Mam'zelle Nitouche" nor in the style of its performance to explain why any lady should step out of the aristocratic sphere to produce it . . .

Miss Yohe's own extraordinary artificial contralto had so little tone on the first night that it was largely mistaken for an attack of hoarseness; and her sentimental song, with its aborted cadence which sought to make a merit and a feature of its own weakness, was only encored, not quite intentionally, out of politeness. Her sustaining power seems gone: she breathes after every little phrase, and so cannot handle a melody in her old broad, rich manner; but doubtless the remedy for this is a mere matter of getting into condition.

As a comic actress she has improved since the days of "Little Christopher Columbus"; and the personal charm and gay grace of movement, with the suggestion of suppressed wildness beneath them, are all there still, with more than their original bloom on them. But with every possible abuse of the indulgence of which Miss Yohe can always count on more than her fair share, it is impossible to say that she removes the impression that the day for opera-bouffe has gone by.[20]

May must have found Shaw's critique especially biting. But she also respected what he had to say. By late 1896, she withdrew from the stage production as actress and singer—but she continued as manager and producer of the Court Theatre. She then, as she was wont to do, proved George Bernard Shaw wrong. Under May's management, the theater was "remarkably successful from a financial point of view" and she was soundly praised for her accomplishment.[21]

Given her series of starring roles, managerial responsibilities, and continual battles in the press, it was time for May to take a break. Another American woman, Lady Beresford, currently in favor with Queen Victoria, was in the limelight. Conan Doyle was working on a theatrical comedy. Gilbert and Sullivan were fighting with each other. Socialists were stirring up passions in London and on the continent. And Lord Francis was incurring more staggering debts. And though May was committed to star in a short-running production of *The Belle of Cairo* by year's end, she said she was through with the theater.

✣ ✣ ✣

May then did the thoroughly unexpected over the next two years. She started to do charity work with the poor. There was precedent: she had performed in benefit concerts in the United States, and in 1895 she'd sung in a charitable matinee for St. Mary's Hospital, held under royal patronage. But her interest became more serious and time-consuming. First May took up the cause of peasants living in the area of Castle Blayney, Lord Francis' mansion in Ireland, originally purchased by Henry Thomas Hope. A few months later, she started working with her mother-in-law, the dowager duchess Henrietta Adéle Hope, ministering to the poor in London's Whitechapel. These were no idle pursuits, for both locales were rough and tumble places in the midst of dramatic social change.

Castle Blayney (more like a manor house in size) was built on Hope land in County Monaghan, south of Ulster. Land and governance reforms were in the forefront of Irish politics in 1897–98, with local people gaining more say in their affairs.

We don't know why May got involved, but she may have taken her cue from author, philanthropist, and woman's rights activist May Augusta Ward. Yohe shared a name with this fiction writer of considerable repute and a profession with one of her characters. One of her books was about a theatrical figure. Another was about Marcella Maxwell, an independent-minded "new woman," who, while married to a wealthy husband, yearns to help the poor. Ward was also close to the very charitable Rothschild family, who supported many social reform causes among Jewish and Irish settlers in London's Whitechapel district.

May Yohe in The Belle of Cairo, *1896.*

May Yohe as a boyish soldier in The Belle of Cairo, *1895.*

Castle Blayney, the Hope estate in Ireland.

May also could have been influenced by Consuelo Vanderbilt. An American from a prominent, wealthy family, Vanderbilt had recently married the duke of Marlborough and was intent on helping the tenants on her husband's ducal estate. Yohe and Vanderbilt were often linked as the two most prominent Americans associated with the British aristocracy, and May could have sought to follow Vanderbilt's lead.

For whatever reason, May helped open up Hope's land for use by impoverished Irish peasants. While her effort met with some amusement in the London press, May apparently stayed with it for several months. Her work in Whitechapel was more intense. A teeming, squalid, urban slum, it was a dangerous place. Poverty bred crime, disease, and vice; police thought that there were more than a thousand prostitutes in the district. A decade earlier, Whitechapel was the scene of Jack the Ripper's infamous serial murders. George Bernard Shaw's socialist Fabian Society met in the slum in an explicit symbolic statement of the social ills and contradictions that beset Victorian England.

May worked with her mother-in-law, who maintained a humble residence at St. Anthony's House in the midst of the slum. Henrietta lived there most of the time. The dowager duchess, a rather striking, well-outfitted woman in her own right, sponsored charities, gave talks, and awarded prizes for good works. She was

May Yohe, c. 1898.

a Catholic English duchess who had joined the Tertiary Order of Franciscans, and thus taken a vow of poverty. She happily served the community to improve their lot "within their own class," and often said the rich got more out of serving the poor than the other way around.[22] She was a favorite of Queen Victoria.

May helped her mother-in-law raise money to rebuild the Whitechapel School by giving benefit performances, including one at the Aldegate public baths hall—a far cry from the Strand. According to press accounts, May was said "to be greatly beloved by those for whom she works."[23] Moreover, May gained the good graces and won the heart of her mother-in-law who had so opposed the marriage of her son to this American showgirl.

Forsaking the theater, working on her husband's Irish estate and with her mother-in-law in Whitechapel, even putting on weight, May, now about thirty-two, seems to have gone through a domestic phase. Rumors, perhaps started by her, suggested that she might be pregnant. If the rumors were true, she and Francis would have an heir, likely to become a succeeding duke of Newcastle, given that Archibald, the current duke, was childless. May's good works and attention to her new family evidently reached the palace, for a report suggested that Queen Victoria would be inclined to receive her at court should Francis succeed as duke and May become his duchess.

Despite the initial chilly reception from British society, May developed a cadre of distinguished friends, a mixture of theater people and aristocrats who gathered for Sunday afternoons or took trips to the nearby countryside. She tended to be the life of the party, outspoken, vivacious, and charming in a spirited way. As one of the group recalled, "May Yohe was one of the most amusing women one could meet, and she could keep a dinner table in roars of laughter for hours."[24]

❖ ❖ ❖

While May was doing charitable work and rehabilitating her image, Francis was squandering more and more money he didn't have. In July 1898, Francis was given permission by the court to sell off a valuable collection of eighty-three Dutch and Flemish paintings including Rembrandts, Rubens, and others to settle his debts. He appeared to be paying off his relatives to avoid their opposition. In 1899, again with a mountain of debt, he asked the Chancery Court for permission to sell the Hope diamond. He had a buyer lined up; L. M. Lowenstein & Co. had agreed to purchase it for about £18,000.

Hope's lawyers argued that he needed the proceeds to meet the demand of his creditors. Francis' brother, the duke, and his sister, Lady Beatrice Lister-Kaye, argued that the gem was a family heirloom and had come into Francis' possession only for his lifetime use, not for sale. It was unique and famous and bore the family name. It was willed to Francis with the explicit intention that it would be passed down in the family. There was no necessity to sell the heirloom save the extravagant spending of Lord Francis. His failure to control his appetite should not be enough to negate the intention of Lord Francis' grandmother in making him the heir to the diamond and her fortune. Should other relatives, like Lady Beatrice, one day inherit the diamond, they would surely do justice to its name and reputation, the Newcastle lawyers confidently predicted.

Francis' lawyers argued that the diamond was too big to wear and thus useless as an ornament. It should be sold, they said, rather than just sit in a safe for decades. It was a "mere curio" rather than a genuine heirloom, and besides, it hadn't been in the family all that long. It wasn't even that rare—other blue diamonds had recently been discovered.

Francis' lawyers pointed to the precedent of the court having allowed Lord Francis to sell off his Dutch and Flemish paintings for the benefit of the estate just the year before. They reminded the court that the permission of the other Pelhams and Hopes—the "remaindermen" as they were technically called—was not needed as the sale would benefit the tenancy in life by bringing cash into the inheritance. The Newcastle lawyers countered that, given Lord Francis' spending habits, he would quickly spend any cash the sale brought in.

Judge Byrne noted that the prior sale of Hope's paintings was justified because the paintings needed substantial funds for their constant upkeep, and would, if not sold, be endangered by Francis' bankrupt situation. The Hope diamond, on the other hand, was safe in a bank and required little or no care. The judge sided with Lord Francis' relatives and denied permission for the sale. Lord Francis appealed the decision to Lord Justice Romer and the Master of the Rolls, and lost again a few months later.

May, never shy about overstatement, mused that she might set the Hope diamond in a tiara.

❖ ❖ ❖

By the fall of 1899, the pressure on the marriage was building. Francis was overspending, and his brother and sister were outraged at his excesses. Despite May's good works, they probably put some of the blame on her. For her part, May increasingly found Lord Francis to be distant and unromantic; she would sometimes refer to him as "it."[25] The love in their marriage was clearly on the wane. May wrote:

> *I was happy, however, with my husband, despite certain shortcomings, of which, I suppose, every good man must have his share. Lord Francis liked to read a great deal—he used to read a book when I thought he ought to be reading me. He liked to hunt, too—and I often felt that he might have spent some of the time hunting ways to enamor me that he spent hunting ways of trapping animals or catching fish.*[26]

In September 1899, the London papers reported that the couple had separated. But by November, they were off on a so-called world tour; May called it a second honeymoon. For May, it was an attempt to revive the marriage. For Francis, it may have been a means of avoiding his creditors and his contentious family. They raised some money during their absence by renting Castle Blayney to the duke of Connaught, Queen Victoria's son.

The trip started aboard the Hope yacht at Cowes. Captain James Holford of the House Guard was among Lord Francis' guests for the send-off party. In the evening, he sidled up to May. He was clearly enamored, telling her, "you are the most beautiful little woman I have ever seen, Lady May. If your husband wouldn't object, I should like to send you a little souvenir to remember the evening by."[27]

With permission from the oblivious Francis, Holford later sent May a lovely diamond necklace with a large brilliant pendant and a note saying, "Wear it and think of us who love you for the splendid little woman that you are."[28]

The couple then traveled to South Africa, Ceylon, and Australia, where they took a house in Sydney's fashionable Pott's Point for about six months. They attended the theater there and in Melbourne, and May offered to sing in various benefits and patriotic

May Yohe, 1899.

matinees. Given their aristocratic standing, which was fairly uncommon in Australia, they were lauded and feted.

   In August 1900, they reached the United States. Whether for
want of money or fondness for the stage, May sought to return to
the theater. She and Francis negotiated an agreement to appear in
New York's Savoy Theatre later in the fall, and then at the Columbia Theatre in Boston, for a thirty-week run of an English musical
comedy. Newspapers reported her salary at more than $1,000 per

week and maybe as high as $1,750. This was astronomical for the times. Broadway's finest star, Lillian Russell, typically made about $1,250, and perhaps only the internationally acclaimed Sarah Bernhardt made more.

May and Francis then sailed from New York to England, and further apart. For Francis, it was a voyage back to respectability and for May the wildest ride of her life.

That instant I became the property,
body, soul and mind, of Putnam
Bradlee Strong!
—*May Yohe's recollection*[1]

CHAPTER EIGHT

New York's Finest Lover

H E WAS A STRIKING FIGURE in his dapper uniform, very military and romantic."[2] So wrote May about Captain Putnam Bradlee Strong, who was a fellow passenger of the Hopes on the Atlantic crossing to Southampton. Strong was the son of William L. Strong, the former Mayor of New York and mentor of Teddy Roosevelt.

May and Francis were accompanied by May's cousin, Thomas Parke, a Philadelphia broker. Strong befriended Tom and, through him, May. According to May, Strong became the "life of the ship." May spent time with him and heard from Tom that Strong greatly admired her. May was flattered, especially given Strong's youth; he was perhaps five to eight years her junior. As she later wrote, Strong was "a fascinating man, with a suave gallantry which charmed women. I never have known a woman who, after being thrown in Captain Strong's company for a while, did not fall in love with him—wife or maid or widow, it was always the same."[3]

Strong's courtship was masterful, something May herself recognized in the years to come. "Strong was a splendid conversationalist. He drew me out about my early experiences, and was

Putnam Bradlee Strong, c. 1900.

wonderfully sympathetic when I told him of my early troubles and enthusiastic when I recounted my successes."[4]

As the ocean liner made its way across the Atlantic, Lord Francis was oblivious to Strong's courtship of May and May's obvious delight in the attention. "Captain Strong was most respectful to him, and seemed to know just how to humor him," May wrote, and added:

He made no advances to me at all during the trip. Had he done so I would have repulsed him without hesitation. Instead though, he [Strong] talked to me of my husband, and congratulated me for keeping "an English Lord" in love with me. 'They are so careless about their women usually, you know,' he said, echoing just what was in my heart, 'and once they have caught them think the romance job is done.'[5]

Strong verbally seduced May, telling her that "a man should be a sweetheart always, planning to humor his wife, to surprise her with little unexpected attentions, to keep her on the same plane she occupied as his fiancé." He declared "You should be happy to have found a Britisher who still remains your lover."[6] For May, this was the clincher:

Of course, Captain Strong knew I hadn't found a Britisher who thought it worthwhile to still be my sweetheart. He just acted as if he thought that, knowing that he was hitting me in a vulnerable spot, without my realizing he knew. Unconsciously, I began to think how much happier I would be and how much brighter the world would be if my husband were as attentive and thoughtful as this Captain Strong evidently would be if he were in my husband's shoes.

When a woman begins to think of that comparison between her husband and another man, she is slipping. If the other man is clever, he will land her for the fall. And Captain Strong was beyond all things else clever.[7]

May recognized her own romantic vulnerability, and she knew she was about to land in England where her career was in shambles and her husband faced increased tribulations from his bankruptcy. Rather than restoring their marriage, the trip around the world confirmed its bankruptcy as well. She was indebted to Lord Francis and felt a true fondness for him. But she needed more. She was an attractive, vivacious, talented and accomplished woman in her early thirties. Strong's charms revealed a love-deprived heart yearning for true romance—and also provided the cure. May was clearly infatuated with Strong by the time they arrived on England's shore.

Lord Francis and Lady May were met in Southampton by Francis' elder brother Archibald, the duke of Newcastle. Archibald had arranged a special train to take them to London. Francis asked Strong to come along, telling the duke that he was "a good friend who made the trip across very pleasant for us."[8] In London, the party had a glorious dinner at the Carlton. May unpacked all of her jewels and picked the best among them to wear.

> *Something prompted me to want to look my best, although at that time my thoughts of Captain Strong never had strayed from the boundaries imposed upon a good wife. Yet, somehow, I wanted to impress this gentleman of the world who had been so attentive to me.*[9]

May wore a gown that was a replica of one worn by the French Empress Eugénie. May later recounted that she wore the Hope diamond for the occasion. Once again, she was almost certainly exaggerating: "With the big diamond shining at the bodice and my own jewels, more than half a million dollars' worth, supplementing it, I must have been very impressive."[10]

That evening, Lord Francis invited Strong to stay with the couple at their country place at Folkestone for a few days. Strong took him up on it. At Folkestone, Strong largely ignored May and spent an inordinate amount of time with Francis. Recalling that, May thought it was part of Strong's game—whetting her own appetite for attention while undermining any suspicious thoughts her husband might have.

It worked. May announced she had to go to Paris to review theatrical contracts. Strong said that he, too, had to go to Paris. Francis insisted that May and Strong travel together.

On the trip, Strong was kind and attentive to May:

> *In Paris he sent me candies and flowers every day. My cousin [Tom Parke] came over to help me with the contracts, and Captain Strong . . . took us to all the best restaurants and theaters. He just showered me with his courtesies, and as we saw more of each other I began to notice more and more a sort of sadness in his eyes, an ineffable, wistful, longing, whenever he looked at me. Tom saw it too, and joked to me about it. I began to feel sorry for the Captain; for I thought perhaps he really had become smitten with me during our many hours together, and was trying to hide his feelings.*[11]

Later, May also recalled her feelings about the difference between Strong's attentions and her husband's behavior:

Captain Strong pulled the strings that tugged at my heart. Always he stood before me, my ideal of the devoted, impulsive, romantic man I would like my husband to be. Meantime Lord Francis was paying little attention to me—letting me go about my affairs, always kind, but never exhibiting any of the little tendernesses which are so dear to a woman.[12]

Back in London, Strong again joined May and Francis. May then had to return to New York to manage her American contracts for theatrical performances. Lord Francis could not go. He had to attend to family business; he and his brother were involved in a lawsuit over the disposal of some family land. May said her good-byes to Strong and Lord Francis and boarded the ship for New York. Then, as she later wrote:

What was my surprise when the boat sailed to meet Captain Strong on deck. He laughingly said he could not bear to say goodbye to me so shortly, and that he was going as far as Cherbourg and stretch the ceremony of parting that far anyway. This just struck me as a rather delicious escapade, and I entered into the spirit of it.

'Why Captain,' I said laughingly, 'you make me feel quite like a guilty wife—as if I were doing something delightfully wicked. I just tremble at the thought of what my husband would say if he knew you had stolen back aboard the boat.'

Captain Strong sobered immediately. He looked at me with the familiar sadness and longing in his eyes. 'I wonder if being so wicked as you play at being would really be delightful—with me as the other part of the wicked bargain?'

I was startled.

'I mean it, Lady Maysie,' he said. 'I'd like it awfully if you and I were eloping now, and you were leaving your husband behind and were to become my wife. But I mustn't talk that way. Forgive me. I'm getting off at Cherbourg, and you mustn't think of what I've said again.'

But I did think of it again. I couldn't help it.[13]

In New York, May found cables from Strong that he'd sent every day while she continued across the Atlantic. Strong sent flowers to her which filled her hotel room. Every morning and every afternoon there was another delivery simply saying "Good morning," or "Good afternoon" from Strong.

> *Presently, I found myself thinking more and more about Captain Strong's whereabouts, what he was doing, what he might be thinking about, etc., than of the same things in connection with my husband. When I caught myself at this errantry I put such vagrant thoughts aside, but it was such a joy in my life, this having someone who seemed to be thinking of me all the time, that I was not as firm with myself as I should have been.*[14]

May had serious business to do in New York. Her agreement with Harry Chamberlyn to appear at the newly built Savoy Theatre in Manhattan's Herald Square on Thirty-fourth Street, opposite Macy's, and at the Columbia Theatre in Boston was falling through. Chamberlyn was grappling with a dispute over the management and rental of the theaters. His failures didn't stop him from later suing May for $50,000.

May pursued other deals and settled on one that would bring her back to the United States quickly. Willie Hammerstein, the son of theatrical entrepreneur Oscar Hammerstein, signed May for $1,500 a week—an exorbitant amount—to appear in a burlesque variety show, *The Giddy Throng,* scheduled to open in December at the New York Theatre. Then May returned to England, where she joined Lord Francis.

In November 1900, Lord Francis and Lady May were invited to the seat of the duke of Newcastle, Clumber Castle. Lord Francis joined the men in a shooting party. It was the first time May was formally received at the castle, and the newspapers made much of the fact that she was "finally recognized."[15] There are several possible reasons for the family's change of attitude. The dowager duchess had been impressed with May's charitable work, and pleased that she was no longer on the theatrical stage. The duke and Francis had just prevailed in a complicated lawsuit with an uncle over control of the estate's lands. Duke Archibald was also intending to take a trip to America, and sought help from Francis and May in making the arrangements.

Ironically, one article noted, "now that the Duke of Newcastle, a pillar of the high church party, has received her [May], society will quickly open its doors to her."[16] If May read the story, she might have thought of Strong and contemplated how very quickly those same doors could slam shut.

Francis and May sailed to New York aboard the *Minneapolis*, he to ready plans for his brother's visit, she for rehearsals for her theatrical appearances—which she continued to deny in the English press in order not to stir things up with the Newcastle clan.

On December 18 the *New York Times* ran a story, "Duke of Newcastle Here," noting that the duke was heartily greeted by his brother and joined for dinner at the Savoy by the "radiant" Lady Francis Hope.[17] Archibald was spearheading an important religious effort—he was working on reconciling the American Episcopal Church with the Church of England. He was also in the United States to see New York, go fishing with his brother in Florida, and visit the Pacific Northwest.

May and Lord Francis probably didn't bring up her forthcoming show premiere—the duke wouldn't have reacted well. Francis, though, was enthused that May was resuming her career in *The Giddy Throng*, and at the New York Theatre, no less.

The New York Theatre was part of the famed Olympia, built by Oscar Hammerstein in 1895 as the first theater in what was to become the Broadway theater district. Hammerstein also built the Victoria in 1899 and the Republic in 1900, to further develop the area between Broadway and Seventh Avenue, from Forty-second to Forty-fourth Street. The Olympia was the length of a whole city block, constructed of Indiana limestone, and ornamented in French Renaissance style. Hammerstein called it an "amusement palace," with three houses, the Music Hall, the Concert Hall, and the Theatre with a capacity of about 6,000. So grand was the Olympia that one of its houses, the Music Hall, had 128 boxes in eleven ascending tiers, offering seating for 2,800. It was devoted to vaudeville.[18] In 1899, the Music Hall was renamed the New York Theatre.

Lord Francis took delight in being in May's dressing room in the extraordinary building, watching her don her costume and set the numerous gems that adorned it. Hammerstein's contract with May included the stipulation that Francis also appear in the theater lobby, so that he could be seen by the audience as it entered and during intermission. It was part of the flash that Willie Hammerstein planned for the place. He was paying top dollar to attract

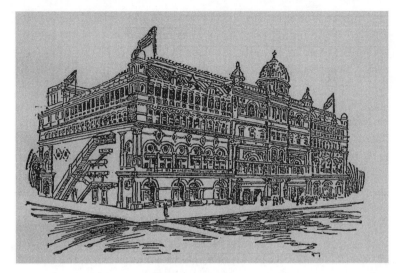

Olympia Theatre on Broadway, later renamed the New York Theatre, 1895.

audiences, and May's name and story were an attraction meriting the large weekly price tag.

May's first performance was scheduled for Christmas Eve, 1900. She would appear in the second part of the bill, after the "Floradora" girl's chorus line and the intermission. May would play Lady Muriel Despair. It wasn't really a dramatic role, but rather a stage label for her in a routine marketed as a "new burlesque" review.

The marketing worked. The *New York Times* reported that so many crowded into "Willie" Hammerstein's

> *to pay homage to the British peerage, or so much of it as is represented by May Yohe, who is billed in the mess of a nonsense produced last evening as Lady Francis Hope . . . When May Yohe left here she was said to have three notes in her voice.*
>
> *She has apparently lost two of them in her journey across the Atlantic. But with a fore front—which in this case means from the neck to the waist line—blazing like the show window of a Broadway store in which are massed thousands of "Parisian diamonds"—your choice for $1—she displayed a*

May Yohe wearing the Hope jewels, including a facsimile of the blue diamond, for a performance, c. 1901.

couple of dresses and almost paralyzed the crowd with that one tone of her voice that is left when she tried to sing. The crowd applauded her because she was Lady Francis Hope. Rather sensibly she refused to try and sing again.

Besides her dazzling display of diamonds—the press agent says they are the family heirlooms of her husband's noble ancestors—she wore a liberal allowance of grease paints and a handsome gown of white crepe de chine over yellow silk, a handsome opera cloak of white satin with elaborate gold appliquéd work, and a huge picture hat of yellow silk illusion with immense yellow roses and green leaves. Altogether, she was a stunning picture.

May Yohe was on the stage for ten minutes at the most in the second scene of "The Giddy Throng." She was on again for two minutes in the last scene to show another gown of some pink stuff. She did not try to sing then, and so the crowd went away after the play better pleased with the last appearance than the first one.

> *Aside from Lady Hope's appearance there was a bur-*
> *lesque-review which was a hodge-podge . . . It was without*
> *plot, and much of it was so pointless that about half the au-*
> *dience left before it had ended. It was one of those things*
> *that was unworthy of criticism, hardly of comment.*[19]

Other critics too panned the show and May's performance. One lamented the fact that she had come back to "her native land to show primarily that she has not lost her histrionic ability, and incidentally to replenish the family exchequer, which is said to be at a low ebb, and also to display the one note that she still possesses."[20]

May might have argued otherwise on both counts. *The Giddy Throng* had a run of 164 performances, the fourth-longest-running show of the year. Over the course of the five-month run, May would have earned about $30,000, an amount equivalent to over $800,000 today.

❖ ❖ ❖

May used some of her ample earnings to buy a lovely house for her mother in Hastings-on-Hudson, just north of New York. Hastings was a retreat for writers, artists, and producers. The house, a Queen Anne-style cottage, rested on a hill and had a domed tower, an open turret, and a wrap-around veranda offering panoramic views of the Hudson River. Its interior featured five fireplaces with blue and white Delftware tiles, an oak-paneled entryway and staircase, trent-pavement tiles, sliding pocket doors, and colored glass windows.

May and Lizzie may have chosen the location in part because of Dewitt Clinton Boutelle, a prominent Hudson River landscape painter who had lived in Bethlehem from 1858 until his death in 1884. Boutelle resided at the Eagle Hotel and his paintings hung on its walls. His vivid depictions of the wide-open Hudson Valley and its vibrant colors likely inspired the mother and daughter.

❖ ❖ ❖

May performed in *The Giddy Throng* until the show closed in May 1901, while taking off time to also perform in Boston. A com-

May Yohe, c. 1901.

Lord Francis Hope, c. 1901.

mentator there noted that the audience at the Columbia Theatre was stunned by Lady Hope's display of jewelry—"she was an impressive picture." But when it came to singing, she received only polite applause for a pleasing song that could be duplicated by "many a girl in this city less known to fame." The reviewer noted that something was clearly wrong and that May was "very nervous and her arms trembled noticeably."[21] The audience tossed May only two bouquets, and she came into the stage wings angry—though she did come out to sing another verse for an encore.

Both May's career and marriage were clearly on the wane. Back in New York, May became ill and was hospitalized with pneumonia. Lord Francis was tarpon fishing in Tampa Bay, Florida. One of Strong's friends let him know May was in the hospital. The Captain returned to New York to see her and brought with him an enormous bouquet of flowers. The nurse assured Strong that May would recover and that there was nothing he could do. May remembered what happened next:

> He asked if he might not come each night and sit on a bench
> in the hall outside my door—just to make sure, he said, he

Queen Anne-style house in Hastings-on-Hudson purchased by May Yohe for her mother Elizabeth Batcheller.

would be close if some emergency should arise. The nurse smiled and told him she was afraid his presence, watching, waiting, would worry me. When he had gone, the nurse said to me, 'That is the kind of man God ought to give every woman.'

I only laughed a little, but I found myself agreeing with her. The Captain's apparent deep concern over my condition, his eagerness to sit on that bench outside my door all night long, willing to just sit there with the knowledge that he was close to me, even if not with me, was more soothing to me than I would admit. I thought of it all that morning—and then that afternoon came the reply to a telegram my physicians had sent during the night to Lord Francis.

They had wired him:

Wife dangerous condition.
Recovery not assured.
She asks you hurry here.

The reply read:

Sorry can't come now. Midst of fishing
season. Departure would seriously
disarrange trip. Advise of developments.
HOPE.

*I dropped the telegram to the floor. That instant I became the
property, body, soul and mind, of Putnam Bradlee Strong—
although neither he nor I knew it yet.*

*Captain Strong read the telegram. He came over to me,
put his arms around me for the first time, and said, 'Poor
Maysie—I'm sorry. But I knew it all the time. When you are
well you are going with me.'*[22]

❖ ❖ ❖

If May was being abandoned by one father-figure, lover, and
friend, Lord Francis, she was now propelled toward another, Captain Strong.

Francis returned to New York in March 1901 with the duke.
He stayed at the Savoy Hotel, not at May's apartment on West
Thirty-fourth Street. Apparently she'd been sharing her apartment
with Strong. Her friends and even casual acquaintances knew. As
her servants John and Louisa Blanche were later to testify, not only
had the couple slept together, but they had set up rendezvous to
enjoy each other's company in Baltimore, Boston, Chicago, and
even in Washington the week before Francis' return, during the
inauguration of President McKinley and Vice President Roosevelt.
The typically unmindful Francis sensed a change in May and their
relationship. Finally, he got the message. "Out you go or out I go,"
May told him.[23] The press got wind of it and put out a story, "Lord
Leaves His Lady."[24]

Lord Francis and Duke Archibald left for Atlantic City. May
referred inquiring reporters to her lawyer, Emanuel Friend, who
said the Hopes had had a misunderstanding, a small tiff. He was
confident they would get back together and muted any speculation
about divorce, saying, "I know of no suit for divorce or separation. No papers have been served on me, and as I am Lady Hope's
lawyer, I ought to hear of any proceedings as grave as a divorce
suit."[25]

Lord Francis returned to England. May was increasingly seen out and about in New York with Strong, enjoying dinners with his group of friends. Strong, a sometimes heavy drinker, probably encouraged May to drink more than she should to still her nerves, especially in light of her separation from Lord Francis.

May was evidently trying to build up her cash reserves and secured a contract to perform at an old haunt, the site of her first success, the Chicago Opera House. The papers there advertised May's triumphal return.

Especially engaged
MAY YOHE
Well Remembered as the Bright Particular Star of
Henderson's Extravaganzas—Now
LADY FRANCIS HOPE
Proud in the Possession of England's Most Honored
Family title as Well as Being the Beautiful Queen
of Song—Lady Hope will at Each
Performance Wear the Celebrated Hope Diamonds[26]

May's train from New York to Chicago was delayed by floods. May knew she was going to be too late for her first scheduled performance, and certainly too late to rehearse. When she finally arrived, she told the Chicago Opera House producers that she was too unsettled to perform. Instead of heeding her warning, they rushed her to the Opera House and induced to get into her gown wearing the Hope jewels. A master of ceremonies told the audience that May had had no time to rehearse with the orchestra, and then led her to the center of the stage where, according to the *Chicago Daily Tribune* report, "he abandoned her."[27]

What followed was an unmitigated disaster that made front page stories in the *Chicago Tribune* and the *New York Times*— "Yohe Faints on Stage." The *Tribune* reported,

> *She [May Yohe] was trembling visibly, and the hand which held the sheets of music shook. She began a love song, and though she faltered several times the audience was good humored enough to applaud, and the sign of forebearance seemed to encourage her. At its conclusion, however, she hurriedly left the stage, returning only for a bow.*[28]

Somehow May agreed to do an evening show that day as well. This too ended badly:

> *Her nerves, however again refused to aid her, and the rise of the curtain disclosed her in the same state of agitation witnessed in the afternoon. She sang one verse of the song, and was about to begin the second when she fainted.*
>
> *May was helped off the stage and revived.*
>
> *The audience seemed sympathetic, and applauded when informed that the actress was in no danger.*[29]

May then, according to the news story, "went to the business office of the theater and insisted she would appear" in the next day's performance.[30] The doctor disagreed. But May went on anyway.

May then performed as scheduled, completing a two-week run at the Opera House. But as she'd found in London, New York, and Boston, her time for great performances had passed. Her voice was no longer strong and intriguing. The theater was changing; her brand of comic opera no longer pleased the paying customers. A more serious type of drama was taking hold. And May was ready for what was to be her metamorphosis in a tale in that would indeed capture the attention and imagination of a much larger, worldwide audience.

*It was because I got tired of Hope
that I became Strong.*
—May Yohe[1]

CHAPTER NINE

Exotic Romance

ESCAPE TALE THAT SHOCKS TWO CITIES" declared one July 13, 1901 front page story.[2] "San Francisco Excited," announced another, while yet a third proclaimed "Romance in New York."[3] Despite an article the week before in the *New York Times* that Lady Francis had patched things up with Lord Hope and was sailing back to England, the opposite was true. May Yohe had run off with Captain Putnam Bradlee Strong. The couple had checked into a San Francisco hotel on July 4th, as Mr. H. L. Hastings and wife, and were intending to sail to Japan.

May carefully planned her exit. She had to, traveling as she did with twelve trunks and other assorted luggage, one or two servants, and five dogs. She had informed the papers of her intention to go back to England. She had called her lawyer, Emanuel Friend, a few days before, saying "The white dove is flying over Castle Blayney. The trouble is all over—we have buried the hatchet, and I'm going to him."[4] The couple's alias was probably May's idea, derived from Hastings-on-Hudson, where her mother lived.

Nonetheless, when discovered, their "elopement" created a furor. Strong's family refused to comment. His mother Mary, the recently widowed wife of New York City's mayor, was a prominent figure in the city and in the public eye. Strong himself was under official Army orders to return to the Philippines and take up his duties as a quartermaster. He had previously served there in the Spanish-American War, earning his spurs in the Manila campaign when he bravely carried out a mission for General Arthur MacArthur, the leader of the U.S. forces (and also the father of Douglas MacArthur).

Because of his desire to be with May, Captain Strong resigned his commission in the Army, sending a cable directly to President McKinley. The secretary of war, Elihu Root, initially refused to accept the cabled resignation, insisting it be submitted by the book. May believed that the Strong family asked Teddy Roosevelt, then vice president of the United States, to intervene by invalidating the resignation. Strong would then have to go to the Philippines as ordered. If he didn't, and stayed or traveled with May, he would become a wanted man, subject to arrest. This would, of course, force the couple apart. Given the "notoriety of the escapade," Secretary Root at first wanted to court-martial Strong for "conduct unbecoming an officer." But the thought of an unseemly investigation and trial soon led him to accept Strong's resignation.[5]

Publicity about the escapade created further tribulations for May and Strong, who, despite the Hastings pseudonym, did a very poor job of keeping quiet about their identities. First, in New York, Strong hosted a "goodbye" dinner for May and his friends at which he gave each a small diamond ring. They then left New York for California. Strong took a room at the luxurious Palace Hotel for himself and the, largest, most expensive suite of rooms at the California Hotel for himself and May, falsely registering as husband and wife. May showed up for dinner at the Palace bedecked in her jewels and was recognized by some diners. Strong met some New York friends and introduced them to May. Both Strong and May perused jewelry shops in the city, over-tipped everyone, and made public shows of their affection.

It was just a matter of days before the press was alerted and leaked the story. When the story reached the California Hotel management, they ordered May from their premises, forcing her, Strong, and the valet to pack up the twelve trunks and other baggage within the hour. Strong asked for more time and breakfast. The assistant manager sent a bellboy up to check on their progress.

He reported, "The room was in a frenzy of disorder. Lady Francis Hope was throwing all manner of wearing apparel into trunks." The bellboy also told Strong, "The management says you ain't going to get no breakfast."[6]

One of the detailed newspaper accounts included the rumor that Strong had been previously engaged to the late Princess Kaiulani of Hawaii. We don't know if May saw that, but if she had, she might have been a bit more apprehensive about what was to follow.

In England, the press was subdued in their coverage, as divorce and affairs in Victorian England were still talked about quietly and through innuendo. Lord Francis expressed his desire for divorce—to be rid of his "giddy and unfaithful wife" —but recognized that English law made it complicated.[7] Furthermore, his brother Archibald, the duke, was adamantly opposed to divorce in general on religious grounds, and would often attend divorce proceedings just to object in principle to the practice. May was less judicious, almost flippant about the whole affair, and when cornered by a reporter quipped, "It was because I got tired of Hope that I became Strong."[8]

May and Strong sailed on the *Nippon Maru* to Japan and rented a "beautiful little palace bungalow" on the bluff outside Yokohama. With seven stories it was not so little; it had been built for Edward, Prince of Wales when he visited Japan. The rent was $300 a month, and it came with staff including, as May wrote, "the cutest little Japanese maid servant I had ever seen." Her name was Yori Komatsu. May later brought her back to the U.S. and wrote that she always treated her like her "daughter."[9]

Even though Strong's family was quite well-to-do—his father, the mayor, had made his money in the dry goods business, first in Ohio and then New York—the couple lived off of May's money. She had managed to bring about $50,000 in cash with her. The New York papers noted at the time that Mrs. Strong sold her house and her husband's house, but Captain Strong claimed that the two sales were merely coincidence and his mother's wish—and he didn't get any of the proceeds. Instead, he told a friend, "I have plenty of money. I am worth $200,000 in cash today, which I made in Northern Pacific when it made its famous jump. I got in on the deal at the right time, and I got out at the right time."[10]

The couple indeed lived lavishly. The pagoda palace was wonderfully furnished, but supplemented by "rare ivories, carvings and other beautiful things" bought by the pair. May later described their lifestyle:

> *We gave many beautiful banquets at our house on the bluff. Captain Strong liked playing host. He had many friends in Japan. Our house became the Mecca of diplomatic officials and tourists.*
>
> *One of our entertainments was a wonderful Roman dinner—served after the vogue of Nero, beginning at sundown and lasting through three whole days and nights. To this we invited many fascinating people. We all dressed in Japanese costumes. The rarest of wines and cordials were served, and to each guest Captain Strong and I gave a little diamond as a favor. The dinner cost us something like $20,000.*[11]

May and Strong were tourists and enjoyed themselves, running about in *jinrikishas*, visiting old temples and being entertained. They often dressed in Japanese clothing, May even made her hair up in the local style.

For May, more than anything else, Strong was her lover, providing her with the attention, romance, and sexual satisfaction she'd hankered for and failed to get with Lord Francis. She wrote, simply and demurely, that "Strong was everything a sweetheart-husband should be."[12]

❖ ❖ ❖

Meanwhile, back in England, Lord Francis returned to bankruptcy court, trying again to sell the Hope diamond. He and his lawyers regarded the diamond as a *damnosa hereditas*, a destructive inheritance that was more of a burden than an asset. It was useless to him, save as something to be sold to help relieve his massive debts. Those debts continued to grow with the expenses of his and May's trip around the world, other travel, and gambling. Nothing, it seemed, could stop Lord Francis from frittering away everything he owned.

This time the court and the Newcastle Pelhams acquiesced to the sale of the diamond for a sum given in conflicting reports as either $168,000 or $250,000. The buyer was London diamond merchant Adolph Weil, who served as an intermediary for the New

May Yohe and Putnam Bradlee Strong in Yokohama, c. 1901.

York jewelry firm Joseph Frankel's Sons & Co. In November 1901, while May Yohe and Captain Strong were in Yokohama, the Hope diamond departed the British Isles for America.

As the extensive court testimony and affidavits in the Chancery Court hearings attest—especially from gemological authority Edwin Streeter—there was no mention of any bad luck or curse associated with the forty-four-carat blue diamond at any time it was in Hope's possession. Nor, despite erroneous suggestions in articles about the gem a decade earlier, had it been cursed in what was presumed to be its previous state as the 67-carat French Blue and 112-carat Tavernier violet. The Hope diamond was regarded as valuable and important, something to be celebrated, not shunned. Indeed, replicas of the Hope diamond were made by collectors such as the duke of Brunswick and Napoleon III, and by several museums. May Yohe also had several replicas made, and at least one for her bejeweled dress-up performance in *The Gilded Throng*.

❖ ❖ ❖

In Yokohama, May and Strong were piling up bills just as fast as Francis was in England, and the solution was also the same— sell the diamonds. "Strong could not hold himself from spending money, and I gave him freely of what I had," May later said. According to May, it was all her money. When they began to run out of cash, Strong asked if he could take one of her jewels to pawn with a friend as a loan until his money came from the States. "I told him to take whatever he wanted," noted May. "He took the $50,000 diamond necklace Captain Holford had given me."[13]

Occasionally over the next few months, reports of friends, acquaintances, or visitors to the couple would make their way into the press. In one report, May was pregnant and planning with Strong to return to the stage in Manila. Others noted Strong's indebtedness and his strange, aggressive behavior and boorishness. One speculated that he showed evidence of paresis—a symptom of untreated syphilis. Another suggested alcoholism.

While neither reports of May's pregnancy or Strong's advanced syphilis were true, alcoholism was a problem for both. Their Roman dinners and entertaining were replete with days and nights of nonstop drinking. Without much to do, with no demands for the stage, extravagant entertaining and inebriation became a daily pattern. The couple's indebtedness also quickly grew. More of May's jewels had to be pawned.

> *I parted with my pearl and diamond coronet, which I had purchased shortly after my marriage to Lord Francis to wear upon formal occasions . . . The willingness with which I allowed Captain Strong to take it out for pawning indicated that I was ready to make any sort of a love's sacrifice. This coronet represented the attainment of my ambitions— wealth, power, love and position. And now I allowed the man who had wrecked all these hopes to pledge it for money with which to buy the excitement he craved and I submitted to.*[14]

May and Strong were growing fat, lethargic, and increasingly moody, caught in a downward spiral fueled by their drinking. While they loved the refuge Yokohama and the house on the bluff provided them, they sensed their lifestyle was unsustainable. By early March 1902 the couple headed back to the United States via Europe, sailing westward to Ceylon and through the Suez Canal to Genoa and Naples. In Italy they pawned another jewel.

As they sailed, Lord Francis's divorce was being granted in London on the grounds of May's misconduct and intimacy with Strong. It would be finalized in September of the next year. Claims still had to be settled, and May's lawyer had filed for £9,187 that she said Lord Francis owed her.

May Yohe and Putnam Bradlee Strong, c. 1902.

Lord Francis' life had become increasingly complicated since May had left. In a terrible hunting accident, a servant had shot him in the foot, shattering his ankle, Gangrene set in and his foot had been amputated. Francis had also been declared bankrupt again and put on an allowance of £2,000 per year—more than adequate for an ordinary person, but paltry for a lord. Not only had the Hope diamond been sold, but Clumber Castle, the Newcastle home estate, was being sold off in parcels at bargain prices. Despite these troubles, and while the divorce was being finalized, Lord Francis was also planning his engagement to his eighteen-year-old second cousin, Beatrice Ricketts.

From Naples, May and Strong sailed back to New York, arriving in Hoboken on the steamship *Kaiserin Maria Theresa* on April 28, 1902 with thirty-three trunks filled with collectibles picked up along their journey. The entourage also included Yori the Japanese maid, Strong's African American valet, a pair of parrots, four Japanese spaniels, two Great Danes, a Persian cat, a flying squirrel, and several other pets, including a large chimpanzee purchased in

May Yohe at her Hastings-on-Hudson cottage.

Colombo, Ceylon, which, according to May, "kept the ship's passengers in an uproar with his antics."[15] If there was any chance that the mass of reporters assembled at the New York pier to meet the scandalous couple upon their return would miss them, the menagerie collected by the pair assured instant recognition.

Strong and May gave "every outward appearance of bride and bridegroom," to reporters and offered only the briefest responses to questions, leaving more complete answers to their lawyer, Emanuel Friend.[16] They said they would stay with May's mother, that May would return to the theater, and that Strong would start a business in the city. Strong referred to May as his wife, saying that the couple had a "contract" to live as a married couple even if they could not legally do so.

They settled into Lizzie's house in Hastings-on-Hudson. Lizzie, long familiar with her daughter's behavior, told May she accepted the relationship "as long as he gives you happiness."[17] Strong's mother Mary, ill at this time, was neither supportive nor forgiving. He tried to reconcile with her, but she refused, holding out until he fully repudiated the relationship with May.

The couple enjoyed their time in the Hudson River village and planned to marry formally on September 26, the day they thought May's divorce would be finalized, and hence the first day they could legally wed under British law. Most evenings, they sat and talked on the wrap-around veranda of "Home Villa," the name they gave to Lizzie's beautiful house perched on a rising slope above the river. During the day, they enjoyed decorating the house with items brought back from Japan—silks, a table and tea service, weapons, and even suits of armor. Outside they planted Japanese cuttings. As an observer noted, "The Japanese idea prevails throughout in the decoration and the interior of the cottage looks as though some residence from the land of the Mikado had been transplanted to the banks of the Hudson."[18]

May and Strong played with the dogs on the lawn, sat in the house's open turret enjoying a panoramic view of the Hudson, and walked through town, always showing a great deal of affection toward each other. They took day trips to New York City, often at Morris Park, Gravesend, and the Sheepshead Bay races where Strong would, according to various reports, typically lose $200 to $300 per race.

Strong feared having all of May's jewelry—worth almost $300,000 (close to $8 million today)—in the relatively insecure house. He suggested that they rent a safety deposit box at a company in New York. This they did, in his name, at the Knickerbocker Trust Company on Fifth Avenue at Twenty-seventh Street. He kept the key. Sometime later, at her request, Strong took May to the premises to see that her jewels were safe and secure.

According to their acquaintances at that time, May would call Strong "Putty," "Dearie," "Lovey," and "Pettie," terms of endearment that irked him, especially when she said them in public. For several of Strong's friends, the match was a somewhat curious one. Their difference in age was amplified by their looks. Strong, though athletic in build, had a youngish, effeminate face and a manner that tended to repel men but attract women. May, on the other hand, had gotten a bit stout; she used a lot of makeup, was typically well-perfumed and "togged out," and had a boisterous, forward, and ornery manner, as is common among alcoholics. As some of Strong's acquaintances cruelly said, "She looked old enough to be the young man's mother."[19]

I vowed to myself that he should
come back to me.
—May Yohe[1]

CHAPTER TEN

Betrayed, Again

W HAT STRONG AND MAY DID NEXT IN 1902 was more
sensational than their elopement and hit the front pages of
every major paper in the nation. The drama began with headlines
such as these in the *New York Times*:

MAJOR STRONG IS MISSING
Left Miss Yohe on Tuesday, Wrote
He would Kill Himself
PAWNED SOME OF HER JEWELS
Brooch on Which He Got $10,000 Located
In Pawnshop—Deposit Vault to be Opened [2]

Strong had been with May in New York on Tuesday, July 15.
She had seen the doctor, and then they lunched at Delmonico's—
the same place May had originally met Lord Francis. Strong said
he had to go see his mother, who was gravely ill and probably
needed surgery. He packed some things from Hastings for his trip
to Lenox, Massachusetts, where she was staying, and dropped May
off at the 125th Street train station to return home.

The next day, she received a note from him. So did Mrs. Strong. The note to May was succinct:

Dear Maysie,
When you have received this I will have committed suicide. I have stolen all your jewels—the tickets you will find at the Knickerbocker. BRADLEE.[3]

The note to Mrs. Strong apologized for his failures and also mentioned suicide. Additionally, it included a number of pawn tickets and a key to a safety deposit box. The receipts indicated that about $10,000 had been received for what was roughly $100,000 worth of pawned jewelry. Strong's note suggested that his mother should redeem them for May.

May sent one of her servants to look for Strong with the message that "all would be forgiven if he returned" and that he could be "assured of May's undying affection."[4] Mrs. Strong and her son-in-law Albert Shattuck hired the Pinkerton Detective Agency to track him down.

The press got wind of all this and descended on Hastings to interview May. "Attired in a wondrous kimono of soft silk, and surrounded by the collections of queer looking dogs, birds, and other things that she brought back from Japan," May spoke in measured language about the disappearance and tried to shield her beloved Putty from any shame, "refraining from saying anything unkind about Strong," according to the *Chicago Daily Tribune*, even though "her sorrow was apparent . . . She sat on the porch of her cottage at Hastings all day looking up and down the road as though expecting Strong to come around the curve at any moment." The *Tribune* quoted May:

> *"All I can say is that Captain Strong, my husband, has gone away. There is no denying that and I don't mind admitting that I don't know where he has gone. I will say, though, that I believe he will come back again. We were going to sail for Japan in September and we may yet."[5]*

Neither May nor the Strong-Shattuck family seriously thought Putnam Bradlee Strong would commit suicide. But they were concerned about his whereabouts. When, by the second and third day,

May Yohe on the porch of her Hastings-on-Hudson cottage, with (right to left) her maid, Yori Komatsu, her mother, Lizzie Batcheller, and her lawyer, Emanuel Friend.

neither May nor Strong's family nor anyone else could locate him, May grew more despondent.

According to the *Washington Post*, "while talking Miss Yohe toyed with two lockets attached to a chain about her neck. Each bore a likeness of Major Strong." May mused,

> *"Why even my parrot calls 'Bradlee, Bradlee' all day long. My private opinion is that he met some friends whom he fell in with while we were on our way back to this country . . . Now, they have probably been wandering about together and the Captain is ashamed."*[6]

Lizzie told reporters that her daughter was "heartbroken and in danger of total collapse." "May loved him devotedly. She would readily forgive him if he would return."[7] May was also concerned about what may have become of her jewels—how many of those not pawned by Strong remained in her vault. But his return mattered more to her than the jewels:

> *"If the Captain only knew that I would forgive him everything! The jewels are nothing, if he would but return. Why,*

if I saw him now coming up the garden walk, I would run to
meet him and bid him welcome home!"[8]

May's lawyer, Emanuel Friend, explained the situation with regard to the supposed stolen jewelry:

"Mrs. Strong will bring the key to New York on Monday
along with the pawn tickets. We will then go to the safe de-
posit company, open the box, and see."[9]

Given the situation, reporters pushed May to reveal details about her life with Strong, especially with regard to his spending and any prior history of pawning her jewelry. She readily told them all that she had supported Strong. To the *New York Times,* she said, "Why this whole thing began a year ago almost. You see, I was like a child. You wouldn't think it of me, with all my experience: but I was just the same."[10] In another interview, she added, "Since his father died and left him bankrupt, he has been mainly supported by me."[11] She told the *Atlanta Constitution* that "ever since we reached Japan I have supported that man, though he kept assuring me that he possessed a fortune in his own right."[12]

Describing how they lived in Japan, she said:

"We'd been living in Yokohama and we got behind in our
bills. He didn't have any money, and I gave him three pieces
of jewelry to pawn . . . With what we received on them we
lived beautifully for a time and paid all our bills. When we
sailed for England, Bradlee gambled heavily on the way and
when the vessel reached Genoa, we were broke."[13]

And on their return to New York, she said nothing had changed: "When we arrived here from Japan, Mr. Strong desired to entertain his friends and he gave many luncheons and dinners, but I paid for them."[14]

The drama played out in the press over the rest of the week. Emanuel Friend speculated that Strong ran off because he was at the end of his rope with financial losses. He also suggested that Strong finally fell victim to his family's pressure to abandon May. Rumors abounded. Sightings of Strong were widely reported. One even had Strong telephoning May, apologizing for everything, saying he was coming home, and claiming that all her jewels would be returned that day. None of these proved true.

A rumor spread that Putnam Bradlee Strong was seen with another woman. At first May didn't believe it. "Miss Yohe pooh-poohed the idea that another woman had 'cut her out' and stolen her captain from her,"[15] one reporter wrote. But when the rumor started to acquire more detail, May was infuriated:

> *May Yohe had just finished telling how she would forgive Strong when the report that he had left her to go to the home of another woman was brought to her. The metamorphosis was sudden and startling. Miss Yohe jumped from her chair, bumped into the diminutive form of Lawyer Emanuel Friend, made two circuits of the veranda in a dozen strides, and then said things that would have made Putnam Bradlee's hair curl if he could have heard them. The last lingering tenderness that the former Lady Francis Hope had for her captain disappeared at that moment, and from now on Miss Yohe says that she will be out for revenge.*[16]

The papers closely followed May's change in attitude toward Strong. "Until yesterday I believed that I loved him, but now I know him as a coward and worse."[17] She proclaimed,

> *"Yes, I'm indignant. Why shouldn't I be? I have been outrageously treated. It was bad enough to be deserted this way without being held up to ridicule. Why didn't he come to me and tell me he had done wrong? If he had taken the jewelry he needn't have been afraid of the consequences. I would have hollered about it. I'm not that kind. I'd just have made the best of it, and if there was no other way, for it I'd have gone back on the stage and earned a living for us both."*[18]

On Tuesday, July 22, a representative of the Strong-Shattuck family turned over the pawn tickets and safe deposit key to May and Friend. Friend promised that if indeed there were jewels missing from the box, he would seek an arrest warrant for Strong for grand larceny unless Strong came forward with the stolen jewels. May confirmed that approach, and said that she hoped Strong would bring back any gems he might have taken. That afternoon,

May, Lizzie, and Friend went to the Knickerbocker Company to inspect the safe. Met by the company's vice president, Joseph Brown, they made sure all of the paper work and permissions were in place.

They stood in front of the deposit box, number 35, with May visibly nervous and trembling as Friend worked the combination and turned the key to open the box. As the *Chicago Tribune* reported,

> *When the box was drawn out of its niche and Miss Yohe saw that three little cardboard boxes were all that it contained, she fell back with a scream . . . "I'll be even for this. I'll have my revenge for this dirty work. That man will get in jail this night if I can get him behind the bars. O[sic], if I could only put my hands on him now!"*[19]

She then cried out, "My God, My God! He left me nothing. All my jewels are gone. All gone. Why?"[20]

May and Friend had come prepared for the worst. She had a typewritten list of the jewels that were supposed to be in the box, as well as other items Strong had pawned and not redeemed. There are some inconsistencies between the list May gave to the police, which was published in the papers, and another list May included in her 1921 book *The Mystery of the Hope Diamond*, but the following captures the sense of what she had. It also reveals a who's who of May's admirers, including an Indian Maharaja; the British banker and financier Alfred Rothschild; Barney Barnato, who sold his Kimberley diamond mines to Cecil Rhodes to form DeBeers; and the personally smitten admirer, Captain Holford, who was arrested years later for pilfering jewelry.

    diamond and turquoise bracelet, in safe deposit in New York (gift of
        Henry Guest, $15,000)
    cluster diamond broach with immense emerald set in centre, in safe
        deposit in New York (from Mr. Walters, $12,000)
    turquoise and diamond arrow, in safe deposit in New York (from Mr.
        Alfred Rothschild, $8,000)
    diamond brooch set with twenty pure diamonds, in safe deposit in
        New York (from Mr. Barney Barnato, $20,000)
    diamond and sapphire "dog collar," in safe deposit in New York (from
        the Maharaja of Cooch Behar $80,000)

black lace fan with tortoise shell frame studded with diamonds, in
    safe deposit in New York (from Charles Rose, $8,000)
a score or more of diamond rings—dinner rings, banquet rings,
    clusters and solitaires, in safe deposit in New York ($95,000)
ruby bracelet, in safe deposit in New York ($17,500)
diamond and turquoise necklace, (gift from Captain Holford, $25,000)
32 stone diamond necklace pawned in Yokohama
pearl and diamond tiara, pawned in Genoa[21]

May and Friend went to the police station to ask that Strong be arrested. An arrest warrant was issued. Friend also put up a $1,000 reward. Some two dozen police officers were assigned to the case and fanned out around the city to see if they could locate Strong. Friend then went to the pawn shops indicated by the tickets to see what remained and determine their redemption value.

May, Friend and Lizzie adjourned to the Sturtevant House café. Hundreds of people came to the window to try to get a glimpse of May. Reporters surrounded her. May was furious and lashed out at Strong during the makeshift press conference. "Here is the ring with which we were to be married," May said to reporters as she exhibited a small diamond solitaire ring. On the same finger was a larger diamond. She was asked how it happened that Captain Strong left it. "I guess he could not get it off my finger. He took about everything else that I had," a writer for the *Atlanta Constitution* reported. She added,

> *"He left me two cheap fans. I suppose that was to suggest that I keep cool. I will keep cool enough. I wish I could cool him.*
>   *"It is bad cricket for a man to fawn upon a woman and profess to love her, and then steal from her. Just think! While he was caressing me and telling me that he loved me, Captain Strong was sneaking my jewels and 'soaking' them."*[22]

To the *Chicago Daily Tribune*, she fumed,

> *"I did not think the man could be so base. I did not think there were such low instincts in his nature . . . I am through with Captain Strong. This thing has ended it. I am ruined. Everything that I had is gone. You can depend upon me*

getting justice for this outrage if justice is to be had in the land."[23]

And to the *New York Times*, she said, "They say that hell hath no fury like a woman scorned. Well, I've been scorned and I've got a right to be furious. Now I want justice."[24]

The next day, July 23, Mrs. Strong and the Shattucks offered to settle with May rather than see Putnam Bradlee Strong possibly arrested for grand larceny—even though their lawyer indicated that since May and Strong were living as husband and wife and the vault was rented freely in his name, she didn't have much of a case. Still the scandal had taken its toll on Mary Strong, who was now in New York, ill, and disgusted by the stories of her son's ignominy and May's daily rants to reporters.

May and Friend visited the offices of Job E. Hedges, the former private secretary to Mayor Strong and legal advisor to the family. They came to an agreement. Though it was not publicly disclosed, the family would pay May about $22,000. This would cover the cost to redeem the pawn tickets for jewelry worth ten times that or more, plus interest, plus money for jewels pawned in Yokohama and in Genoa. In return, May agreed to drop the charges against Strong and rescind the reward offer.

May, Lizzie and Emanuel Friend then went to the police station to do just that. Their next stop was Goldstones Jewelers at 234 Sixth Avenue, where most of May's jewelry had been pawned. It took about half an hour to locate all the pieces and redeem them. May was reported to be carrying a roll of cash about six inches in diameter. She paid about $7,500 in cash.

May's next stop was the telegraph office. Strong was said to be headed back to Japan. May was worried that he was carrying some of her jewels and would try to pawn them in Yokohama. She sent a telegram to one of her contacts there.

To Wood, Yokohama
Look out for diamonds. I sail on the next
steamer.
MAY YOHE.[25]

In the following days, rumors started cropping up in the papers that even though they might be departing separately, May and Strong were arranging a rendezvous in Japan.

Reporters asked May about this. "Reconciliation? Ugh!" was May's reply. Friend was more articulate, but the message was the same: "Never, I can tell you. If ever a woman hated a man, she hates that man."[26]

The affair occasioned a great deal of commentary and editorializing around the nation about relationships between men and women. It was a transformative time, with questions of gender roles and women's rights rising to the fore of American social consciousness.

One widely distributed commentary was especially biting.

The worst thing about this May Yohe—"Putty" Strong mess is that it will probably furnish the lady with an excuse to get back on the stage. Even the columns of slush being unloaded upon their readers by the newspapers of New York do not constitute an affliction comparable to that.

There is no end of sympathy for the poor mother of young Strong, whose notorious affair with the wife of Lord Francis Hope has been a scandal from one end of the world to the other, and who has succeeded in dragging the honorable Strong name into the dust, but there can be no sympathy for either of the principals.

Young Strong deliberately threw away an honorable position in the army that he might bask in the smiles of a woman whose pose has been that of a man-devourer, and it was his inevitable fate to go down to ruin.

With the woman it is the familiar story of age throwing away everything in its fascination for youth, the young lover soon tiring and seeking other fields. An older woman takes long chances when she undertakes to hold the love of a man much younger than herself. When she deserted Hope, who was apparently foolish enough to put faith in her, and ran away with the young army officer, the Yohe woman went into a game in which she had scarcely a chance to win. There is absolutely no ground for sympathy for her.[27]

The writer took the view that May's vanity and illusion caused the affair—her misguided attempt to keep a younger man. Because of Strong's thievery, deception, and cowardice, May and many women might have challenged that interpretation, seeing instead her loyalty, her willingness to support her man, and her steadfast sense of justice, had not the story taken another, decidedly strange, and totally unexpected twist.

❖ ❖ ❖

A few days after the settlement, on July 25, reports came out of London that Strong had arrived in England, not Japan. He claimed he had "pawned about $8,400 worth of May's jewelry at her request and for her benefit, and she had received the entire proceeds." He said, "I have never had one dollar of May Yohe's money . . . As to the story that I rifled her safety deposit box, that is absurd on its face. May Yohe never had any safety deposit box that I know of . . . I had one in my own name at Knickerbocker which I suppose my family has opened as I gave them full authority to do so."[28]

May, in New York, reacted to these reports, "I'm not saying anything. Just watch me."[29] The same day she boarded the steamer *Fürst Bismarck* under the name Mrs. Batchellor and headed to London. Newspapers reported that May had set out to give Strong a "horsewhipping." In London, Strong was said to be switching hotels, trying to hide from May, and worried that she would take out a warrant for his arrest.

May arrived in London on July 31 claiming that Strong's denial "is all a batch of lies."[30] She also said, "Strong's story that he paid back anything is another lie." When told that Strong had said he had got his money from the sale of his library, May responded, "Well, he brought all his library to my house in an old steamer trunk; it must have been valuable. He is the greatest liar I have ever known."[31]

May noted that she had "suffered all this outrageous treatment to save his mother and my own." May said she was determined to travel to any and all places Strong had pawned her jewelry. "I am anxious to get to Genoa, where I have tickets for a tiara diamond heart and other things he pawned . . . I may land in Kamchatka before I get through."[32]

May then checked into the Great Western Hotel in Paddington, intending to stay the night and continue on to the Continent the next day. But she received a messenger who brought with him a packet of letters from Putnam Bradlee Strong. May decided to check into the Savoy under the name Lady Francis Hope. She spent the day reading and re-reading the letters. Strong urged forgiveness and professed his love. He also intimated he might commit suicide unless May joined him in Paris.

Dear Maysie,
Excuse the shakiness of my writing, but I'm nearly crazy. My nerves are all unstrung. Oh, Maysie, how could you accuse me of stealing? You know I'm no criminal. This will be delivered by a man who knows my address and who will send me your answer by mail or wire. If you still love me, write or telegraph, preferably the latter, as the letter might reach me too late. Remember that I'm yours even until the next world. Yours lovingly,
BRADLEE[33]

Then, despite her outrage, sense of indignity and humiliation, despite her reaction in New York to the idea of reconciliation, May dropped a bombshell. She told reporters, "I care only for Bradlee. Where is he? Why don't they bring him to me? Why does he write me if he does not love me? I would forgive him in a minute if he would only say that he is sorry." She added, "He can have everything I have got if he will only come back."[34]

She wrote a note to him:

Come back immediately. I forgive all.
MAYSIE[35]

May's dramatic turnaround, for her, the triumph of love over distrust and revenge, was not seen quite so charitably by others. The press proffered its speculation. How could she so easily and quickly reverse direction? Had the drama in New York been a scam—a plot by Strong and Yohe to soak his family for funds?

Strong was thought to be near Paris. Apparently he was still unsure about May, thinking she might file a warrant against him. There were rumors that she'd been in contact with Scotland Yard. May decided to head to Paris. She stumbled leaving her carriage to catch the train to the continent, was hobbled, and had to be carried to the coach. In Paris on August 3, she had to be ferried in a litter and chair. Strong, however, was not there. He'd been ill in Lisbon and was still there when May found him. By mid-August, the newspapers revealed the startling turnabout in Lisbon:

May Yohe and 'Major' Putnam Bradlee Strong are united once more. They are living happily together in the apartments at the Avenida Palace Hotel here and are registered as Mr. and Mrs. Atkinson.[36]

Said Strong in an interview,

Miss Yohe and myself are perfectly happy together. We intend to get married as soon as her decree of divorce is made absolute, which will be September 25.
Where we will be then I don't know.
Miss Yohe is thoroughly disgusted with all of this fuss. There has been no collusion between Miss Yohe and myself. She had no idea of following me and did not know where I was until I wired her on Monday in Paris.[37]

When an American correspondent asked, "Do you intend to return to the States," Strong replied emphatically, "No." May Yohe joined in, "We will never return to America."[38]

What the press did not hear was the account of the couple's actual reunion. Years later May wrote about the finale of her trans-Atlantic and cross-European quest to track Strong down:

I walked straight up to him. He held out his hand, caught mine and pulled me to him and kissed me just as if nothing had ever happened and as if this were a reunion after a lonesome separation. I wanted to begin scolding him right away, but he merely smiled at me.
"Don't get fussed up—Maysie," he said. "There's no use fighting when it is so hot. Have you any money? I'm broke."
When I reproached him for the theft of my jewels, he merely laughed. "Oh, why bring it up," he said. 'Both of us needed a little excitement—we were stagnating."[39]

Whatever anger and trepidation May might have felt, her romantic side won out. As she euphemistically put it, they checked into the same hotel and stayed together for the next week.

Following their Lisbon recoupling, the pair sailed for Argentina, arriving in Buenos Aires the first week of September. They rented a place, lived as a married couple, and, shunned by some, welcomed by others, they joined the city's most exclusive club, the Jockey Club, and awaited word from England that the divorce from Lord Francis was finally official. According to May, when word did come, Strong again tried to delay the scheduled marriage. May would not stand for it.

> *Bradlee . . . you swore to me when I eloped with you that come what might, whether we were happy or whether we tired of each other, you would go to the ends of the earth, if necessary, to marry me the minute I should be freed by Lord Francis. Every time you have deserted me and I have taken you back, you have made the same promise. Now you will have to make good.*[40]

May invoked a local code of male honor to threaten Strong. She told him that if he didn't marry her, she would tell other gentlemen at the Jockey Club that he'd deceived and dishonored her. She threatened that he'd be posted a cad. Every member would regard this as a dishonor. First one, then another, would challenge him to a duel. It might be with pistols, it might be with swords. He might win the first, and even the second, but at some point he would lose and "be killed."

In the face of May's onslaught—marry or die—Strong had no choice. The cowardly but gracious Strong responded, "Maysie dear. You know I can hardly wait when I realize you are going to be my wife at last. Come, let's hurry."[41] The wedding, a civil marriage, took place on October 3, 1902, a week after May's divorce from Lord Francis was final. May sent a dispatch to her New York lawyer which was widely circulated to U.S. newspapers:

Married; Buenos Ayres; 2nd.
MAY STRONG.[42]

It wasn't clear whether "2nd" referred to the mistaken date or whether May considered this her second marriage to Strong.

Lord Francis Hope, too, was waiting for the divorce to become final. He wanted to marry his young second cousin, Beatrice Ricketts, but his mother and his brother opposed the marriage. They thought the idea further evidence of Francis' foolishness—marrying a family member, and such a young girl at that. They were also opposed on religious grounds. Father Black, a clergyman of the Church of England, joined them in their opposition. He and the duke of Newcastle had appeared at numerous weddings to object to the marriages of divorced brides or grooms as being contrary to the "canons of the church and the laws of God."[43] The pair could hardly continue their work if the duke stood with his brother on this remarriage. In the end, Lord Francis abandoned his plans. Two years later, he married Olive Muriel Thompson, who was the daughter of an Australian banker and closer to his own age.

May was also waiting on the disposition of her lawsuit against Lord Francis. Francis had given May a promissory note during their marriage. Under the terms of his bankruptcy, his estate was paying off creditors at ten shillings on the pound (i.e., five percent), but had refused to pay May. She said, "The money is due me, and I'll fight for it until I get it."[44] She did fight, in the English courts, and won at a ten percent rate, double anyone else, receiving about $5,000.

By December, May and Strong arrived back in New York on a Cunard liner, the *Umbria*. Accompanying them were twenty-two pieces of luggage, two wicker chairs, a barrel of pineapples, a Japanese poodle, and a monkey. They avoided the voracious press, and settled back in at Lizzie's house in Hastings-on-Hudson. Rumors suggested that Strong would explore business opportunities and May might return to the stage. There were also rumors of a reconciliation with Mary Strong and the Shattucks.

None of that happened. In the spring of 1903, the couple returned to Argentina. Strong wanted to buy a ranch but became an automobile salesman instead. The couple was outwardly living the good life, as they always did, and running out of money as well. In 1904, they were back in New York looking for work.

❖ ❖ ❖

May had to return to the stage, and her comeback was promoted in Boston, Atlanta, and New York. While she was already famous, her notoriety with Strong added to her public appeal. In Boston, the papers promised, "there will be a stampede to see and hear the erstwhile Lady Hope and friend of Captain Putnam Bradlee Strong."[45] May was going to sing a few old songs. But her talents had completely slipped away.

May tried another tack, seeking performance venues in Great Britain. She garnered bookings for major music halls—the Brighton Hippodrome, the Royal Hippodrome in Liverpool, the London Music Hall, Newcastle Pavilion, and the Glasgow Pavilion. Unfortunately for May, her presentations were no better than they'd been in the United States earlier in the year. Reviews reflected her poor performance:

> *The recent appearance of May Yohe in the Royal Hippodrome, Liverpool and its pitiful denouement, has caused considerable comment . . . She was to appear in a selection of her old-time favorite songs. When the curtain was raised Miss Yohe was evidently greatly agitated for some reason and her voice seemed to have lost its former power . . . but it soon became painfully evident that she was in a very overstrung condition, and after a futile attempt to sing, she exclaimed, 'Oh, I can't do it,' and with some difficulty left the stage. The curtain immediately fell.*[46]

It was now back to New York for May and Strong.

In 1904, Broadway was booming. The theater district north of Forty-second Street had become known as the "Great White Way," named in this case for the lights on the marquees. The intersection of Broadway and Forty-second Street, then called Longacre Square, had become the city's symbolic center, at the crossroads of the new subway system's north-south and east-west lines, which were just being completed. Adolph Ochs had purchased a triangular piece of land at the intersection and built the headquarters of the *New York Times*, prompting the mayor to rename the intersection Times Square.

Vaudeville was popular with the huge crowds that passed through the newly constituted Times Square, and now May once again had a chance to shine. She was booked for Willie Hammerstein's Theatre of Varieties at the corner of Forty-fourth and Broadway, the new epicenter of the city. The theater offered a potpourri of off-beat and colorful entertainment—anything that Willie thought could fill 1,350 seats. Over the years, it hosted Harry Houdini, Will Rogers and Irving Berlin.

May was booked to appear on New Year's Eve, December 31, 1904. This would be the first time the transition from one year to

Hammerstein's Victoria Theatre with its Roof Garden in newly named Times Square.

the next would be celebrated in Times Square. Ochs and the *New York Times* staff had arranged a fireworks display to draw a crowd. Some 200,000 turned out, initiating a tradition that continues to this day, albeit with a descending ball rather than pyrotechnics.

While the New Year's celebration was a success, May was a flop. The audience gasped at Yohe's ungainly, stout appearance. Her husky, raspy voice failed to elicit even polite applause. "It was a disastrous return, for there was more than a suggestion of hissing," reported the *Los Angeles Times*.[47]

May, who had become a heavy drinker, started an even more precipitous decline. She would get nasty drunk. Her stomach would become particularly bloated. She would curse a lot. She would become sick. The alcohol took its toll on her theatrical capabilities and finally on the relationship with Strong as well.

May continued to seek stage success. She tried to link her madcap reputation to Times Square by performing a new song, "Down in the Subway," by William Jerome and Jean Schwartz, which appealed to young people and New York City's innovative transportation system:

There's a new place at last to go spooning
Now the man in the moon looks deserted
Where lovers can love with delight
His face wears the smile of despair
In the future just cut out your mooning
Underground it is broadly asserted
And banish the stars from your sight. . .
Oh what a place, under the
Isle of Manhattan speeding through
Space, just the place for spooning.
All the season round. Way
Down in the subway
Underneath the ground.[48]

But she found that her reputation and following were fading. John Drew, Ethel Barrymore, Maude Adams, George M. Cohan, and John Philip Sousa and his band were the big headliners.

May came up with a novel idea: why not incorporate Strong into her act? Their premiere was at Keeney's Fulton Street Theatre in Brooklyn on April 24, 1905, in what was labeled as a dramatic sketch titled "The Actress and the Detective." By June, the vaudeville sketch made it back to the Victoria Theatre on Broadway, the only draw being the couple's fame.

At 10 o'clock, the curtain went up . . . The audience waited almost breathless to hear his (Strong's) first words—for the voice of him had been chronicled around the world—and then, it settled back and waited for the woman . . . she came too, timidly at first, speaking later with more confidence . . . They talked together for a few moments, they quarreled, they called one another names, they kissed—the audience watched them eagerly—and then the curtain came down at 10:20.

All through these twenty minutes of "entertainment" the spectators had sat seriously browed, silent, the men puffing sagely at their cigars and the women with curiously intricate expressions . . . The curtain was down. A minute's silence and then a few friends applauded in a half-hearted way . . . High up in the gallery a man hissed loud and long.[49]

May Yohe and Putnam Bradlee Strong performing as a married couple in a vaude-ville act, 1905.

Another review was less kind: "If May Yohe were not the former Lady Francis Hope, and if her partner were not the former Capt. Strong, their services wouldn't be accepted as a gift."[50]

One night deputy marshals showed up at the theater, bought tickets, and called for Willie Hammerstein to secure his cooperation. They had come to serve a summons on Strong and collect any of his property that might be at the theater and any salary he was due. Strong was being sued by a tailor, Charles Wetzel, for nonpayment of $143. The marshals surrounded the stage and guarded the exits, collected Strong's things, and served him the summons as soon as he finished his sketch with May.

Two weeks later Strong filed for bankruptcy. The money, the fame, and the passion had left the marriage. On November 27,

1905, the anniversary of May's marriage to Lord Francis, Strong deserted her, leaving for Japan.

May, who is credited with saying, "When a woman marries she pawns her liberty and then loses the ticket," was ready to redeem herself.[51] She lined up a lucrative tour of Europe with the help of theatrical friends.

> *On this tour I made a great deal of money. Somehow I began to see the differences between the men I met—the real, world-experienced men and Bradlee. Many men made love to me. I began to realize, too, what a difference there was between their love and his. I determined again to divorce Strong and free myself of him forever.*[52]

May filed for divorce while in Berlin. Opined the *Washington Post*, "The country will be the better off if May and the Captain are compelled to live together."[53]

Strong took up residence in Japan, and then lived in China and Malaya for several years. Given his foreign residence and May's own peripatetic career, it took years for her to divorce Strong—an action that finally took effect in 1910.

Though Strong and May would physically meet only once more during their lifetimes, their paths would also cross for an encore that no one expected. In the 1930s, in one of the strangest court cases ever adjudicated, their marriage was examined in order to determine the fate of their alleged son.

A woman is not old until she
is dead!
—May Yohe[1]

Independent Woman

MAY BANKED ON HER FAME allowing her to appear on stage after Strong left. Her performances were universally regarded as awkward and amateurish, drink no doubt contributing to her slide.

May's descent from venues such as Hammerstein's Roof Garden on Broadway to cheap, ten-cent vaudeville theater, restaurant and café shows around the U.S. paid the bills, but were a far cry from the success and acclaim she'd achieved on the London stage when she drew praise from the likes of George Bernard Shaw. Willie Hammerstein noted he was able to book May at $75 a week rather than the $1,500 he'd paid just a few years earlier. The *Los Angeles Times* reported, "Now she has returned to her original name, save that now it illumines on the grime and slime of the slum theater."[2]

The years following Strong's departure were harsh for May. She was virtually destitute. She sold the house in Hastings-on-Hudson in 1905 to Oliver Gribben, an Oriental rug and tapestry buyer for Macy's. May had loved the house and the artistic, creative community that was sprouting in Hastings-on-Hudson. Architect William

Sanger had designed the house next door and was about to move in with his wife Margaret. Broadway impresario Florenz Ziegfeld, who had been inspired by May's performances in Chicago decades earlier, was planning to build his mansion, Burke Estate, there.

May auctioned off some of her treasures and memorabilia. She said at the time, "To be quite frank, I am out of money and must work. I love the theatrical life anyway and may stay in vaudeville for a long time."[3] She never settled her financial claims with the Strong family; she confessed with her typical candor, "They'd rather see me dead." She knew she was paying for her own willfulness, because, as she said, "I divorced him, he didn't divorce me."[4]

May reflected on her life, "Certainly I was happy with Lord Francis, until I became infatuated with Captain Strong. My mother always calls it hypnotism. We speak of him in our home as Svengali." To one interviewer, she said,

> *People often ask me how I can bear it. People who knew me when I was Lady Francis Hope, and I had my own yacht and my beautiful homes, the jewels and al the rest of it. But really, I'm not unhappy. I realize that I have made a terrible fool of myself. I have lost everything. I was sick for a long time after my trouble with Captain Strong. Now I have to face it and go back to work. Sometimes the papers and people have been terribly unkind, and I have to bear that too. I just have to begin all over again.*[5]

She was quite candid about her stage career:

> *What do I do here? What could I do? They don't want to hear me sing. They just want to look at me. So I just go out there and sing a few little songs. Meanwhile I have pleasures in my own way. I crochet and embroider.*[6]

To say May's only avocation was home crafts would be an exaggeration. She still had some of her "Madcap" verve. A performance at Hammerstein's Rooftop Garden in 1906 drew some praise, with *Vanity Fair* opining, "She's full of life and energy."[7]

May considered appearing in a review, *Mam'zelle Champagne*, slated for Madison Square Roof Garden in the summer, but was in London instead. At the fateful premiere, millionaire Harry Thaw walked up to Sanford White, America's preeminent architect, drew a revolver, and shot and killed him. Thaw was accompanied by his wife, Evelyn Nesbit, a beautiful former model and chorus girl, who had been White's lover years earlier. Jealously enraged, Thaw maintained that White still had an influence over Nesbit. May was an older friend of Evelyn Nesbit; they both shared difficult family upbringings in Pennsylvania, and Evelyn, as a "Floradora" girl, performed in the chorus on some of May's bills.

The shooting and subsequent news and trial consumed New Yorkers and the theatrical community. The show, though, went on. May joined the cast to play the lead role when *Mam'zelle Champagne* moved to the Berkeley Lyceum Theatre in the fall.

May was linked romantically with several men, all rumored to be married to her, engaged to her or living with her in a common-law marriage. One was Newton Brown, reportedly a childhood friend of May's from Philadelphia. Out on a date late one April night in 1907 in New York, they tried to get married, perhaps half seriously. They couldn't get the hotel chaplain or a clergyman to officiate, and dropped plans to cross the river to New Jersey to find a justice of the peace. Nonetheless the story persisted, probably with May's encouragement. The *New York Telegraph* reported that the couple were married at May's Hotel Dunlap apartment in the presence of her Japanese maid and then enjoyed a bridal supper at Churchill's. May supposedly owned up, "Yes, we're married."[8] Another newspaper sought Newton Brown's view on any marriage to May. "Nothing doing, do you think I'm crazy?" he was quoted as saying.[9]

After reading about May's theatrical decline in the California papers in early 1908, another suitor, this one an unnamed San Francisco millionaire, became intrigued by May's story. He started courting her, and reportedly gave her $5,000 worth of diamond jewelry on their first date. Though rumors swirled, there was no marriage.

❖ ❖ ❖

While May was sliding toward obscurity, the Hope diamond was back in the news, tempering her fall. A 1907 *New York Times* gossip column had reported that ladies were decorating themselves with colored gemstones: "Diamonds in black, yellow, blue, topaz, green, and gray are highly prized."[10] The column cited the Hope diamond as the world's most famous blue diamond and noted the special attention it had received in London as a result of May Yohe's marriage into the Hope family.

Despite the Hope diamond's fame, Frankel's had apparently been unable to sell it at a good price after acquiring it in 1901. In the ensuing years, rumors circulated that J. P. Morgan, Charles Schwab, J. J. Hill, former Senator William A. Clark, and even Lord Francis Hope's older brother Duke Archibald were interested in buying it. A banker's panic in 1907 occasioned a tough recession. Wealthy Americans were not buying diamonds in the amounts and sizes seen in earlier years.

By New Years Day 1908, Frankel's as well as several other jewelers faced severe financial challenges, even bankruptcy. They could not pay off loans used to build up their inventories. Frankel's debt amounted to about $4.5 million, and even though the firm claimed assets of over $6 million, it was faced with potential liquidation as creditors began to call in their loans.

A January 7, 1908 article in the financial pages of the *New York Times* lamented the woes of Joseph Frankel's Sons & Co., which had much of its capital tied up in the Hope diamond. On January 19, the *Washington Post* published an item in its "Gossip of Society" column:

> *Buy the famous Hope diamond and besides getting one of the world's greatest jewels you will help the multimillionaire firm of Frankel's Sons out of its financial difficulties. It is said that this jewel, valued at about $250,000, was partly responsible for the troubles of Joseph Frankel's Sons, whose inability to pay pressing bills resulted in the appointment of trustees for it and three correlated concerns.*[11]

This was followed by a commentary, "All that Glitters is Not Gold," which appeared in the *Los Angeles Times* and directly connected bad luck to both the Hope diamond and May Yohe, who was then at her low point, performing in cheap vaudeville theaters on the West Coast.

> *It is interesting to note that a contributing cause of the liquidation of one of the firms was the possession of the Hope*

diamond, which May Yohe wore in the days when she and the gem were scintillating rivals. That jewel . . . has been found to be . . . dead capital, for, in these dull days, the New York firm cannot find a purchaser for it. Even the Pittsburgh chorus girl chasers are keeping their hands in their pockets when it comes to diamonds.

The Hope diamond . . . has brought some of its possessors bad luck. No doubt the woman [May Yohe] now appearing before the footlights of a Main-street vaudeville house wishes she had never seen the bauble, but as she says, she "played her own dope."

This much is certain, the possession of diamonds is not necessary to happiness . . . Diamonds came to May Yohe . . . and what girl in Los Angeles would change places with her?[12]

These articles led to further elaboration and a much more fanciful article in the *New York Herald* republished in the *Washington Post*, "Remarkable Jewel a Hoodoo—Hope Diamond has Brought Trouble to all who have Owned It:"

Deep behind the double locked doors hides the Hope diamond. Snug and secure behind time lock and bolt, it rests in its cotton wool nest under many wrappings, in the great vault of the great house of Frankel. Yet not all the locks and bolts and doors ever made by man can ward off its baleful power or screen from its venom those against whom its malign force may be directed.[13]

According to the author,

Every gem has its own power for good or evil, and this power never dies, though it may wax or wane under the circumstances, may lie dormant for centuries only to reappear with redoubled energy when terrestrial and celestial conditions combine to bring into play the mysterious forces hid beneath its glittering surface.[14]

The article presented a fractured history of the Hope diamond, beginning with Tavernier's original acquisition of the gem. The diamond was implicated in bringing Louis XVI's "head to the ax," or rather the guillotine. The article falsely claimed that May had worn the diamond in her tiara, errantly stated that Lord Francis Hope sold it only months after his divorce from May Yohe, and incredulously suggested that it was to blame for his "marital and financial difficulties." The author also recognized the recent troubles of the jeweler, Simon Frankel. "There are those who say they will never regain their old position of supremacy in their trade so long as the Hope diamond remains in their ownership."[15]

May's own decline, her leaving Lord Francis, his bankruptcy, the failed relationship with Strong, and now her own hard times were all fodder for the stories. May was back in the news, but it was as a victim of the unlucky Hope diamond.

❖ ❖ ❖

In 1908, May was performing vaudeville in venues in the Pacific Northwest, accepting bookings on the Sullivan-Considine circuit, one of the syndicates that organized the cheap but popular theatrical performances across the country.

May made Portland, Oregon, her home base, living at the Perkins Hotel. She was again linked to various lovers in the region, among them a former English army officer, John Baxter Rowlands, who lived in Creston, British Columbia, just over the U.S. border. Later that year, Rowlands was shot and wounded by an irate husband, Lord Sholto Douglas, when the latter unexpectedly returned to his home from travel abroad only to find Rowlands bedding his adulteress wife. Such was May's sexual notoriety that she was rumored not only to have had an affair with Rowlands, but also with Lord Sholto.

May found a lover and benefactor who enabled her to move from the Perkins Hotel into a five-room cottage on Northrup Street and set up a household with staff.

By year's end, May was signing her name as "Mrs. James Fellows." James Fellows, a Canadian from Vancouver, would come down on weekends and stay with her. He paid the bills. As court documents would latter reveal, they were intimate. May and Fellows lived as man and wife and were known as such around town. But because May had not officially divorced Strong, they could not be married. About the same time, there were numerous newspa-

May Yohe in Oregon.

per reports that May had married a Canadian lumberman named Murphy and even had a son with him whom she put up for adoption. As such stories emerged, May abruptly decamped from Portland and, using the pseudonym "Mrs. Bellinger," embarked on a tour of the Orient.

❖ ❖ ❖

A half a world away, the Hope diamond's story became even more complicated in 1909. Frankel's had sold it to a mysterious gem collector, Selim Habib, who, running into his own financial difficulties, was reselling it in Paris. An article published in the *The Times* of London on Friday, June 25, 1909, declared [the Hope diamond's] story "is largely blended with tragedy . . . murder, suicide, madness, and various other misfortunes."[16]

The article was a fanciful one, asserting new fictional claims about the history of the Hope diamond. It falsely claimed that Tavernier had lost all his money after selling the diamond to Louis XIV. It apocryphally blamed the diamond for the downfall of Louis XIV's mistress and his chief of finance. Both Marie Antoinette and her bosom friend supposedly lost their lives because they wore the diamond. Fictionalized thieves who stole the diamond faced ruin, starvation, and suicide.

The Times article blamed Lord Francis' bankruptcy, his rocky courtship of concert hall singer May Yohe, May's divorce, and her tribulations with Strong on the evil influence of the blue gemstone. The article invented new, totally fictionalized victims of the stone—a French broker gone insane, a Russian prince who was assassinated, a Greek magnate driven off a cliff, and a Folies Bergère star who was shot. The fantastic account blamed three major revolutions—the French Revolution, the 1905 Russian revolution, and the revolt of the Young Turks in Ottoman Turkey, on the blue brilliant.

The tongue-in-cheek story, chock-full of clearly erroneous, easily-dispelled material presented in the guise of news, declared the unlucky diamond's alleged adventures to "beggar the wildest fiction."[17] It wasn't until some eighteen months later, in 1911, that T. Edgar Wilson, the editor of the *Jewelers Circular Weekly* wrote a general rebuttal published in the *New York Times,* and another corrective article in the *Metropolitan* came out. By then, it was too late. The story took on a life of its own.

❖ ❖ ❖

May's 1909 tour of the Orient took her to Yokohama, Japan, where for a few hours she saw Strong in her hotel suite in a thoroughly chaperoned visit. May thought the meeting cordial and cold.

May next visited Hong Kong for a theatrical appearance, and was then off to Singapore, where she performed at the Victoria

Theatre. She went on to India to visit her "old friend," the Maharaja of Cooch Behar, and gave several somewhat private "drawing room entertainments." From there, she visited Ceylon and Australia before returning to the United States.

By late 1909 May was appearing in a routine called *Silk Attire*, which was basically the old monologue about her adventures with Hope and Strong. She played Atlantic City and other venues. She settled back in Oregon to establish residency so that she could formally divorce Strong. She filed papers, and without any response or dispute from Strong, the divorce was ordered by the Circuit Court of the State of Oregon on April 25, 1910.

That summer, May got help and encouragement from Evelyn Nesbit Thaw to get back on the stage. Said May, "I'm going back to the stage to show them I'm not a has-been."[18] She lined up appearances in San Francisco. They were in small venues, cafes, and restaurants. Performing in one she was singing "Bring me a Rose" and had reached the words "I'm so tired of violets; take them all away" when she was stricken with a paralytic attack and literally fell off her chair. Physicians came to her aid, and though the effects seemed temporary, she was incapable of performing. Public attention again came her way, pointing to the unlucky diamond and to her failed marriages. One newspaper, heralding her demise, headlined its story "May Yohe nearing the end of a career speckled with sin."[19]

May recovered and rumors of another marriage surfaced almost immediately. Now she was supposed to have married F. M. Reynolds, a musician in a touring musical comedy company. Reynolds denied the marriage.

❖ ❖ ❖

In 1910, another chapter in the Hope diamond tale was added when it came into the possession of the Cartier brothers. Pierre, Louis, and Jacques were prominent Parisian jewelers with a prestigious list of royal and wealthy customers from Europe, India, and America.

The brothers were at the center of yet another Orientalist period of jewelry design, fashion, and cultural movement in Europe. Things Indian were all the rage. The brothers were familiar with the Indian origins of the Hope diamond, Tavernier's diaries, and

May Yohe as a vaudeville actress, c. 1909.

May Yohe on the vaudeville circuit, c. 1910, with a 1926 inscription and signature.

Indian gemological texts recently translated from Sanskrit into French. The Cartiers were also intrigued with Wilkie Collins' *The Moonstone.* They took the tale of the cursed yellow moonstone and grafted it anew onto the 1909 London *Times* article about the unlucky blue diamond to craft their exotic story of the Hope diamond for one of their American customers—Evalyn Walsh McLean.

Evalyn and her husband Edward ("Ned") were vacationing in France, staying at the Hotel Bristol in Paris in September 1910.

The couple was in their mid-twenties, alcoholic, very spoiled, and very wealthy. Ned McLean was the son of the affluent owners of the *Washington Post*. Evalyn was the daughter of Thomas Walsh, a gold miner who struck it very rich and was called "the Colorado Monte Cristo." Pierre Cartier knew the couple; his firm had sold them the "Star of the East," a 94¾ carat diamond, for $120,000 during their honeymoon two years earlier.

Cartier came into the McLeans' suite at the Hotel Bristol carrying the Hope diamond in a package tightly closed with wax seals. He recounted the history of the diamond, describing how Tavernier brought it from India and sold it to Louis XIV. In a new twist, according to Evalyn:

> He told us that Tavernier had stolen the gem from a Hindu god. My recollection is that he said Tavernier afterward was torn up and eaten by wild dogs. Marie Antoinette wore it, so we understand. Marie Antoinette was guillotined and the Revolutionists seized all the wealth.
>
> I might have been excused that morning for believing that all the violences of the French Revolution were just the repercussions of that Hindu idol's wrath.[20]

The stone disappeared after the revolution. According to Cartier, it was stolen. Cartier recounted how the diamond had later appeared in London in the possession of the Hope family. Lord Francis Hope's fortune as well as his marriage to May Yohe dissolved. Cartier asserted that the diamond was then sold to Selim Habib and the Turkish Sultan. He said the Sultan was deposed and his paramour, who'd been wearing the diamond, had her throat cut.

Evalyn could wait no longer. "Let me see the thing," she implored.

Cartier unwrapped the package with great flourish, revealing the Hope diamond. As Evalyn later wrote:

> Cartier told me things he did not vouch for; that it was supposed to be ill-favored, and would bring bad luck to anyone who wore or even touched it. Selim Habib is supposed to have been drowned when his ship sank after he had disposed of the gem. We all know about the knife blade that sliced through Marie Antoinette's throat. Lord Hope had

*plenty of troubles that a superstitious soul might seem to
trace back to a heathen idol's wrath.*[21]

Wrote McLean,

*You should have heard how solemnly we considered all
those possibilities that day in the Hotel Bristol.*
  "Bad luck objects," I said to Cartier, "for me are lucky."
  *"Ah, yes," he said. "Madame told me that before, and I re-
membered. I think, myself, that superstitions of the kind we
speak of are baseless. Yet, one must admit, they are amusing."*[22]

Despite the alluring story, Evalyn and Ned did not purchase the
diamond. Evalyn was disappointed with the setting.

Later that year, Pierre Cartier sailed for New York on the *Lu-
sitania*, carrying the Hope diamond with a new setting. He visited the McLeans in Washington and came to terms on January
28, 1911. Cartier valued the purchase at $180,000. The agreement
included the condition, "Should any fatality occur to the family of
Edward B. McLean within six months, the said Hope diamond is
agreed to be exchanged for jewelry of equal value."[23]

The story of the cursed diamond, as told by Cartier to the
McLeans, circulated quickly and widely. The *New York Times* re-
ported the sale on its front page the next day. "J.R. McLean's Son
Buys Hope Diamond" read the title, with an ominous subtitle,
"Credited with Bringing Ill-luck to Its Possessors."[24] Newspapers
around the world picked up the story.

❖ ❖ ❖

The next day, the *Chicago Tribune* notified May Yohe about
the sale of the famous "hoodoo" gem to the McLeans, looking for
a reaction. May responded bluntly,

*It may be worth a lot of money, but I wouldn't give anyone
a tin nickel for it.*
  *Superstition never has been anything more than a word
to me. I was born in room 23 in my grandmother's hotel at
Bethlehem, Pennsylvania, and I am not afraid to walk under a ladder or open an umbrella in the house. Still, I firmly*

am convinced that the diamond once held an evil influence over me, as well as everyone who owned it.[25]

May wrote to Evalyn McLean urging her to give up the diamond lest its influence harm the McLean family. Some years later, May even reported on a conversation that she and Lord Francis reportedly had about the diamond only a few days after their marriage. The story is certainly apocryphal, but nonetheless reveals May's willingness to keep the curse story alive:

> *Tell me truly, Francis, do you believe the Hope diamond curses those who wear it? . . . A shade of anxiety passed over his face; then, quickly recovering, Lord Francis Hope replied with a smile:*
> *'It certainly hasn't cursed me, Maysie dear, because it has brought me the greatest good luck a man can have—the dearest little wife in all the world, your own precious self"*
> *. . . Of course a diamond could not bring bad luck. What nonsense! . . . And yet there was a sinister shadow over the lives of every person who had ever owned this diamond.*[26]

As the Hope diamond curse story circulated ever more widely, the press and the public permanently associated May with the diamond. Much of what she did—her divorces, her failings, her ills— all invoked the baleful influence of the diamond.

❖ ❖ ❖

While on the vaudeville circuit through 1911, May became romantically linked to Jack McAuliffe, a former boxing champion known as "Little Napoleon." McAuliffe told the press that he'd known May for decades and had been engaged to her before she'd left the United States to marry Lord Francis. McAuliffe embraced the idea of marriage, as did Yohe:

> *Just think, he's carried my picture for twenty years! We're having a vaudeville sketch written called 'The Uplift.' You've seen in the papers that we're going to be married. Maybe we are. Anyway, why not try once more? First I had a peach, then a lemon. This time at least there may be a good pair.*[27]

May Yohe depicted as May McAuliffe, 1911.

McAuliffe seems to have had a good effect on May. His own emphasis on physical fitness, exercise, and diet served May well. He put her on a buttermilk diet. The *Philadelphia Inquirer*, commenting on one of her appearances, noted that May looked great, had lost a lot of weight, wore a Worth gown, and was most entertaining. May's performances during the year occasioned fine reviews—she performed *Silk Attire* in Chicago, headlined a variety show in Minneapolis, and received no less than four curtain calls at Brooklyn's Olympic Theatre. She started to look for better venues. In New York, appearances at the Casino and the Palm Garden were filled to capacity and drew fine reviews.

> *Costumed in an up to the minute evening gown, Miss Yohe's appearance caused an excited flutter in the capacity audience. She sang two songs and proved that she has not lost*

her voice. She was greeted with a storm of applause at the close of her act.[28]

By September, the press was announcing nuptials. In November, May and McAuliffe were staying together as man and wife at the Saratoga Hotel in Chicago. *Variety* reported their marriage at Christmas time. May and McAuliffe did not in fact marry, but the possibility seemed to enliven May. "I'm on the upgrade!" she publicly confided.[29]

May planned, among other things, a return to England in a sketch satirizing British society. She even auctioned off more of her things to help finance the tour herself. She reveled in her independence: "I've learned that the only really independent woman is the one who can rub a few hundred dollars of her earnings and savings together."[30]

May was back at the top of her game. She became more outspoken about women's issues. "Two things that are most worthwhile are my mother and my work," she told a reporter.[31] She railed against those who thought she was beyond her prime and could not stage a comeback. "A woman is not old until she is dead," she wrote in a *Washington Post* column. "We are in our mental prime at 40 years of age. We have just begun to live . . . and realize, what is life? At 40 we have suffered. And suffering makes the stage player."[32]

Through her comeback, May sought to generate more appearances and a higher salary. She hyped the Hope diamond connection, ordering a fine blue crystal copy to be made in Paris and then having it placed in a new, Cartier-like setting by a New York jeweler in order to wear it regularly for her performances.

When bookings looked slim in the summer of 1912, May staged her own disappearance as part of a publicity stunt. Some of her clothes and a handbag were found in Central Park, along with a note suggesting suicide. May's maid, Josephine Scott, was questioned. May was nowhere to be found. For several days articles speculating about May appeared in the press. The police were searching for her body. The lake in the park was about to be drained. Just then, May reappeared in Atlantic City; she'd been on a business holiday with friends, she claimed, performing in two-or three-act shows in some small "jay towns" and "cleaning up a few hundred a week."[33]

May's ruse worked. Offers came pouring in. Hammerstein upped her fee and she "packed them in" at his Roof Garden Theatre. The papers also complied, "May Yohe is proving herself to be not merely a freak act, but a genuine entertainer," declared the *National Telegraph*.[34]

May resented attempts to curb her ambition, or, for that matter, the ambitions of any woman. "Ambition," she said, "should be encouraged in every human being. Only the depraved and degenerate are without it. Ambition is forcing me back to the stage. Ambition is the essence of hope and without hope we are beasts."[35]

But many disagreed. May's arguments inspired her former brother-in-law, the duke of Newcastle, to rail against the woman's suffrage movement when he came to the United States. "This woman-suffrage movement is a perfectly senseless one," Archibald declared. "To be a good wife and mother is a far greater honor. The place for the woman is in the home. If she succeeds in being a vote caster and a legislator she will put herself out of the sphere in which nature designed she should direct all of her efforts."[36] May retorted, "Most people think the bonds of matrimony are the only bonds for a woman. But they never paid me a dividend. Of course," she added, "I didn't play by the rules."[37]

Little could anyone, including May, imagine how that sentiment would animate the next, surprising chapter of her life.

*The pal I have been searching for
through all the world is by my
side and I am content.*
—*May Yohe*[1]

CHAPTER TWELVE

War Bride

MAY AS A CARING NURSE, a housewife, a janitor, a chicken farmer? It is hard to imagine anything more unlikely. Yet these were the roles the former stage queen and lady of the realm came to play. And, to hear her tell it, she was never happier.

This unlikely plot twist in May's life began when she met John Smuts in 1913.

❖ ❖ ❖

That year, May and her mother Lizzie headed back to England, now twenty years after their first visit, and with a renewed confidence. May had a strong sense of herself as a woman, fueled not by youthful bravado, but by maturity born of experience. She was also well along the theatrical comeback trail, having signed on to appear in a musical revue, *Come Over Here,* at the London Opera House.

The production included an extraordinary, well-paid, all-star cast. As the papers said, there were "fat envelopes changing hands."[2] May sang some of her old-time pieces like "Oh Honey, My

May Yohe, 1912.

Honey," but in a more "jazzed up" way, backed by a robust modern band. May was quite a success, despite the fact that in one scene she looked almost comical, dressed in a costume reprising her *Little Christopher Columbus* role, with her large bosom overflowing her chemise and waist.

Newspapers noted that Lord Francis was in a house box, coming twice to see the show and, presumably, May. Though she avoided looking in his direction while on stage, rumors suggested that he'd been touched by the performance, and headlines followed. "May Rewed May Yohe" screamed one.[3] The next day another headline, "Lord Francis Hope Emphatically Denies London Yarn" put them to rest.[4] May and Francis were never to meet or see each other again.

During the show's run, May became enmeshed in a dispute launched by scathing attacks in the press on chorus girls. The *London World* railed against the rising incidence of English youth— "young dogs of the age"—being taken in by the "limitless greed of some young harpy of the stage." The paper excoriated the "cult of the chorus girl," referring to such women as "expensively-clothed Amazonian armies." The attack went further:

> *We are faced with the edifying spectacle of young England doing obeisance to scullery-maids who do not possess humanity. The chorus girl, selected for her physical attributes, is often drawn from the uneducated class. Her only training is in the curses of musical comedy. She learns to dance a few steps and bleat commonplace vulgarities.*
>
> *[The chorus girl] centers her few brains on catching one or more of those raw young men who will provide her with the clothes, pocket-money, and food which she covets so intently.*
>
> *The young men of today must know they are merely being exploited, regarded as a banking account, and identified with a gilt-edged menu.*[5]

As the London press proclaimed, it was "May Yohe to the Rescue."[6] In what was described as "spirited language," May took the attackers to task. "The attack is cruel and unjust, and uncalled for," she said:

> *The public goes to the theater in comfort and has no consideration for the girls on the stage. They don't think of the hours of hard work which have to be put in before the show can be produced. They see pretty faces, and they wouldn't go to the theater at all if they didn't, but paint and tinsel doesn't do everything. The girl has got to be pretty behind the*

> *tinsel, and bright and vivacious and just because a young*
> *man falls in love with one of these girls when his people*
> *want him to love some society girl, it is no reason why re-*
> *venge should be taken on all chorus girls.*[7]

May was an articulate defender of working women, and of course, as everyone in London knew, she spoke from profound experience. The one-time *prima donna* now seemed wise and compassionate.

❖ ❖ ❖

The success of May's London appearance led to a performance tour in South Africa. There, May met Captain John Addey Smuts, said to be a cousin of the famous Boer general, Jan Smuts. John had served the British in the Cape Police and fought with the Dennison's Scouts against the Boers in the Anglo-Boer War. By 1913, Jan was a government minister and perhaps the second highest ranking official in the relatively new Union of South Africa, a dominion of the British crown.

John Smuts, nine years younger than May, was a tall, broad man with rugged features, kind brown eyes, and a reassuring grin. May wrote that the courtship went very quickly between her and John. She found him "a man set apart for me."[8] Smuts provided an alternative to both the carefree Strong and the doting Hope. Strong was totally undisciplined. May thought Hope overly generous, treating her as a golden goddess and gratifying her slightest whim. May reflected on her own personality: "Spirited, untamed, headstrong as I was, I needed a firm hand on my reins."[9] Smuts, with his military bearing and experience, was her man.

May returned to New York in January 1914 and told the press that she would soon be married—but refused to name her future husband. She then returned to South Africa, opened an inn near Cape Town, and was prospering. Later in the year, according to May, her wedding to John Smuts took place with great state fanfare, with numerous Boer officials and luminaries in attendance.

May and John then planned to travel, but World War I intruded. German South-West Africa (now Namibia) was a colony adjacent to South Africa. With Great Britain and Germany at war in Europe, conflict also erupted between these neighboring states in southern Africa. Jan Smuts formed the South African Defense Force and cousin John Smuts took command of a unit.

John Smuts went to battle under the command of General Botha against the German colony garrison, and May followed him and his troops as a British Red Cross nurse. According to newspaper accounts, May "behaved with exemplary patriotism and public spirit . . . The former actress and society woman was now transformed into an earnest soldier's wife and friend of all good Allied fighting men."[10] As May later recalled, "I was in the thick of the fighting, never far from my husband's side."[11] Fighting was brutal and care wanting in Southwest Africa.

May became "a proficient war nurse, skilled in treating the soldiers' wounds, in preparing food for the sick and ever ready to endure all the horrors of war without flinching . . . while she has become a thoroughly devoted and skillful nurse, her old talent as an actress and singer is of great value in cheering up the sick and convalescent."[12]

John regarded May as "my little trooper," so loyal and so devoted was she in the war effort. More than one reporter editorialized about May. She has "changed so that her friends of reckless Bohemian days would scarcely have known her," said one. "May Yohe has regained her own soul. She has paid nobly for the sins of the past."[13]

John Smuts was wounded several times. May and others treated him at the front, and after his repeated injuries, he was sent to a hospital back home. May tended to him there as well. Apparently the most serious of his injuries affected his foot, making walking difficult and painful. He became an invalid, and in 1915 he was sent to India with May to recuperate.

May and Smuts fell into a familiar spousal relationship for her. Smuts was the stalwart hero, the father figure who could keep May safe and secure. He was also the son she could care for and who could tag along while she played the starring role.

"His American wife nursed the captain tenderly back to health," reported a newspaper.[14] In India, they lived off of his meager pension, and May was able to line up several performances to generate additional income. Smuts ineffectually looked for business opportunities, but found nothing promising.

They headed for Burma, apparently strapped for cash. In Rangoon, Smuts ran into trouble paying his boarding house bill and was arrested by the police. They then traveled to Singapore, where May knew the Sultan of Johore from earlier tours and performances across the Orient. Singapore was still in shock over a mutiny of its Indian colonial troops. Many of those troops were Muslim and had reacted violently to rumors that they would be sent to fight fellow Muslims—Ottoman Turks—in the Middle East, where Turkey was allied with Germany against Britain. The mutiny was put down and several hundred troops arrested and imprisoned. Nonetheless, it had unnerved colonial authorities and local Malay allies in the region.

Among those British allies was the Sultan of Johore, whose Malay Peninsula domain abutted the island of Singapore. As May reported, the Sultan asked her to sing "Oh Honey, My Honey" and offered to employ Smuts in return. May sang, very movingly, and the Sultan apparently made Smuts the manager of one of his rubber plantations.

Rubber production was on the rise in the region. The industry had its beginnings in Charles Goodyear's accidental discovery in 1839 of the key to vulcanizing latex to make durable rubber. Convinced that rubber trees would grow well in the region, and that labor could be organized in the form of plantations to tap the latex sap on a massive scale, the British, in 1877, sent twenty-two seedlings from Kew Gardens (grown from the seeds of a Brazilian species) to Malaya. Those seedlings resulted in a thousand trees that formed the basis of the Malayan plantations. As automobiles—and the rubber tires they rolled on—proliferated in the early 1900s, the market for rubber skyrocketed. In Johore, a railway and improved transportation with adjacent Singapore allowed for dramatic increases in rubber exports.

Smuts and May experienced the industry's heyday, and though they did not seem to greatly benefit financially, they enjoyed the stability the plantation provided. May called Singapore "a tiny paradise on earth."[15] She liked the freedom the colony provided, "the right to do as one pleases without apology or excuse."[16] Living there also worked domestically for the couple. Said May, "Oh, I'm satisfied with my husband. It was like vaccination—I had to try three times before it 'took.'"[17]

After three years in Singapore, with World War I still raging in Europe and the couple essentially out of the fray in the Malay Peninsula, Smuts became increasingly anxious to get back into the military. Though he'd been ruled too infirm for British military service in South Africa, he'd heard that he might be able to reenlist through the "back door" in America. The couple concocted a plan to travel across the Pacific to the United States, en route to the front in France. But they had to raise the funds to do so.

May arranged for a benefit concert at Singapore's famed Victoria Theatre. Her concert was scheduled for March 20, 1918. Patrons lined up to support her effort. Advertising was aggressive. Public notices in the newspapers made the case:

> *Mr. Smuts, who has been planting, is eager to go on active service, and has been accepted by the military authorities, but the only way his wife can go with him is via America, and the heavy cost of that journey has decided her to face the footlights again, and show us how she won the heart of London audiences.*[18]

Other local entertainers joined May for the variety show at the Victoria. The concert became a cause célèbre for British colonials in Singapore. May drew a full and enthusiastic audience to the concert. The evening was stellar:

> *The artiste [May Yohe] had a great reception when she appeared and she quickly proved that she retains all her old charm in giving the songs which she made so popular. Her voice was full and effectively used, and every number was rendered in a way which betokened the true artiste. At her second appearance she wore the famous chic "coon" costume and the audience was still more enthusiastic. Her last contribution was the famous "Oh Honey, My Honey," which was freely sung and encored to the echo.*[19]

Others on the program sung patriotic and rousing songs, including "Over There," composed just the previous year by George M. Cohan after America's entry into the war.

The concert was a financial success. The couple sailed to Yokohama and then on to San Francisco aboard the *Seiyo Maro*, arriving on June 10, 1918. Entering the United States, they listed their permanent residence as Cape Town. Smuts declared his occupation as "planter," while May listed hers as "housewife." On the immigration form, in the box for listing their closest relative or friend, they wrote "Sultan of Johore."

The couple traveled to Seattle, where Smuts' visit to the British recruiting office proved disappointing. His injuries were deemed too severe—he would never serve again.

May and Smuts were broke and broken. May, ever the energetic optimist, took off to perform and give concerts in San Francisco to earn money. While there, she received a letter from her husband. He had found a way to do his part for the war effort. Seattle's mayor had called upon citizens to work in the shipyards so that vessels might be readied for transporting needed materials for the war. Smuts had gone to the Seattle North Pacific shipyard to ask for a job. Thankfully, he succeeded in getting one. Given his lack of experience, he was taken on as a laborer, riveting and punching for $3.96 a day. May came back to Seattle to take care of him.

> *We settled down then to a home-y life. Captain Smuts came home to me each evening, very dirty and tired, and found a hot dinner waiting for him—cooked by May Yohe, of "Little Christopher" fame, who once had owned the Hope diamond and who might have been a duchess!*[20]

The seemingly idyllic working-class poverty of the couple took a turn for the worse later in 1918 when Smuts, like one-third of all people on earth, fell prey to the influenza epidemic. He couldn't work for three months. Afflicted by the dreaded disease, his health degenerated. May and Smuts were desperate for income.

Of that crisis, May later wrote, "What was I to do? I could not earn money on the stage and remain in Seattle taking care of my sick husband." She did the unexpected.

> *I put on a gingham dress and a cotton apron, tied my hair in a knot on top of my head, wrapped an old shawl about me and went to the shipyards. 'Please let me help a bit,"I said, 'even if I have to scrub the office floors."*
>
> *They asked me who I was and I told them, "Mrs. Smuts." The name meant nothing to them. They asked me if I were experienced with the mop. Once I had played the part of a slavey in a comic opera [Lady Slavey], and during one of my*

May Yohe as a scrubwoman.

songs waved a mop back and forth over the stage floor. So I
said I was an adept scrubwoman.

I was told to report for duty at seven o'clock that evening—night shift—and that I was to be the office janitress
at $18 a week.

So every night for many long weeks I scrubbed those office floors. The night force of clerks and managers sat at their
desks all around me. Some were gentle and thoughtful of
the 'janitor woman' and dropped kindly greetings to me as
I mopped around them. Others were curt and overbearing.
Quite often I would hum while I worked, and sometimes if
the office were quiet I would sing snatches of my old songs—
especially the one which helped me to become famous, "Oh
Honey, My Honey."

*Many times while I swung that mop I wondered what
these men would say about me if they knew their janitress
was May Yohe, who had been Lady Francis Hope, and
whose throat, now covered with grime and perspiration had
glistened white behind the great Hope diamond and count-
less other gems men liked to hang upon it.*[21]

May's role as scrubwoman was publicly discovered after about
five or six weeks. She was inadvertently exposed by John Considine, a major vaudeville circuit producer who had booked her
to perform at Seattle's Coliseum in 1907. He'd paid May $1,000 a
week. Recognizing May at work he yelled, "My god, Maysie, is this
a farce comedy or what?"

Without missing a beat May shook out her dust mop and replied, "It's what!" Considine then shouted out to all those about,
"Do you know who this is?" When met by silence from the puzzled
shipyard workers, he answered, "She is Lady Francis Hope—May
Yohe!"[22] The incident became well-known and widely published.
May's story about the vicissitudes of life and the elasticity of human fortune received a lot of attention.

One editorial had it exactly right. May's life "reveals the stretch
of human emotion and the possibilities of the human heart."[23] For
her part, May told reporters, "The Maysie of the stage, the Maysie
of scandals is gone. The former Madcap May insisted that this May
is now going to live a quiet life."[24]

Smuts recovered and went back to work. A reporter noted,
"The plucky woman [May] had fought the desperate battle for her
husband's life and won," as May said, "the greatest happiness I have
ever known."[25]

May's beloved mother Lizzie, who had been living with relatives in New York, died on May 17, 1918 and left some money to
her daughter. The armistice that ended World War I was signed
on November 11, 1918. In 1919, the couple moved to Los Angeles
where the climate was better for Smuts. With the inheritance, they
bought a modest chicken farm in Lomita, then on the outskirts of
the city, now in south-central Los Angeles. May fell into the routine of a farm wife:

*I am up early in the morning cooking breakfast while my
husband stirs around in the garden. While he attends to*

business I am sweeping and dusting and chatting with the neighbors about our chickens. Saturday nights we go to the movies and Sundays we take long walks, hand in hand, out along the boulevards—and Mrs. John Smuts, housewife, is happier than May Yohe ever was![26]

May was apparently a good sport, finding rural life on the chicken farm incessantly fascinating. She was humble with neighbors. No one knew who she was, and she didn't put on airs. May would daily walk to the grocery store, more than a mile from their home, and sometimes she'd get a ride with neighbors, white and African American. Yet, despite it all, the chicken farm was quickly going bust financially.

May was at a loss about what to do next. Just then, fate sadly provided a new opportunity, bringing the former Lady Hope and the famous blue diamond back into the public eye.

The Hope diamond?
It looked like a bum sapphire. Why, I
gave the old stone more publicity than
it ever had before or since.
—May Yohe, reflecting on the diamond[1]

CHAPTER THIRTEEN
Cursed

THOUGH SHE MAY NEVER HAVE ACTUALLY WORN IT, May helped make the Hope diamond the well-known icon it is today.

May repeatedly contended that she had worn the Hope diamond twice, the first time at the Rothschild dinner in January 1895, the second at the duke of Newcastle's dinner in September 1900. In 1911, Lord Francis denied that May or anyone else had worn the diamond. He asserted that it had been sitting in a vault at Parr's Bank since 1894. Whether this was true or not, May nonetheless made good use of the diamond—wearing a replica of the famous gem in her performing career and tying herself and her failed marriage to Lord Francis to the diamond's infamous history.

May was not the only one to flaunt her association with the diamond. Evalyn Walsh McLean, who had recently bought the diamond from Cartier, did her part to promote the curse, sharing its story with her high-society crowd in Washington, wearing and showing it off provocatively, and even having it blessed by a priest.

❖ ❖ ❖

Whether playfully considered or not, the reputation of the Hope diamond changed on May 18, 1919. Ned and Evalyn McLean were in Louisville for the Kentucky Derby. Their eldest son, nine-year-old Vinson, who had been termed the "hundred million dollar baby" when he was born, was playing near the road in front of the family's northwest Washington, D.C. estate. A former gardener had pulled over to the roadside. He had some ferns in his car. Vinson playfully grabbed a few and was making his getaway when a Ford, coming down the road at about eight miles an hour, banged into him. Vinson was knocked to the ground and his head hit the concrete. The boy was carried into the house. An army surgeon who was in the area was summoned.

Vinson's condition was serious and declining. The McLeans were called in Louisville. They left immediately for home via a specially chartered train. A specialist from Johns Hopkins University in Baltimore, a brain surgeon from Philadelphia, and another physician from Washington all joined to help.

Despite an emergency operation, young Vinson died. A *New York Times* report noted,

> *When news of the death of the boy spread throughout Washington tonight, it was at once remarked that this was another tragedy to be added to the long string of misfortunes that had followed the successive owners of the Hope diamond.*[2]

Ned went on a drinking binge, devastated by the death of his son. Florence Harding, wife of Warren Harding, then still a senator, tried to console her friend and mentee Evalyn. And family, friends, and the public wondered if the Hope diamond was truly cursed.

May and others commented on the tragedy and consoled the McLeans. May noted the effect upon her own life. "Its curse fell upon both of us [her and Francis]. It was under the malignant influence of the gem that I committed the most tragic and unhappy mistake of my life. Far better that a millstone be hung around my neck than that I should wear it again."[3]

Evalyn Walsh McLean and Edward Beale McLean with their oldest son Vinson and his brother John.

✤ ✤ ✤

May and Smuts spent the summer of 1919 in Quebec at the vacation home of cousin Adeline Parke (aunt Anna Yohe's girl) and her husband Harry Cummings. The couple's daughter Dianne, eight years old at the time, remembers May and Smuts as a couple "very much in love, with never a cross word spoken."[4]

Clearly affected by Vinson's horrific death, May decided to take on a big project, and to tell, in her own dramatic fashion, the story of the Hope diamond. She had time on her hands to do it, especially because the chicken-farming operation was going belly up.

May, capitalizing on her fame and her own brief history with the diamond, was able to secure a deal to write a nationally syndicated series of articles under the title *The Hope Diamond Mystery*. Her stories would appear in Hearst newspapers across the country. That deal enabled her to convince producer George Kleine, a German

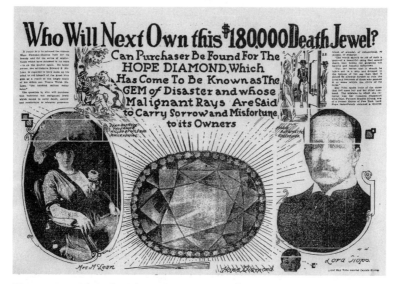

Newspaper article in the Atlanta Constitution, *July 13, 1919.*

American from New York, to take the lead in making a silent movie serial as well.

The newspaper series was published weekly for months in 1920 with the byline given as "May Yohe (Lady Francis Hope)" even though May was now Mrs. John Smuts. Articles typically took up a full newspaper page and were quite boldly produced. They included images from May's original photographs, copies of historical paintings, and original illustrations.

Each week an editorial lead-in promised,

> *The story of May Yohe's career will be told from week to week in these pages by May Yohe herself. Few plots in drama or fiction equal the extraordinary real life experience of this remarkable American girl. And the curse of the Hope diamond? Something indeed seemed to cast its sinister shadow over her life and pursued her relentlessly in America, in Asia, in Europe, and even in South America. She follows its sinister trail down through the centuries to the shocking death of little Vinson Walsh McLean, whose parents now own the 'cursed' stone.*[5]

Much more fanciful than either the London *Times* or Cartier's account, the articles offered fictional history, May's recollections, and bizarre imagination. The plot roughly followed Collins' *Moonstone* story. In Yohe's ethnographically puzzling account, Tavernier is supposed to have discovered the blue diamond in the breast of Brisbun, a Tibetan jade statue of Buddha in a Sita Ram temple in Burma. A "cult of pagan priests" is "bent on recovering the stone." Its agents wreak havoc on the owners of the Hope diamond as they try to steal it back in order to restore it to the "jade idol in the wilderness."[6]

Yohe liberally inserted her own biography in the tale, including her own, seemingly fictionalized experiences with the diamond. For example, she describes meeting with an ascetic in India who is supposed to have revealed the unknown, early history of the gem.

May found in her failed marriages with Lord Francis Hope and then Putnam Bradlee Strong the long reach of the Hope diamond curse. Appearing to run out of steam at several points, she inserted all sorts of fictional elaborations about the Hope diamond and its owners. One week, for example, she totally made up an account of how the diamond had been loaned by Frankel's to J. P. Morgan, who was mysteriously stricken by illness until the deadly diamond was returned. In another piece, she fabricated an episode in which the Marquess of Queensberry owns the diamond and evil befalls his family.

Through the series, May offered her own life as a lesson in humility exacted by the curse of the diamond. It is she, bedecked with the Hope diamond and other jewels, who is reduced to working as a scrubwoman in the Seattle shipyard. With many dramatic flourishes, she places herself among the high and mighty brought low by the cursed gem.

As May was writing the articles, Kleine formed Kosmik Films, Inc., to produce the silent film serial. Kosmik's treasurer, Jack Wheeler, put together financing, and Kleine signed up Stuart Paton to direct the series. May started writing the script, but the film took a turn away from her story as Kleine hired other writers to finish the screenplay for what became *The Hope Diamond Mystery*. Paton lined up William Marion to play the owner of the Hope diamond, a Lord Francis figure. Vamp Grace Darmond played the heroine. May Yohe played herself—Lady Francis Hope. The most interesting figure was the turbaned Indian, Dakar, the priest of the cursing deity Kama-Sita, played by a young Boris Karloff.

May Yohe as a janitoress in the newspaper serial "The Hope Diamond Mystery."

Poster for the movie The Hope Diamond Mystery, *1921.*

May Yohe in a promotional photograph for the 1921 movie, The Hope Diamond Mystery, *Brown Brothers BB–17597–172J.*

The plot was incomprehensible. Its episodes, played out over a 15-week period, included "Hope Diamond Mystery," "Vanishing Hand," "Forged Note," "Jewel of Sita," "Virgin's Love," "House of Terror," "Flames of Despair," "Yellow Whisperings," "Evil Eye," "In the Spider's Web," "Cup of Fear," "Ring of Death," "Lash of Hate," "Primitive Passions," and, finally, "Island of Destiny."

The episodes made an unrecognizable hash of the history of the Hope diamond. May's flighty fictionalizations obscured the series' occasional historical facts. Nor did the film story bear even the

A scene with Boris Karloff, William Marion, and Harry Carter in The Hope Diamond Mystery.

slightest resemblance to the fantasies about the diamond perpetrated by *The Times* of London or the Cartier account.

The newspaper series also fueled a book in 1921, unimaginatively titled *The Mystery of the Hope Diamond* and published by the unknown International Copyright Bureau. The book was written by H. L. Gates, who acknowledges on the title page that the story comes from the "personal narrative" of Lady Francis Hope. The book also has photographic images of stills from the movie, somewhat less extraneous material, and a lot more of May's biography than the newspaper story.

The book ends with a chapter called "I Escaped the Curse:"

*In every episode the Hope diamond has played its part . . .
leading to tragedy, to tears, to terrors, and to heart-breaks.*
   *Does it retain its pagan curse? Does it sparkle only with
reflected evil? Does it bring death, dishonor, disgrace?*
   Is there any escape from the curse of this stone?
   The answer lies in the fact that I have.[7]

A fanciful magazine illustration of May Yohe as Lady Francis holding the blue diamond with Lord Francis Hope, 1947.

How does May escape? By divorcing Lord Francis, divorcing Strong, putting her jewels and life as Lady May behind her, and enjoying the poverty and humility of life with John Smuts—at least as of 1921. Though she is now free of the "pagan curse," she expects the diamond to continue to exert its evil upon others.

✜ ✜ ✜

May Yohe's fractured history was the most elaborate version of the tale of the supposed curse of the Hope diamond to date.

In subsequent years, bits and pieces of her story found their way into magazines, books, and newspapers, including such legitimate news sources as the *New York Times*, *Newsweek*, *Time*, and, more recently, a variety of websites. May's fantastic assertions and misinformation have been repeated over and over again until they have become part and parcel of the Hope diamond story. For example, decades later, the *Washington Post* falsely reported that "hundreds of years of legends surround the curse of the Hope diamond." [8] *Life* magazine, in a photo-essay featuring a Michelle Pfeiffer photo shoot with the gem at the Smithsonian's National Museum of Natural History, accepted May's imaginative assertion that the Hope diamond came from the blazing eye of the statue of Ram Sita, and guide books for tourists repeat as fact May's designation of a temple in Burma as the original home of the diamond.

With the death of Vinson McLean, the publication of H.L. Gates' version of May Yohe's story, and the release of the film series, the curse of the Hope diamond became enshrined as a popular modern legend. It was then elaborated, spread, and touted by Evalyn McLean, who had a unique ability to keep the story before an interested public before she too died in 1947. Two years later, her estate had to sell the Hope diamond to pay off debts. Harry Winston bought it at a bargain price, and then in 1958 donated it to the Smithsonian.

I was never so happy in my life.
—May Yohe[1]

CHAPTER FOURTEEN

Domestic Tranquility?

MAY'S PUBLICITY PUSH ALMOST WORKED. The newspaper and film serial generated some interest. *Variety* reported that John MacArthur would sponsor, Ned Doyle would produce, and Paul Ash—the "Rajah of Jazz"—would musically direct a revival of *Marrying Mary* with May Yohe in the lead.[2] That never came to be, and so, despite the Hope diamond productions, the Smuts still had their financial problems. They sold the farm for a $500 profit. May said she and her husband were going to return "home" to Singapore. But they didn't have enough money to do so. They headed East. May had no real choice. She now had to try another comeback on stage, not so easy for a woman over fifty-five.

May held an auction on Fifth Avenue in New York in 1921, earning $4,329 selling off a mat of rare feathers given to her by the President of Chile, a bronze clock given to her by the duchess of Marlborough, and an ancient gold-embossed Japanese mirror given to her by the British actor-theatrical producer Sir Henry Irving.

She returned to the performing circuit in 1922, updating her old repertoire with jazzy newer music. The newspapers were kind this time around. "May Yohe is on the upgrade again," said the *Chicago*

Daily Tribune.[3] May was singing "If I Were Only You" and "That Old Girl of Mine," in their more traditional versions and then with the more spirited and syncopated arrangements of the "roaring 1920s." "The years since her sensational escapades earned her the title of "Madcap May" have not deprived her of the colorful personality and engaging frankness that captivated English nobility, American Bohemia, and theater goers of both countries," said the *Tribune.*[4]

As she moved around the country, she was, of course, asked about her husbands. May was always laudatory about her first husband: "I can't say anything too good about Lord Francis Hope," she'd begin, "and I can't say anything too bad about Putnam Bradlee Strong. But my present husband Captain John Smuts is a dear."[5]She was also asked about the Hope diamond and its infamous curse. Usually, she played up the melodrama of the story—her leaving Hope for Strong, Lord Francis' money troubles, and her descent from fame and fortune. Sometimes she'd make light of it. Talking about her chicken farm, for example, she'd say, "I found out since that the man I sold it to struck oil on it. Isn't that just my luck?"—and blame it on the diamond.[6]

May was at the Bushwick Theatre in Brooklyn one week, the Colonial on Broadway the next, then it was off to B. F. Keith's in Boston, returning to New York, then back to Bowdoin Square, Gordon's, and Boston Theatres in Boston. Her new act was regarded as entertaining, setting "nerves a tingling." A *Boston Daily Globe* review captured the spirit of her performance:

> *An old-time gem in an ultra-modern setting, May Yohe linked up with the jazziest of jazz bands, is the unusual combination at B.F. Keith's . . . May Yohe is the headliner this week of a bill that is good all the way through, with excellent dancing, snappy singing, and keen humor marking the various acts.*[7]

May still grabbed some headlines and good notices on the entertainment pages, though her show style was receding. The prominent names in live entertainment were the Ziegfeld Follies, Al Jolson, and Sophie Tucker. Interestingly enough, Florenz Ziegfeld, as a youth in Chicago, had been heavily influenced by the lavish David Henderson shows—such as *The Arabian Nights* and *The Crystal Slipper*—with none other than May Yohe in a lead role. But

John Smuts and May Yohe at the Blue Diamond Inn, 1922.

more than shows, it was the silent movies that were drawing audiences, and they, too, would soon give way to the "talkies."

May and Smuts opened a tea room in Manhattan's theater district. The eatery closed within weeks, a total failure. In 1923, they opened an inn in Marlow, New Hampshire called "The Blue Diamond," catering to tourists visiting the White Mountains. The place included a modest house for the couple and an inn on 600 acres of farmland wooded with sugar maples. Smuts did the cooking, offering South African dishes quite rarely sampled in the United States. May was the hostess and manager. But, as if to prove the bad luck of the Hope diamond, after which it was named, the inn burned down the following November. Arson was suspected; the fire was thought to have been set to cover up a burglary.

Only two weeks later, the Boston police were called to the Smuts' recently rented rooms at 129 West Concord Street. John Smuts had been shot in the chest. His condition was touch and go. A suicide note was found that read "I am going to shoot myself because I have been unkind to my wife."[8] It was signed with Smuts' name, but the text and signature were in different handwriting.

To the police it was obvious that Smuts could not have shot himself. Besides, the handwriting on the note clearly wasn't his. When questioned at his City Hospital bedside, Smuts said, "It makes no difference who shot me. If you make trouble for my wife I will maintain that I shot myself no matter what you may say. I'm a game fellow. I can stand this. I love my wife."[9]

Smuts claimed the shooting was an accident—he'd been cleaning the gun when it went off. The police couldn't figure out how it happened and May claimed she'd found her husband stricken after the gun had fired. She also professed her love for her husband. The shooting was a mystery. Some newspaper stories implicated the curse of the Hope diamond. Smuts recovered and no charges were ever filed.

May continued to perform in the Boston area and sometimes in New York through the 1920s. She also engaged in various charitable causes, including dressing and distributing dozens of dolls to orphaned and motherless girls for Christmas. She liked working with young women. As one newspaper reporter, Carl Warton, noted, May attracted their attention because, despite her age, she was "extremely youthful in spirit." May offered some wisdom about her role:

> *Advising young people, particularly young girls, is a rather precarious business, especially unless it is sought. The ideas of one generation are different than those of another.*
>
> *They don't see things from the same slant, so you have to keep that in mind and be tactful if you expect to exert any influence. But even then there is a factor you can't control. You may say ten words to one girl and it may change the whole course of her life for the better. To another, you can talk until you're black in the face and it won't mean a thing.*
>
> *Both of them may have the same ideas of life, the difference being that one has that something in her which tells her that there is much to be learned from older people, in other*

May Yohe and John Smuts, 1924.

words that experience can't be wholly discounted; the other believes that the past doesn't solve any problems for us and that we must deal only with the present—taking things as we find them and acting accordingly. The latter seem to be in the majority today.[10]

In August 1925, May appeared on the "Herald Headliner," an evening radio show on WBZ out of Springfield, Massachusetts. It was relatively rare to hear a woman talking on the radio, as many people in the industry thought their vocal frequency was not suited to radio transmission. May, though, embraced the challenge. She spoke of her life, dramatized elements of the Hope diamond legend, and sang a bit of "Oh Honey, My Honey" accompanied by Elgard's orchestra. Her performance was a huge hit. The orchestra and studio audience applauded. The station fielded numerous congratulatory telephone calls from listeners. Telegrams poured in, including cablegrams from Australia and South Africa where admirers had picked up the broadcast on short wave. For a moment, May again had thrilled a crowd and enjoyed their praise.

Buoyed by her reception and offers for performances, May had facial surgery performed by Dr. H. B. Bernstein in Baltimore.[11] She said she had it done it to appear younger and more vital in her performances. She may also have been concerned that the age difference with the younger Smuts was beginning to show.

May continued to perform sporadically and to sell off her treasures to support herself and her husband, who worked for a cement company in Boston. She was also rumored to have gone into the hotel business with Consuelo Vanderbilt, a fellow American whose marriage to the duke of Marlborough had been long annulled.[12]

May was still feisty. In 1927 she sued the Winter Garden Hotel in Lawrence, Massachusetts, after they failed to return promotional material she'd given them to market her performance there.

❖ ❖ ❖

Though she and Smuts always professed their love for each other, his shooting—probably by May—and a series of other mishaps raise some question about their relationship.

In January 1935, May reportedly fell in her home and cracked a rib. It was not the first time she'd fallen. Years before she had injured her back so badly in a fall that she had to cancel a Carnegie Hall appearance.

In June 1935 she suffered a broken arm, a fractured jaw, internal injuries, and possible brain damage, again from a reported fall in her home. Doctors sent her to the Boston State Hospital for observation. For several weeks many newspaper articles appeared reporting that May was thought to be near death and linking the calamity to the baleful influence of the Hope diamond. Despite the warnings by doctors that she might not survive, May managed to recover. Smuts then sent her to a nursing home in Maine, presumably to help her convalesce.

Whether May's frequent injurious falls were caused by her proclivity to faint—documented from the earliest days of her career—or something more nefarious is now impossible to tell. It is possible that Smuts had long been physically abusing May. He was an army man whose career was cut short in the early days of World War I. He only worked short-term jobs and depended upon May to be the breadwinner. May could be obstinate, rambunctious, and insultingly obnoxious. May probably shot Smuts in 1924, and it could have been in retaliation for his abuse. With Smuts essentially homebound in 1935, his frustration with himself and May could have again come to a head.

Because of her diagnosed brain injury and erratic behavior, May was placed in the psychiatric ward. She escaped and went back home to Smuts. Neither incarceration, a possibly abusive husband, or a cursed diamond could keep her down.

Preposterous . . . false . . . rubbish.
—May Yohe, on hearing that someone
claimed to be her son[1]

Mother?

M AY YOHE WAS HIS MOTHER, claimed one very determined young man in 1935. Was it true—and did she have
other children?

One claim was a bald misstatement. In 1925 Warren Doble,
vice-president of the Doble Steam Motor Company, announced
his wedding to Audrie Hope. He claimed she was the daughter of
Lord Francis Hope and May Yohe. He was misinformed about a
lot of things—declaring, for example, that Putnam Bradlee Strong
had died in Shanghai and that May was living in New Orleans.
When May read the announcement, she quipped, "As I never had
a daughter, I find this a most interesting story."[2]

Doble's wife was the daughter neither of Francis and May nor
of Francis and his second wife Muriel. Neither Dobie's marriage
nor his credibility seemed solid. The couple later divorced and his
steam car company folded.

A decade later, in July, 1935, another woman, Mrs. A. J. St-
reit of Waukegan, Illinois, whose maiden name was Hazel Potts,
claimed she was the daughter of May and Lord Francis. "The adoption papers in the possession of my foster mother give my mother's

name as May Hope," she said. Her foster mother, Rose Potts, told the press,

> *We adopted our daughter, Hazel Potts, at a Catholic found-*
> *ling home in Minneapolis 33 years ago. At the time we took*
> *her we were told her true name was Olive Hope. The sisters*
> *told us they could not reveal the parents' names to us, but*
> *they did tell us that the baby's father was a prominent Eng-*
> *lishman and that the baby's mother was a talented concert*
> *singer.*[3]

The father's name was not filled out on the adoption papers. A friend of Hazel's sent a telegram to Smuts and May, asking May if she was interested in knowing the fate of her daughter. Hazel herself told the press that she just wanted to see her mother.

May and Smuts did not take Potts' claim seriously, for it was the second claim that had popped up that week. The first claim, made by Robert Edgar Thomas, a bit player in Hollywood movies, was much more serious and was to result in a complicated and protracted legal battle.

Thomas claimed he was born to May Yohe in Portland, Oregon, in 1908 while she was still legally married to Putnam Bradlee Strong. Thomas' mother, Rosa, declared, "My late husband [Edward R. Thomas] and I adopted Robert in Multnomah County on May 5, 1909. Until the death of my husband eighteen months ago, Robert did not know Miss Yohe was his mother." She continued,

> *We were going through my husband's papers and Robert*
> *came across a packet inscribed 'Papers about my son.' He*
> *found clippings and a picture of Miss Yohe which she had*
> *autographed to me.*
>
> *After Robert's birth Miss Yohe did not plan to place him*
> *for adoption. I'm sure Mr. Thomas and I talked her out of*
> *the baby, who was only 6 months old. She was a beautiful*
> *and fascinating woman.*[4]

The Thomases ran the drug store in the Perkins Hotel where May lived before she rented her own cottage in Portland from 1908 to 1909. May came into the store regularly to make purchases.

Smuts responded that while they would like to hear from Robert Thomas, now twenty-six, the assertion that he was May's son was "bosh." Smuts opined, "This is obviously a publicity stunt, and it's too silly to talk about."[5]

While Smuts may have honestly believed his statement, May must have known there was more to be told. Back in 1909, a Portland newspaper headlined a story, "Oft-Married Actress Becomes Mother" and asserted that May Yohe had given birth to a boy, placed him for adoption with an "Edward R. Thompson (*sic*)" and then "left town." *Variety* had picked up the story, as did scores of other publications. The *Los Angeles Times* had written,

> *May Yohe, one of the most notorious women of the stage, gave birth to a child in Portland Oregon. It has been adopted by a family in that city and will be reared as the son of Edward Thomas and wife.*[6]

Once again, in the twilight of her life, May was back in the news. Newspapers and magazines ran full-page features about Thomas' claim. These stories recounted Madcap May's life in the Naughty Nineties, her stage career, her escapades with Strong, and her association with the Hope diamond. In several, Rosa Thomas offered the reason why May had put her baby up for adoption. "She talked a great deal about the curse of the Hope diamond, saying that she feared it would descend on the newborn baby."[7]

Rosa's attribution of May's motive was probably apocryphal, since accounts of the Hope diamond being unlucky were just starting to emerge in the newspapers in 1908, and had not yet been articulated as a "curse." An old photograph of May with her autograph which Rosa Thomas showed to reporters was also problematic. Supposedly, it was from 1908 and inscribed to Rosa with "affection." However, it was signed "May Yohe-Smuts"—a name May did not have until 1914.

In December 1935, Robert Thomas filed a lawsuit in New York's Supreme Court, claiming that May Yohe was a callous mother who had hidden the birth of her child, and then, some six months later, handed him over to the Thomases, thus depriving him of his birthright. Despite public statements by Robert Thomas about the chance discovery of his adoption papers and his desire to meet May and get to know her as a "warmly affectionate friend," the lawsuit was really an effort by Thomas to establish the right to

Robert Edgar Thomas and Rosa M. Thomas, 1935.

inherit a portion of the estate left by Mary Urania Strong, Captain Strong's wealthy mother.[8]

Mrs. Strong had died in 1921, leaving an estate reputed to be worth some two million dollars. If Robert Thomas was born to May, who was at the time married to Putnam Bradlee Strong, he could claim to be their legal offspring. Thus he would be the rightful grandson of the deceased, and entitled to a portion of the estate. While maternity was the means of proving his case, Thomas was after the Strong money.

Rosa Thomas, the adoptive mother said, "There is no doubt that Robert is the son of Miss Yohe and her former husband Putnam Bradlee Strong . . . We have all of the necessary proof. All that is required is for the courts to pass upon it."[9]

Thomas' suit claimed he was born on October 1, 1908 (even though some of the documents mistakenly said September 1). He asserted his rights to the estate of Mr. Strong probated in 1901, the estate of Mrs. Strong, a trust fund she'd established, and the benefits due as the son of both May Yohe and Captain Strong.

"It's all rubbish . . . It seems funny to me that he didn't get in touch with me when he learned he was supposed to be my son," said Yohe.[10] Instead, Thomas talked to the newspapers and filed a lawsuit. May accused Thomas of looking for fame and "a share in the Strong fortune." "We'll fight it to the end," she declared.[11] John Smuts even went so far to say, "We'll testify for Putnam Bradlee Strong, if he wants us to."[12]

The suit took two and a half years to resolve, including an appeal. Strong, now graying and in his sixties, testified in front of court-appointed referee Jeremiah Connors in New York. He denied parentage, claiming that he had only seen May Yohe once since their separation in 1905, in Yokohama, for one day, in 1909—months after Robert Thomas was born. He reasserted before the court that he and May had been married in 1902 in Buenos Aires and divorced in 1910 in Oregon.

Strong's testimony provided highly convincing evidence that he was not the biological father. Indeed, even under appeal, the judge in the case opined that there was not "one scintilla" of evidence that Strong was the father. But was May the mother? And since they were still legally married at the time, if May was the mother, did Thomas then have a claim on the Strong family estate, given a legal presumption that any offspring of the mother are the legitimate children of the marital union?

Robert Thomas supported his contention with several documents filed at the time of the adoption. One was the Petition for Adoption signed by the Thomases on May 4, 1909. It read in part,

In the County Court of
the State of Oregon
for Multnomah County

Your Petitioners E. R. Thomas and Rosa M. Thomas, his wife, respectfully represent unto this Court that they are husband and wife, residing in the City of Portland, Multnomah County, State of Oregon, and that they are desirous of adopting Robert, a male child, born on the 1st day of September, 1908; that Mrs. Mary Strong is the mother of, and the surviving parent of the said child, and we further say that we have sufficient ability to bring up the child here referred to and furnish him with suitable nurture and education, and that the consent of the mother, through her attorney, is herewith given, and that your petitioners desire to have said child's name changed from Robert Strong to Robert Edward Thomas.[13]

A companion Power of Attorney document was duly signed by May on the same day. It said,

I, Mary Augusta Strong, mother of the minor child referred to in the petition of E.R. Thomas and wife, to which this consent is attached, do hereby and by my attorney in fact consent in writing to the adoption of such child by the said E. R. Thomas and Rosa M. Thomas, his wife.[14]

While the petition indicated May was the mother, it also referred to her as the "surviving parent," implying the other parent was deceased, and thus weakening the claim that Strong was the father. In May's 1910 petition for divorce from Strong, she stated that there were no children of the union—further evidence against the Thomas' assertion.

But if Strong was not the father, who was? At the time May was maintaining a Portland household as Mrs. James Fellows. James paid the household bills and came down from Vancouver on the weekends, staying in her bedroom. There was little doubt they were intimate and living as man and wife. However, Fellows was alive in 1909. If he were the father, May could not have stated in the adoption petition that she was the sole "surviving parent." And what about the mysterious Murphy, the Canadian lumberman May was said to have married in Portland? Was he, perhaps, the father?

Nothing in the court case or appeal answered the question about paternity. In a surprising twist, the determination of maternity turned out to be equally difficult, despite the 1909 petition and affidavit for adoption. In short, was May really the mother?

One way to answer that question would have been to call May to testify under oath. The court issued summonses to bring her to the court referee handling the case. She avoided all of them, making good use of the fact that while the case was filed and heard in New York, she was living in Boston. She had been in the hospital after a bad fall, she said, and preferred not to travel, but was willing to provide a deposition at home. But that never happened. Time after time, one excuse after another was offered; and when servers and constables tried to locate her, somehow she always managed to disappear—much to the consternation of Thomas' attorneys.

Other testimony, however, gave credence to the Thomas's charge that May was the mother. The elder Thomases got to know May in 1908 as a result of her visits to their drugstore. According to testimony, May browsed the store as a customer and made purchases related to a pregnancy and the care of a baby. Several of May's neighbors and acquaintances from Portland in 1908 confirmed that she looked and seemed pregnant. Her stomach was extended and she said she was pregnant, according to acquaintances Bruce Billings, Louise Glover, and Mrs. Beale.

Rosa Thomas testified that she was called over to May's house on Northrup Street the first week of October 1908 and given a recent newborn baby by May, who'd said it was her child. May had become friends with the Thomases, knew they didn't have a child but wanted one, and offered them the newborn for adoption. They agreed, and May left town the next day or so, purportedly for a performance tour to Australia. The formal adoption petition was filed months later.

The case turned on the testimony of Dr. Harry S. Lamb, May's physician at the time. According to Dr. Lamb, he visited May periodically at her home in Portland, treating her for a variety of illnesses. He addressed her as Mrs. Fellows and sent his bills for service to Mr. Fellows in Vancouver.

At one point May told him she was about five months pregnant. Dr. Lamb took her statement at face value and believed her to be pregnant. A few weeks later, examining her for another ailment, the physician noticed that her abdomen was not as enlarged as he would have expected. He suggested a complete examination. Yohe came to his office, where Lamb conducted "a complete abdominal

and vaginal examination" and ascertained that "she was not pregnant at all at any time."[15] Despite that examination, Dr. Lamb was
aware that May continued to tell people she was pregnant and to
visit the Thomas' store, buying things indicating she expected a
baby.

According to Dr. Lamb's testimony, he was called to Yohe's
home in late September or the first week in October. He found her
alone and she informed him that a baby was about to be brought to
the house. Lamb testified, "After a few minutes, a woman came to
the house with a male baby then about a week old, left the baby with
Yohe and shortly departed. This woman was poorly dressed and
wore street clothes and a hat."[16]Lamb said he had the impression
the baby had been brought from Idaho. May put the baby to bed.

The next day Yohe again telephoned the doctor to come over
to her house. This time, the Thomases were present. To Dr. Lamb,
it appeared that Yohe had already made arrangements with them
to adopt the baby. Mrs. Thomas fondled the baby. According to
Lamb, May didn't hug or breast-feed the infant or otherwise act in
a maternal way. She even said to Mrs. Thomas, "I don't know what
to do with this baby, he is so hungry and all."[17] Then May turned
over the baby to the Thomases.

Other facts came out in the testimony. May did in fact leave
Portland the next day. No certificate was ever filed for the birth
of the child, in contravention of state law. Certainly it could not
have been filed by Dr. Lamb, who, when questioned about the state
requirement, said that he had neither attended nor witnessed the
birth. In his view, the child was clearly not May's.

Despite the Thomases' search, they could not locate a birth
certificate anywhere. No one who witnessed the birth came forward. May employed an almost full-time nurse on her household
staff, but that nurse was excused from her duties while the infant
was in the house. Nor were any of May's other servants present; all
had been given leave. While Louise Glover saw May with the baby
during the "second day," she did not see the birth. Seven months
later, the formal adoption petition and May's statement were filed,
but not by May. Her lawyer represented her.

As the judicial referee, Jeremiah O'Connor, found, "It was not
pregnancy at all; it was a well staged, well acted, imitation of one."
The only reasonable inference to be drawn from all the testimony
is that Yohe wanted it generally believed that she was about to

have a child. She purposefully bought things in the drugstore, said things to people, and distended her abdomen or made it appear large. "At the same time," wrote the referee, "she desired to keep secret certain of the details of her private life."[18] The conclusion of the referee, backed up by the court on appeal, was that Putnam Bradlee Strong was not Robert E. Thomas' father, nor was May Yohe his mother.

The court had two further conclusions. One was that May had avoided testifying because she was still trying to hide what she had done. The court could not determine her ulterior motive, but that was not its task.

The other was that the entire case was motivated by a certain Frank Evans, who had served as the secretary to Putnam Bradlee Strong's sister and brother-in-law, the Shattucks. Evans had been dismissed from his job and was obviously disgruntled, harboring ill-will toward the Strong family. When Strong's sister, Mrs. Shattuck, died in 1935, Evans realized that the estate would now go to Mrs. Strong's surviving son, Putnam Bradlee Strong. If it could be proved he'd had a child, then at some point that offspring would be an heir and come into a fortune. Evans apparently contacted the Thomases and encouraged them to file suit. Evans knew about May's involvement in the 1909 adoption case from a cache of the Shattucks' "confidential papers" that he had unethically kept. Those papers included newspaper clips from 1909 reporting on the birth and adoption of May's baby. Evans probably made a deal to split any resulting funds with the Thomases. As it turned out, they might have been somewhat disappointed with the result. Testimony in the case revealed that the trust fund was not worth $2 million, but rather only about $150,000. The chance of that passing through the hands of the spendthrift Strong to an heir would be most unlikely.

❖ ❖ ❖

If Dr. Lamb's definitive testimony is to be believed, why then did May feign pregnancy and cover up the birth of a baby by falsely asserting she was the mother—and then arrange for the newborn to be adopted?

It is hard to imagine that Dr. Harry Lamb was bribed by May to offer his astounding testimony. He was a solid member of the community. He'd been born and raised in Oregon, attended normal school, earned a teaching certificate, served as a school principal, and received his B.A. and M.D. degrees from the University of Oregon by the time May was his patient. Granted he was only a year out of medical school when he gave her the examination in 1908, but determining pregnancy or lack thereof at five months or so was not difficult. In the intervening decades between that time and the Thomas lawsuit, Lamb had married, operated a successful medical and surgical practice, and earned a completely respected reputation. A few years after the lawsuit, he became the president of the county medical society.

Since she had not been pregnant, who was May helping and protecting?

With the maternity case pending, May planned a trip from Boston to Victoria, British Columbia. She didn't tell anyone why she actually made the difficult trip—she claimed it was to see her lawyers. Perhaps May was heading back west to finally close the door on the mysterious adoption.

May was traveling by transcontinental bus. In mid-February 1937, she was on a Union Pacific stage as it wound its way along the Columbia River Highway between The Dalles and Portland. According to reports of the time, all of a sudden May started screaming. She was shouting that "gangsters had seized the bus and were shooting traffic officers."[19] May apparently tried to leap from the bus—several times—in order to escape.

May was taken into custody by the Portland police and detained in jail. The police believed she was hallucinating. Able to identify her as both May Yohe and Mrs. John Smuts, they cabled her husband in Boston, who then cabled back instructions. She rested, and then, appearing better, was soon released—her secret intact.

❖ ❖ ❖

A tantalizing clue to that secret may be another cross-country trip by one of May's relatives—Dianne Beattie—some six decades later.

May was like an aunt to Dianne Cummings Beattie, the daughter of her cousin Adeline Parke Cummings, the grand-daughter of Anna Yohe Parke. These were May's closest relatives, those with whom she maintained lifelong contact. Ever since they had spent the summer of 1919 together in Quebec, Dianne had looked up to May and May reciprocated with a fondness for the young woman.

Dianne lived most of her life in New York. Her elder brother, Parke Cummings, a sports writer and humorist, died in 1987. After his death, Dianne, at the age of about seventy-six, for no obvious reason, relocated to Portland, Oregon, where she died some sixteen years later.

Dianne may have gone to Oregon to try to solve the mystery of May's adopted newborn, armed perhaps with a clue from reading her deceased mother's papers, which could have been passed on to her when her brother died. She may have suspected that Robert Thomas was actually her half-brother.

Dianne's elder brother, Parke Cummings, was born to Adeline in 1902. Dianne was born in 1911. Though it is purely a matter of speculation and hypothesis, Adeline could have had an affair in 1908, gotten pregnant, gone to the house of her elder cousin May in Oregon, and asked for help in hiding the infant from her lawyer husband. It is difficult to imagine May going through the pregnancy ruse for a stranger but easier to envision her trying to protect Adeline, who was most like a sister to her. In any case, without additional evidence, the true motive and the actual circumstances of May's feigned pregnancy remain a mystery.

I'm like a rubber ball, the harder
I fall, the higher I bounce.
—*May Yohe*[1]

CHAPTER SIXTEEN

Poor, Ill, & Un-American

BEFORE SHE DIED, May had to fight the United States government. Not surprisingly, she won.

By early 1938, May and Smuts were in a desperate financial situation. They lived in a small, sparsely furnished apartment next to the railroad tracks in Boston's Back Bay. The only possession bespeaking May's fame and wealth was a framed photograph of Edward VII when he was the Prince of Wales hanging on the bare wall. It was personally autographed by the future king to May, a keepsake from when she was cheered by London and in line to become a duchess.

Smuts had been hospitalized for six months. He had severe arthritis. The couple had exhausted their meager savings. With the nation still in the Depression, there wasn't much support for an old couple like the Smuts. May, always the fighter, sought work.

Even though she had still not fully recovered from her last fall or the broken bones from the year before, May applied for a job through the Works Progress Administration (WPA). The WPA was created as a centerpiece of President Franklin Delano Roosevelt's New Deal, a way of providing relief to and work for millions of Americans. Normally, only one spouse was entitled to a WPA job, and since Smuts was infirm, May applied.

May was in for a surprise when she did. A check of her citizenship status revealed a problem. Prior to the passage of the Cable Act of 1922, a female American citizen who married a man of another nationality automatically lost her U.S. citizenship, as it was presumed she would become a citizen of her husband's country. May had lost her citizenship with the marriage to Hope, though authorities referred to the fact that when she married John Smuts in 1914, he was a British citizen. May argued that Smuts had immigrated to the United States in 1918 and had become a naturalized citizen in 1928. No matter, said officials. Smuts' becoming a U.S. citizen did not nullify May's loss of citizenship.

May had a long history of being proudly American. She felt this tie and often expressed it viscerally as a core aspect of her identity. It emboldened her as an "outsider" with her female classmates in Dresden and in her interactions with the British aristocracy. Even though she travelled the world, and more than once vowed not to return to America, she always did. Now she needed a job, and she was outraged that the U.S. government had taken away what she regarded as her birthright—no matter what the law said.

May applied to the Naturalization Bureau for the return of her American citizenship. Under the law, May would have to demonstrate she was of sound morals—which may have been a bit more difficult in her youth, but was easier to show in old age.

May also took her case to the papers and generated a broad outpouring of support. Only a few days passed before Mary Ward, the Commissioner of Naturalization and Immigration for Boston, announced that May Yohe would be re-granted her citizenship.

On April 4, 1938, May entered Federal Court in Boston and took the oath of citizenship as Mary Augusta Smuts. On her official documents she indicated her true birth date of April 6, 1866, not 1869.

Two days later, in honor of her birthday, the *Washington Post* ran an editorial about her entitled "Soon Forgotten," and noted that

> *May Yohe enjoyed (that's the word) unprecedented public-*
> *ity . . . and a career that would have filled a score of lives.*
> *[Recently] . . . there was none to do her honor, none to rec-*
> *ognize her, none to detect any traces of that glamour which*

John Smuts and May Yohe in Life *magazine, circa 1935.*

*once cast about her head an aura exceeding the brilliance
of the famous gem she wore to Queen Victoria's court. She,
who had had her cake and had eaten it, too, and in almost
fabulous slices, was just a troublesome old woman.*[2]

On May 4, 1938, newspapers around the country reported that
"May Yohe, once the toast of two continents and a dinner companion of royalty, got up at 6 a.m. today and went to work as a $16.50
a week W.P.A. research clerk." May said, "I'm happier than ever
before."[3]

May's job was to transfer vital statistics from old written led-
gers to card catalogs. After a few weeks of work, she was asked how
she was doing at her job, May responded that she was "holding her
own" with the younger workers.[4]

No. 4 376 820

Name SMUTS,   Mary Augusta

residing at 2 Oakdale Sq., Boston, Jamaica Plain
Apr 6, 1886

Age 71 years. Date of order of admission   April 4, 1 38

Date certificate issued   April 4 1 38   by the

U. S. District   Court at   Boston, Massachusetts

Petition No. 186470

Mary augusta Smuts

May Yohe's citizenship petition, as Mary Augusta Smuts, April 4, 1938.

Less than four months later, on August 28, May lay down to sleep. According to Smuts,

> *Shortly after midnight she wakened me. She said she couldn't breathe well. I got a pillow to put under her head. She slumped forward and died in my arms, just like going to sleep.*[5]

As if attentive to May's stagecraft, Smuts somberly told reporters, "It was a beautiful way to die."[6]

Apparently May was not strong enough to weather the arterial sclerotic heart disease and chronic vascular nephritis that did her in. Her funeral was held at the Thornton Funeral Home in Roxbury and her body cremated at the Forest Hills Cemetery; several days later, Smuts took a boat out on the Atlantic Ocean to spread her ashes as she had requested. "She loved nature and open spaces and abhorred funeral pomp," he said.

The *New York Times, Los Angeles Times, Philadelphia Inquirer,* the Boston papers, and *Time* magazine all carried notices and articles about Miss May Yohe. Evalyn Walsh McLean, the owner of the

May Yohe at home, 1938.

Hope diamond, wrote for "My Say," her newspaper column, "May Yohe may not have been all that the standards of etiquette call for but she certainly proved herself to be a real woman and I salute her memory with sincere admiration and deep respect."[7]

The *Chicago Tribune* reflected on her passing with "A Myth Goes a Glimmering"

> *So May Yohe is dead, after all these years of serving as a heroine for articles in syndicated Sunday supplements about the actress who had once been in possession of the Hope diamond, alleged to carry a fatal curse. It is surprising to find that the touch of mortality has fallen upon a character who seemed to be permanently enshrined in American folklore. We had never thought of May Yohe as a human being—she was like a figure of mythology.*[8]

Amen.

I've done pretty nearly everything
in my life except theft and murder,
but thank God whatever I've done,
my heart's been in it.
—*May Yohe, reflecting on her life[1]*

Epilogue

MAY'S LEGACY, REALLY ONLY A SHADOW of this larger-than-life lady, is still with us today, albeit in various forms.

Most concretely, the Hope diamond that she helped make famous rests today in the Smithsonian Institution's National Museum of Natural History on the National Mall in Washington, D.C. It is, along with the Mona Lisa, the most visited museum object in the world, seen by up to eight million visitors a year, and millions more through television programs, web pages, and other media.

There are other touchstones of her life.

Though May's mother, Lizzie Batcheller, died in 1918, her magnificent Queen Anne-style house still stands in Hastings-on-Hudson, New York, a symbol of history connecting the local community to fame beyond its bounds. While May is much celebrated by the Hastings Historical Society and in the tours it periodically sponsors, her former home is now known as the "Gribben House," after its subsequent owner. The interior has changed significantly since May's time, with a family room and master-suite addition. It is now painted white and has modern utilities. In contrast to the open landscape of May's time, scores of homes now dot the land-scape all around it, but you can still see the Hudson River as clearly as May must have seen it more than a century ago from its distinctive and still extant tower and turret. The house bears witness to May and Lizzie's residency—evidenced by the old wood paneling, a stained glass window, blue Delftware tiles on the fireplace, and built-in panel doors for the living room. The veranda has been renovated, but one can still envision reporters camped out on it, interviewing the kimono-clad May and waiting for the latest news about Captain Strong and her jewels during that infamous summer of 1902. Even though the driveway was relocated from Villard to Edgar Road in the 1940s, traces of the old one remain. It is easy to imagine May yearning to see Strong walking up that drive to return to her.

May's husband Lord Francis Hope became the eighth duke of Newcastle after his brother died in 1928. Due to his profligacy, the Hope diamond, Old Master paintings, Deepdene, and Castle Blayney were all sold off. When he died in 1941 at the age of seventy-five, Henry Edward, his son by his second wife, became the ninth duke. Henry Edward died childless in 1988, and was succeeded by a distant cousin as the tenth duke. When that childless cousin died less than two months later, the dukedom became extinct. Clumber Castle was demolished in the 1930s and never rebuilt. Deepdene was demolished in the late 1960s after serving as a hotel, British Railways wartime headquarters, and office building. Castle Blayney served as a military barracks, hospital, and Franciscan retreat. It is now a small, somewhat run-down hotel, restaurant, and special-events venue in Lake Muckno Park run by the municipality.

After leaving May, Putnam Bradlee Strong was arrested in China and worked in a Macao casino and for the Thai government. He sought to fight against the Turks and join the U.S. Army Reserves. After his escapades with May, his mother paid him to stay out of the United States. They reconciled in Germany, and while she left him money in her will, it was half of what she left her daughter. Strong married divorcée Norma Ashby in 1912 and adopted her daughter Kathryn Ashby Davis from her first marriage to Henry Shackelford Davis. That marriage too ended, and Strong married Mildred Stark Strong. The couple settled down in Culpeper, Virginia, where he died in 1945.

May's last husband, John Smuts, might not have been quite the person May thought he was. Smuts married a young woman, Ethel Wood, in December 1938, just four months after May's death.[2] He died of a heart attack in 1939. By some accounts, Smuts was married and divorced before meeting May and deserted his several children.[3]

Yori Komatsu, May's dedicated maid whom she brought to the United States from Yokohama and who then was with her for years, was reported—by May—to have married a wealthy New Yorker. I have not succeeded in tracking down information that confirms May's account.

Robert Edgar Thomas, who claimed to be May's birth son, had a short career in Hollywood. He appeared as a bit player in the 1936 western, *Ride, Ranger, Ride*, which starred Gene Autry. He is listed in the Burbank City Directory in 1940 along with his wife Eunice M. Thomas. She was a resident of San Diego when she died in 2001. I haven't been able to find out anything else about him.

Solving the mystery of Thomas's birth and May's seemingly extraordinary role in it would be a noteworthy accomplishment. If we could track down Thomas's descendants and the descendants of May's known relatives, including the Parkes, the Beatties, or the Cummings, we could test their DNA to see if they are related, and how. A test of this kind could not only rule out May out as the mother, but might also reveal whether May's cousin Adeline was the mother or not.

❖ ❖ ❖

Photographs of May Yohe are found in Britain's National Archive, in the Victoria and Albert Museum, in the Library of Congress, and in the New York Public Library. The Performing Arts Library at Lincoln Center has scrapbooks that faithful fans put together over the years. May Yohe memorabilia can sometimes be found on eBay—specially monogrammed buttons, a cigarette case, celebrity cards, and playbills.

And what of May herself?

Though May never returned to Bethlehem in life, she seems—at least to some—to have done so in death.

The old Eagle Hotel, owned and operated by her grandparents, the place where May was born and spent her early years, was torn down and replaced on the same site by the Hotel Bethlehem, which opened in 1922. The new hotel was built at the direction of Charles M. Schwab, the president of Bethlehem Steel. He wanted a more modern hotel to host visitors to his company town in its heyday. Schwab had been named as a possible buyer of the Hope diamond when Frankel's owned it in the early years of the 20th century, but he passed on the purchase.

The Hotel Bethlehem is a grand hotel, now renovated several times. Over the past few decades, staff and guests have claimed to have seen various ghosts, including that of May Yohe. The place is thought to be haunted. After a fire in 1989, a priest was even called in by management to assuage any lingering spirits. More recently, instead of trying to "quell the reports, the hotel has decided to embrace them," says hotel historian Natalie Bock.[4]

"Friendly" ghosts are said to be found in different parts of the hotel, and especially in room 932. In this room guests have supposedly heard voices, seen reflections in the mirror that weren't there for real, and have "reported unexplained happenings; papers standing upright, or flying off the desk, lamps flashing, the bathroom wallpaper turning pink."[5] Paranormal investigators conducted examinations in 2007 and again in 2009. They claim to have recorded voices and seen blurry shadows of ghosts and witnessed the door to room 932 shutting itself inexplicably. Though they do not know which 'ghosts' occupy the room, one of the voices heard in 2007 is supposed to have said, "It's Mary."

Bock's speculation is that Mary Augusta Yohe's ghost visits the Hotel Bethlehem because she had her happiest times singing and dancing in the hotel lobby of the old Eagle which preceded it. According to the hotel's account, a youthful May has been seen in the third-floor exercise room and in the lobby areas. Some housekeeping staff have reported imprints of a small hand, like that of a little girl, supposedly May, on mirrors, rails, and other surfaces. Bock has carefully marketed the ghostly May. Staff and guests "say they can still hear May, and when our player piano turns on by itself (as it often does!). When that happens, we think we know who it is!"[6] With hubris and bravado May, it seems, is still entertaining guests and larger audiences today.

Hotel Bethlehem brochure.

❖ ❖ ❖

Fanciful ghost stories aside, May Yohe is a phantom of history, leaving us with barely discernible features of a bygone era, of a life lived that by any stretch of the imagination was bigger than almost any lives we've known.

May Yohe was, as one commentator put it, "an eccentric bit of femininity."[7] She lived enough for several people, did many amazing things, and had many exceptional highs and awful lows. Her activities stretched across the planet, and she experienced life in the limelight of the stage, as well as on her knees scrubbing floors. She sought and relished the cheering appreciation of fans, and felt as well the jeers of a disdainful public fed up with the narcissistic drama of failed romance, an empty jewelry box, and hard times.

May would be disappointed that so few now know her name. She knew she had an amazing life story. As she told a San Francisco reporter, "I should cause earthquakes all over the world with my book . . . but I'm afraid I should have too many libel suits. I shall let some one else rattle the bones in my closet after I am dead."[8] Now, with this biography, we are rattling those bones, and May might take heart from knowing that someone can learn a lesson or two from her triumphs and tribulations. She was a pretty, talented, and smart woman—and one with a long list of foibles—who just wouldn't stay down. She strove to become everything she could possibly hope to imagine, and by overcoming amazing challenges and obstacles, she did. Inside her was strength and fortitude, a perspicacity to succeed that overrode all that she faced. If any of us can be inspired by that most ennobling characteristic, May will have performed her role very well.

MAY YOHE TIMELINE

1866 Mary Augusta Yohe (May) is born in Bethlehem, Pennsylvania to William Yohe and Elizabeth Batcheller, and the next year baptized into the Moravian church.

1866–79 May grows up with her grandparents, the proprietors of the Eagle Hotel in Bethlehem, and with her mother in Philadelphia

1872 William, who had divorced Elizabeth, marries Rebecca Lewis.

1879–85 May attends schools in Dresden, Germany and Paris, France.

1885 William Yohe dies.

1886 May performs in *The Little Tycoon* in Philadelphia and in *Josephine Sold by Her Sisters* in New York.

1887 May appears in *Lorraine* in New York City and Chicago and in *The Arabian Nights* in both cities.

1888 May appears in *Natural Gas* in Chicago. She has her first speaking role in *The Crystal Slipper* at the Chicago Opera House. She runs off with Eli Shaw, causing a scandal, and there are false rumors they will marry. Gossip columns assert that May married actor Jack Mason in Boston.

1889 May performs in a tour of *Natural Gas* and in *The City Directory*.

1890   May is rumored to have married sportsman Thomas
       Williams in San Francisco. May travels to Australia.

1891   May performs in *U and I, The City Directory,* and *Hoss and
       Hoss* in New York and Chicago.

1892   May is rumored to have married a Massachusetts senator.
       She meets Lord Francis Hope in New York.

1893   May makes her London debut in *The Magic Opal* at the
       Lyric Theatre. She stars in *Mam'zelle Nitouche* and in *Little
       Christopher Columbus* to great public and critical acclaim,
       including praise from George Bernard Shaw. "Oh Honey,
       My Honey" becomes her theme song.

1894   May continues in *Little Christopher Columbus.* She stars
       in *Lady Slavey.* Rumors circulate of her marriage to Lord
       Francis Hope. They wed quietly in November.

1895   May and Lord Francis reveal their marriage. She is intro-
       duced to London society as the prospective duchess of
       Newcastle and claims to have worn the Hope diamond. May
       stars in *Dandy Dick Whittington.* Lord Francis is declared
       bankrupt.

1896   May revives *Mam'zelle Nitouche* and successfully manages
       the Court Theatre. May aids Irish peasants at Hope's Castle
       Blayney estate. She stars in *The Belle of Cairo.*

1897   May retires from the London stage.

1898   May does charity work in London's Whitechapel with the
       dowager Duchess of Newcastle.

1899   Lord Francis Hope tries to sell the Hope diamond but fails
       because of the objections of his siblings. Lord Francis and
       May begin a world tour.

1900   May and Lord Francis live in Sydney, Australia, and com-
       plete a world tour, meeting Captain Putnam Bradlee Strong
       on the trans-Atlantic crossing. May claims to have worn the
       Hope diamond for the second time. May signs contracts
       to perform in the United States, appearing in *The Giddy
       Throng* in New York on Christmas Eve.

1901   May appears in *White Rats* in Boston and performs in
        Chicago. She shares an apartment in New York with Strong
        and runs off with him to San Francisco and then Yokohama,
        Japan, where they enjoy local life. Lord Francis sells the
        Hope diamond.

1902   Lord Francis is again declared bankrupt and is granted a
        divorce from May. Strong and May return to New York as a
        common-law couple, living in Hastings-on-Hudson, New
        York with May's mother Elizabeth. Strong threatens suicide,
        steals May's jewels, and flees the country, creating an inter-
        national scandal. May threatens Strong's arrest and follows
        his trail to London, Paris, and Lisbon. The couple reconciles
        and marries in Buenos Aires, Argentina.

1903   May and Strong return to New York and then to Argentina.

1904   May returns to the stage in London, Liverpool, and
        Brighton, and in New York at Oscar Hammerstein's venues.

1905   May and Strong perform vaudeville in New York and At-
        lanta to poor reviews. Strong deserts May in November and
        she files for divorce and sells the house in Hastings-
        on-Hudson.

1906   May performs in vaudeville in New York and in the lead as
        Mam'zelle Champagne.

1907   May continues performing in lesser vaudeville venues in
        Chicago and California; she is rumored to marry Newton
        Brown.

1908   May is associated with an anonymous San Francisco mil-
        lionaire as well as former British Army officer John Row-
        lands. She lives in Portland, Oregon as Mrs. James Fellows,
        the spouse of a Canadian businessman. She gives a baby boy
        up for adoption to Edward and Rosa Thomas.

1909   May is alleged to have married a Canadian lumberman
        named Murphy and to have had an affair with Lord Sholto
        Douglas. She travels to Singapore, Ceylon, and India.

1910   May's divorce from Strong is finalized. She performs in San
        Francisco and is stricken with paralysis. She is rumored to
        have married F. M. Reynolds.

1911   May performs in Chicago, at Hammerstein's Victoria Theatre in New York, and in Washington. She and boxer Jack McAuliffe announce their engagement.

1912   May continues to perform in New York and Boston.

1913   May appears in *Come Over Here* at the London Opera House; she takes up the case of London chorus girls and meets John Smuts.

1914   Smuts and May marry and live in South Africa.

1915   Smuts serves in the British army and is wounded in a World War I battle with the German army in South-West Africa. May serves as a nurse.

1915–17   May and Smuts live in India where he recuperates. They then move to Singapore, where, befriending the Sultan of Johore, Smuts becomes the manager of a rubber plantation and May performs at the Victoria Theatre.

1918   Seeking to rejoin the British army, Smuts leaves for Seattle with May. Denied reenlistment, he works in a shipyard, and when he is stricken with influenza, May works as a custodian. May's mother Lizzie dies.

1919–21   May and Smuts live in Los Angeles and run a chicken farm. She writes a nationally syndicated serial newspaper story on the Hope diamond and works on a book and a silent film. May and Smuts sell the chicken farm.

1921–23   May and Smuts return to the East Coast, auction more possessions, and open a tea room in Manhattan that fails. May performs in Boston and New York. The couple opens the Blue Diamond Inn in Marlow, New Hampshire.

1924   An arsonist burns down the Blue Diamond Inn. Smuts is shot in the chest—the Boston police suspect May, but the couple claims it resulted from an accident while he was cleaning a gun.

1925   May appears on a radio show on WBZ in Springfield, Massachusetts.

1926–34   May performs periodically and participates in charity events; the couple auctions off possessions. They live in Revere, Suffolk County, Massachusetts.

1935   May breaks a rib in January and in June is admitted to the hospital for a broken arm and a brain injury; later, she is admitted to a sanitarium. Robert Thomas files suit claiming he is May's biological son.

1936–37   The maternity case proceeds through the courts. May takes a bus from Boston to Portland and is briefly taken into police custody suffering from hallucinations.

1938   Applying for a W.P.A. job, May discovers she lost her U.S. citizenship when she married a British citizen. The Thomas maternity suit is decided in May's favor. May successfully petitions to regain her citizenship. She dies in her sleep at age 72; her body is cremated and her ashes spread in the Atlantic Ocean.

Currently   May's ghost is said to haunt the Hotel Bethlehem.

ACKNOWLEDGMENTS

I am grateful to Veronica Conkling who, as a Smithsonian research associate, helped bring this book to fruition by investigating various aspects of May's life, researching photographs, securing needed permissions for use of historical materials, and aiding in the assembly of notes. Pat McAndrew, an author and researcher from Bethlehem, Pennsylvania, contributed mightily to discovering information about Bethlehem, the Yohes, and May's early life in the region. Smithsonian interns Sarah Rothenberg and Eva Falls provided dedicated research assistance, carrying out the historical detective work that forms the basis of this book. I also thank colleagues in Bethlehem, Pennsylvania: Charlene Donchez Mowers, the President of Historic Bethlehem, and Natalie Bock, the Hotel Bethlehem historian, for their research help and insights. Closer to home, my daughter, Jaclyn Kurin, helped examine legal documents.

Thanks are due to the readers of the manuscript who made fine suggestions: my esteemed Smithsonian colleagues, Evelyn Lieberman, Alison McNally, and Diana Parker; curators Amy Henderson of the National Portrait Gallery and Dwight Bowers of the National Museum of America History; and director Carolyn Gleason of Smithsonian Books. Smithsonian National Board members Peggy Burnet, Sako Fisher, Patricia Frost, Shelby Gans, Judy Huret, and Phyllis Taylor were encouraging and insightful in their readings of several versions of the manuscript and helped it along. I have tremendous appreciation for their service to, and support of, the Smithsonian. Jaclyn Kurin and other family members, my wife Allyn, and my mother, Mary also read the manuscript and offered useful suggestions.

I am grateful to Christina Wiginton for guiding the manuscript to its final book form. Owen Andrews, who edited the volume, deserves special thanks for his very careful reading of the manuscript and good suggestions for its improvement. Coincidentally, there is a historical connection between his great-grandfather and Putnam Bradlee Strong. The Smithsonian's LeShawn Burrell-Jones and Roberta Walsdorf provided needed support services.

Doing research through on-line databases has revolutionized what used to be tedious work. Nonetheless, it is still a pure pleasure to explore the collections of the Smithsonian, to access the tremendous resources of the Library of Congress, to sit in the reading room of the New York Public Library, and to open up the next set of clippings or an artist's scrapbook at the New York Library for the Performing Arts, Dorothy and Lewis B. Cullman Center at Lincoln Center. I also appreciate the aid of the Moravian Archives in Bethlehem and its assistant archivist Lanie Graf, and the hospitality of Debby Beece and Larry May in Hastings-on-Hudson in letting me into their home to see May Yohe's old house. Finally, I appreciate Clarie Miller and Jeffrey Krinsky letting me use their home as a welcome base for drafting the manuscript.

NOTES

CHAPTER ONE: Bethlehem's Daughter

1. H.L. Gates, *The Mystery of the Hope Diamond* (New York: International Copyright Bureau, 1921), 79.
2. "It is Y-O-H-E Without an Accent," *Chicago Daily Tribune*, April 7, 1895, 41.
3. "Y-O-H-E Without an Accent." May's mother's family were early settlers in the Uxbridge, Massachusetts area where there was a good deal of intermarriage with the Nipmuc Indians, related to Algonquin and Narragansett peoples. So May's assertion, while lacking any empirical evidence, could have been based on family folklore.
4. "Y-O-H-E Without an Accent."
5. "Y-O-H-E Without an Accent."
6. May Yohe, "The Hope Diamond Mystery" (a weekly serial in 17 chapters), *Syracuse Herald*, July 4, 1920 to October 24, 1920, chap. 1.
7. Haidt's paintings are in Bethlehem's Moravian Archives; the one depicted here is in the collection of the Smithsonian American Art Museum.
8. John Hill Martin, *Historical Sketch of Bethlehem in Pennsylvania with some account of the Moravian Church* (Philadelphia: Printed for Orrin Rogers by John L. Pile, 1872), 122.
9. Gates, *Hope Diamond*, 75.
10. Cf. *Bethlehem Globe Times*, 1942; thanks to Pat McAndrew and to Ken Raniere for this discovery.
11. "Why I've Become an Uplifter," *El Paso Herald*, January 5, 1912.
12. Gates, *Hope Diamond*, 74.
13. "Vengeance on a Murderer," *The Sun*, December 28, 1880, 1.

14. "Vengeance on a Murderer."
15. Gates, *Hope Diamond*, 75.
16. Gates, *Hope Diamond*, 75, 76.
17. Yohe, "Hope Diamond Mystery," chap. 1.
18. Yohe, "Hope Diamond Mystery," chap. 1.
19. Yohe, "Hope Diamond Mystery," chap. 1.
20. Yohe, "Hope Diamond Mystery," chap. 3.
21. "Y-O-H-E Without an Accent," *Chicago Daily Tribune*, 41.
22. Gates, *Hope Diamond*, 78–79.

Additional references for this chapter include:
"A Centennial Putz," *New York Graphic*, March 15, 1875.
"Advertisement—Hillside Garden," *Bethlehem Daily Times*, April 9, 1877.
   Bethlehem Directory, 1873.
"Caleb Yohe Passes Away," *Bethlehem Daily Times*, November 10, 1892, 1.
"Calypso Island—a Moravian Invention," *Southern Exposure, Newsletter
   of South Bethlehem Historical Society* vol. 15, no. 1(Spring 2007), 1.
"Child Murder at Freemansburg," November 1874.
"Constable's Sale," *Bethlehem Daily Times*, May 27, 1882.
"Death of W. W. Yohe," *Denver News*, January 30, 1885.
"Detective Yohe Missing," *Allentown Chronicle*, May 5, 1882.
"Eagle Glen," *Bethlehem Daily Times*, November 13, 1873.
"Eagle Hotel Putz," *Stereoscopic Gems of Bethlehem Scenery No. 31*(Beth-
   lehem: H. T. Clauder, Bookseller and Stationer, n.d.).
"Election of a Chief Engineer," *Bethlehem Daily Times*, October 21, 1872.
Aaron Spencer Fogelman, *Jesus is Female: Moravians and Radical Re-
   ligion in Early America* (Philadelphia: University of Pennsylvania
   Press, 2007).
"Funeral of W. W. Yohe," *Denver News*, February 3, 1885.
"Funerals—Mrs. Mary M. Yohe," January 29, 1885.
"Hillsdale Garden of W. W. Yohe", *Bethlehem Daily Times*, April 9, 1877.
Joseph Mortimer Levering, *A history of Bethlehem, Pennsylvania, 1741–
   1892 with some account of its founders and their early activity in
   America* (Bethlehem, PA: Times Publishing Company, Printers and
   Publishers, 1903).
"Looking for a Clue," *Bethlehem Daily Times*, April 26, 1877.
"Married," *Bethlehem Daily Times*, June 12, 1872.
"Married," *Harrisburg*, December 25, 1863.
Donald M. McCorkle, "The Moravian Contribution to American Mu-
   sic," *Notes, Music Library Association*, 2nd series, vol. 13, no. 4 (1956),
   597–606.
"Misbehavior in Church," *Bethlehem Daily Times*, October 21, 1872.
Elizabeth Myers, "Caleb Yohe," September 26, 1928.

"Obituary—Mrs. Mary M. Yohe," *Bethlehem Daily Times,* January 26, 1885.

"Obituary—Samuel S. Yohe," October 1902.

Frederick Clifton Pierce, *Batchelder, Batcheller Genealogy* (Chicago: W.B. Conkey Company, 1898), 501–03.

"Pleasure Grounds, Young Ladies Seminary," 1865–75, stereoscope by M. A. Keckner, item 114, Robert N. Dennis collection.

"Sets of Portraits of May Yohe," *Strand Magazine,* vol. 10 (July-December, 1895), 6.

"The Yohe Forgery Case," *Easton Express,* April 25, 1882.

Raymond Walters, *Bethlehem Long Ago and Today* (Bethlehem: Carey Printing Company, 1923).

"Yohe's Hotel, The Eagle," *Godey's Lady's Book,* October 1858.

Documents:

Baptism of Mary Augusta Yohe, April 6, 1867, Central Moravian Church Register, 1865–1892, MF 22.3, p. 20.

Civil War Veterans' Card File, 1861–65, Pennsylvania State Archives.

Death of Mary Magdealena Yohe, n. 2851, January 25, 1885, Central Moravian Church Register, 1865–1892, MF 22.3, p. 587.

Deed, Caleb Yohe and Mary his wife to George H. Meyers, The Eagle Hotel, Bethlehem, Pa, 1874.

Excise Tax enumeration, State of Pennsylvania, Division One, of Collection District Eleven, May 1865.

Pension Application for Service in the U.S. Army, William Yohe, December 15, 1879. NARA T289.

U.S. Census, Philadelphia, Pennsylvania, 8th Ward, 1st Election District, 1880, 211.

U.S. Census, Schedule l, Inhabitants in 8th Ward, District 22, Philadelphia, Pennsylvania, November 15, 1870, 7.

U.S. Census, South Bethlehem, Northampton, Pennsylvania, 1880.

U. S. Passport Application of William W. Yohe, n. 6021, April 25, 1878.

CHAPTER TWO: Footlights Goddess

1. "May A. Yohé." *On and Off: thirty-five Actresses interviewed by "The Call Boy."* Gilbert Dalziel (London: November 1893), 44.
2. *On and Off,* 75.
3. Gates, *Hope Diamond,* 79.
4. According to the Yardville Inn, May hosted lovers up in her room in the late 1800s as Lady Hope, cf., http://www.yardvilleinn

.com/HISTORY.html. The timing is problematic, and it is more likely that if true, this could have been a location for trysts with Captain Strong in 1900–01. Still, she would have known about the roadhouse/inn from visits in the late 1880s.

5. "Why May Yohe Longed for the Footlights Again," *Washington Post*, August 28, 1910, 8.
6. "*On and Off*," 44.
7. Yohe, "Hope Diamond Mystery," chap. 3.
8. Yohe, "Hope Diamond Mystery," chap. 3.
9. Yohe, "Hope Diamond Mystery," chap. 3; Gates, *Hope Diamond*, 80.
10. Yohe, "Hope Diamond Mystery," chap. 3; Gates, *Hope Diamond*, 80.
11. "Miss Yohe's Serenade," *Chicago Daily Tribune*, August 21, 1887, 18.
12. "Aladdin is Coming," *New York Times*, July 29, 1887, 2.
13. *New York Times*, March 9, 1888.
14. *New York Times*, March 9, 1888.
15. Gates, *Hope Diamond*, 81.
16. "The Theatres," *Chicago Daily Tribune*, February 14, 1888, 5.
17. Gates, *Hope Diamond*, 81.
18. *New York Times*, May 4, 1888.
19. "The Local Theaters," *The Current*, June 23, 1888, 62.
20. 'Theatrical," *Chicago Daily Tribune*, April 27, 1890, 36.
21. Letter to the editor by Russell Thompson: "Youth of May Yohe" in response to James O'Donnell Bennett. Original source unknown.
22. Original source unknown.
23. "Y-O-H-E Without an Accent," 41.
24. "The Sequel to an Elopement," *Washington Post*, July 14, 1888, 1.
25. "They Were Divorced and Reunited," *Chicago Daily Tribune*, September 15, 1889, 9.
26. "Miss May Yohe's Marine: He is heard from After an Absence of Eight Years," *Chicago Daily Tribune*, July 20, 1888, 1.
27. "Cinderella was Angry," *Chicago Daily Tribune*, August 23, 1888, 4.
28. Don Gillan, "An Unsuitable Peer-Bride," www.stagebeauty.net, 2007.
29. "Ought Actresses Wed?" *Chicago Daily Tribune*, October 21, 1888, 27.
30. "Rousing Success," *Boston Daily Globe*, November, 3, 1890, 2.
31. Yohe, "Hope Diamond Mystery," chapters 5 and 6.
32. "Music and The Drama," *The Examiner*, November 24, 1900, 3.
33. "The New Opera House," *The Sydney Morning Herald*, April 7, 1890, 9.
34. "Madcap" is first used to describe May's behavior in 1889 with regard to the escapade with E. B. Shaw; see "They Were Divorced and Reunited," *Chicago Daily Tribune*, September 15, 1889. Frank

Whelan, in "At Turn of the Century, Singing Scandalizing May Yohe Conquered New World and Old" (*The Morning Call*, March 22, 1992), believes the nickname resulted from the scandal over an 1893 episode when May had an affair with a New York state senator. Also, cf., "Two Bewitching Girls," *Los Angeles Times*, May 24, 1891, 5. May refers to herself as a "madcap girl" in "May Yohe is Wretchedly Woefully Disappointed," *The World*, February 12, 1901, 4. In a 1918 interview in Singapore, May suggested that she'd acquired the moniker in London; see "Every Woman Can Come Back Once, Declares May Yohe, Who's Trying Again," *The Evening Telegram*, May 15, 1921. "Madcap May" is taken for granted in "Again the Hope Diamond Blamed for Misfortune," *Atlanta Constitution*, December 21, 1924, F8.

Additional references for this chapter include:
Nicholas van Hoogstraten, *Lost Broadway Theatres*, (Princeton: Princeton Architectural Press, 1997).
"May Yohe's Reported Marriage," *Chicago Daily Tribune*, December 12, 1889, 3.
"May Yohe's Sudden Trip," *Chicago Daily*, July 4, 1888, 1.
Bailey Millard , "Thomas Hansford Williams," *The San Francisco Bay Region*, v. 3 (American Historical Society), 268–70.
Lilian and John Mullane, "Diamonds are [not always] Forever: May Yohe, the Hope Diamond, and Hastings-on-Hudson," *Hastings Historian*, vol. 39, no. 1 (Winter, 2009).
"Says She Was Not Away," *Chicago Daily Tribune*, July 5, 1888, 1.
"Was It An Elopement," *New York Times*, July 5, 1888, 2.

Documents:
Map of Hastings-on-Hudson in Joseph R. Bien, *Atlas of Westchester County, New York* (New York: Julius Bien & Co.: New York, 1893).
Maps of Hastings-on-Hudson in George Bromley and Walter Bromley. *Atlas, Westchester County, New York*, Volume 2. (New York: G. W. Bromley & Co., 1881; Philadelphia, PA, 1907).

Deeds:
Dressner to Yohe, Liber 1598, page 306. Filed and recorded December 18, 1901. Deeds, Westchester County Clerk's Office, White Plains, New York.
Yohe to Gribben, Liber 1635, page 291. Filed and recorded February 2, 1903. Deeds, Westchester County Clerk's Office, White Plains, New York.
Playbills:
The Little Tycoon, Temple Theatre, Philadelphia February 8, 1886.

Josephine, Wallack's, New York, September 20, 1886.

Lorraine, Star Theatre, New York, March 5, 1887.

The Arabian Nights, Standard Theatre, New York, October 22, 1887; Academy of Music, New York, December 5, 1887; The People's Theatre, New York, December 19, 1887; Chestnut Street Opera House, Philadelphia, December 26, 1887.

Natural Gas, Fifth Avenue Theatre, New York, May 1, 1888.

CHAPTER THREE: Nobly Courted

1. Gates, *Hope Diamond*, 90.
2. Gates, *Hope Diamond*, 74.
3. Gates, *Hope Diamond*, 84–85.
4. Gates, *Hope Diamond*, 85.
5. Gates, *Hope Diamond*, 86–87.
6. Gates, *Hope Diamond*, 87.
7. Gates, *Hope Diamond*, 87.
8. Gates, *Hope Diamond*, 88.
9. Gates, *Hope Diamond*, 89.
10. Gates, *Hope Diamond*, 90.
11. Gates, *Hope Diamond*,90.
12. Gates, *Hope Diamond*, 90.

CHAPTER FOUR: Hopeful

1. "What is Life Without Hope?" *Boston Daily Globe*, April 4, 1912, 15.
2. Lord Byron had earlier disparaged Hope's work on furniture, but reportedly cried reading his *Anastasius* in 1819.
3. Henry Philip Hope, *A Catalogue of a Collection of Pearls and Precious Stones*, compiled by Bram Hertz, (London: 1839), 25.
4. Henry and Irene Law. *The Book of the Beresford Hope*s (London: Heath Cranton, Ltd., 1925), 114.
5. Benjamin Disraeli, *Disraeli's Reminiscences*, ed. Helen and Marvin Swartz (London: Hamish Hamilton, 1975), 19–20.
6. "Two Famous Diamonds," *Hawke's Bay Herald*, April 25, 1888, 3 (originally published in *New York World*).

Additional references for this chapter include:

Germain Bapst, *Histoire des Joyaux de la Couronne* (Paris: Libraire Hachette et Cie.), 1889.

Wilkie Collins, *The Moonstone*, ed. Anthea Todd (Oxford and New York: Oxford University Press, 1982).

Marian Fowler, *Hope: Adventures of a Diamond* (New York: Ballantine Books, 2002).

Richard Kurin, *Hope Diamond: The Legendary History of a Cursed Gem* (New York: Smithsonian Books/HarperCollins, 2006).

John Mawe, *A Treatise on Diamonds and Precious Stones* (London: Longman, Hurst, Rees, Orme and Browne, 1813, 1815, 1823).

Bernard Morel, *Les Joyaux de la Couronne de France* (Antwerp: Fonds Merctor, 1988).

Susanne Steinem Patch, *Blue Mystery: The Story of the Hope Diamond* (Washington: Smithsonian Institution Press, 1976); 2nd edition (New York: Harry Abrams, Inc., 1999).

Edwin W. Streeter, *Precious Stones and Gems* (London: Chapman and Hall, 1877, 1882).

Edwin W. Streeter, *The Great Gems of the World* (London: George Bell and Sons, 1882).

Jean-Baptiste Tavernier, *Travels in India*, trans. Valentine Ball [1889], ed. William Crooke (London: Humphrey Milford, Oxford University Press, 1925).

CHAPTER FIVE: My Honey

1. Gates, *Hope Diamond*, 91.
2. "Miss May Yohe at Rehearsal," *Penny Illustrated Paper*, October 27, 1894, 258.
3. "Comic Opera Duchess," *Washington Post*, April 1, 1894, 10; "Lyric Theatre," *The Times*, January 20, 1893, 6; "Senor Albéniz's 'Magic Opal,'" *The Graphic London*, January 28, 1893; "Music and the Drama," *Penny Illustrated Paper*, January 28, 1893, 58.
4. *On and Off*, 44.
5. George Bernard Shaw, *Music in London, 1890–94*, 249. (New York: Brentano's, 1906).
6. "May Yohe. Gallery of Players," ed. Henry Austin, *The Illustrated American Magazine*, No. 7 (Lorillard Spencer, New York: 1895), 28.
7. *On and Off*, 44.
8. "Miss May Yohe at Rehearsal," 258.
9. *The Sunday Chronicle* (Manchester), March 13, 1893.
10. "Trafalgar-Square Theatre," *The Times*, May 8, 1893, 8 Col. A, p. 8.
11. *The Theatre*, ed. Charles Eglington, Vol. 21, London, June 1, 1893, 335–36.
12. Eva Moore, *Exits and Entrances* (London: Chapman & Hall, Ltd., 1923), 36–7.
13. "Comic Opera Duchess," 10.

14. "May Yohe Triumphed," *Brooklyn Eagle*, July 7, 1894, 6. Also quoted in "Actors Rush to Law," *Chicago Daily*, July 8, 1894, 9.

15. "Marriage of May Yohe is Verified," *Chicago Daily Tribune*, January 13, 1895, p. 9.

16. Sir Henry Joseph Wood. *My Life of Music* (Books for Libraries Press, 1971) 67; "Deepdene Dorking," *Penny Illustrated Paper*, October 12, 1895; "The Ghost Walk," *Otago Witness*, January 9, 1907, p. 60.

17. "Comic Opera Duchess,"10.

18. "Oh, Honey, My Honey," composed by Ivan Caryll, words by George R. Sims and Cecil Raleigh, for *Little Christopher Columbus* (London: Hopwood & Crew, 1893), 175–84.

19. Gates, *Hope Diamond*, 91

20. Shaw, *Music in London*, 67.

21. "May Yohe. Gallery of Players," 28.

22. "May Yohe. Gallery of Players," 28.

23. "May Yohe. Gallery of Players," 28.

24. "May Yohe. Gallery of Players," 28.

25. "Miss May Yohe at Rehearsal," 258.

26. "On the London Stage," *Chicago Daily*, August 5, 1894, 9.

27. Review from *The Times,* in Horace Wyndham, *Chorus to Coronet* (London: British Technical and General Press, 1951).

28. Keble Howard, *My Motley Life: A Tale of Struggle* (London: T. Fisher Unwin, Ltd., 1927), 96.

29. "Poem to May Yohe," Sister Olive, in *The Sketch*, March, 20, 1895.

Additional references for this chapter include:
Cranstoun Metcalfe, *Peeresses of the Stage* (London: Andrew Melrose, 1913).
Ernest Henry Short and Arthur Compton-Rickett, *Ring Up the Curtain* (London: Herbert Jenkins, Ltd., 1970).
The Mascot, June 27, 1896.
The Theatre, June 1, 1893.
Playbills:
Little Christopher Columbus, Lyric Theatre, London.
Mam'zelle Nitouche, Trafalgar Square Theatre, London.

CHAPTER SIX: Aristocratic Artist

1. "What's A Poor Girl To Do?" music by Mary Watson, words by Joseph Watson, for *The Lady Slavey: A New Musical Comedy in Two Acts*, words by George Dance, music by John Crook (London: Hopwood & Crew, 1896), 17–20.

2. "Comic Opera Duchess," 10.
3. "May Yohe's Capture Denied," *Chicago Daily Tribune*, August 26, 1893, 5.
4. "May Yohe's Capture Denied," 5.
5. "May Yohe's Capture Denied," 5.
6. "Some Ignoble Types: Blots on the Escutcheon of Britain's Aristocracy," *Chicago Daily Tribune*, October 20, 1893, 13.
7. "Comic Opera Duchess," 10.
8. "May Yohe's Capture Denied," 5.
9. "May Yohe's Capture Denied," 5.
10. "Comic Opera Duchess," 10.
11. "Some Ignoble Types," 13.
12. "Comic Opera Duchess," 10.
13. Comic Opera Duchess," 10; "Anti-English Cabinet," *New York Times*, June 3, 1894, 17.
14. Gates, *Hope Diamond*, 92.
15. Gates, *Hope Diamond*, 92.
16. Gates, *Hope Diamond*, 93.
17. Gates, *Hope Diamond*, 93.
18. "What's A Poor Girl To Do?" 17–20.
19. "She Captures a Coronet," *Washington Times*, January 13, 1895, 5.
20. Gates, *Hope Diamond*, 94–98.

Additional references for this chapter include:
Madeline Bingham, *Earls and Girls* (London: Hamish Hamilton, 1980)
"May Yohe's Husband's Debts." *New York Times*, December 20, 1895, 5.
"May Yohe Married to a Lord," *Chicago Daily Tribune*, March 31, 1894, 5.
R. Caton Woodville, *Random Recollections*. (London: Evelyn Nash, 1914).

Playbills:
Mam'zelle Nitouche, Royal Court Theatre, London.
Dandy Dick Whittington, Avenue Theatre, London.

CHAPTER SEVEN: Destitute Duchess

1. Gates, *Hope Diamond*, 208.
2. "May Yohe's Catch," *Los Angeles Times*, January 20, 1895, 2.
3. "Lady Francis Hope (Miss May Yohe) and Lord Francis Hope." *Chicago Daily Tribune*, January 11, 1897, 3; *Washington Post*, February 1, 1897; cf. Armond Fields and Marc Fields, *From the Bowery to Broadway: Lew Fields and the roots of American Popular Theatre* (Oxford and New York: Oxford University Press, 1993), 130.
4. "Anti-English Cabinet," 17.

5. William Archer, *The Theatrical World of 1894* (London: Walter Scott, Ltd., 1895), 287.

6. Gates, *Hope Diamond,* 98–99.

7. Gates, *Hope Diamond,* 100.

8. "Y-O-H-E Without an Accent," 41.

9. "Y-O-H-E Without an Accent," 41.

10. "Y-O-H-E Without an Accent," 41.

11. "Avenue Theatre," *The Times,* March 4, 1895, 3.

12. "Taken from Truth," *Chicago Daily Tribune,* March 27, 1895, 6.

13. "Drama Over the Water," *Chicago Daily Tribune,* July 7, 1895, 38; "About the Theaters," *Los Angeles Times,* July 14, 1895, 23.

14. "Work for Lady Hope," *Washington,* November 3, 1895, 22; Gates, *Hope Diamond,* 100.

15. "Work for Lady Hope," 22.

16. "Work for Lady Hope," 22.

17. "Work for Lady Hope," 22.

18. Archer, *Theatrical World of 1896,* 282.

19. "May Yohe in Mam'zelle Nitouche," *Chicago Daily Tribune,* June 2, 1896, 1.

20. George Bernard Shaw, *Dramatic Opinions and Essays,* Vol. II (New York: Brentano's, 1906), 23–26.

21. "May Yohe's Success on the Metropolitan Stage," News of the London Theaters, *Chicago Daily Tribune,* July 26, 1896, 13.

22. Curtis Brown, "Home of a Duchess in London Slums," *Los Angeles Times,* February 22, 1903, D7.

23. *Los Angeles Times,* July 3, 1898, 2.

24. R. Caton Woodville, *Random Recollections* (London: Evelyn Nash, 1914), 143.

25. "Langtry and Husband Part," *Chicago Daily Tribune,* October 31, 1899, 1.

26. Gates, *Hope Diamond,* 101.

27. Gates, *Hope Diamond,* 101.

28. Gates, *Hope Diamond,* 102.

Additional references for this chapter include:

"In Re Hope," *The Times,* November 1, 1895, 8.

"Hope Diamond A White Elephant," *Boston Daily Globe,* May 17, 1899, 1.

"In Re Hope; De Cetto v. Hope," *The Law Reports,* Supreme Court of Judicature, Chancery Division, London: Council of Law Reporting, 1899, v. 2, 679–95.

"Marquis de Fontenoy Letter," *Chicago Daily Tribune,* April 4, 1900, 10.

"May Yohe's English Lord Deserted Her," *Denver Evening Post*, September 21, 1899.

"The Affairs of Lord Francis Hope," *The Times*, July 16, 1894, 13.

"The Story of Lord Francis Hope and May Yohe," *Denver Evening Post*, November 13, 1898, 12.

"Will The Iron Molder's Child Be a Duchess," *Denver Evening Post*, September 24, 1899, 3.

CHAPTER EIGHT: New York's Finest Lover

1. Gates, *Hope Diamond*, 210.
2. Gates, *Hope Diamond*, 211.
3. Gates, *Hope Diamond*, 211.
4. Gates, *Hope Diamond*, 212.
5. Gates, *Hope Diamond*, 212.
6. Gates, *Hope Diamond*, 212.
7. Gates, *Hope Diamond*, 213.
8. Gates, *Hope Diamond*, 213.
9. Gates, *Hope Diamond*, 213–214.
10. Gates, *Hope Diamond*, 214.
11. Gates, *Hope Diamond*, 215–216.
12. Gates, *Hope Diamond*, 216.
13. Gates, *Hope Diamond*, 217.
14. Gates, *Hope Diamond*, 218.
15. "May Yohe Finally Recognized," *Chicago Daily Tribune* (Special Cable to the *New York World* and *Chicago Daily Tribune*), November 14, 1900, 3.
16. "May Yohe Finally Recognized."
17. "Duke of New Castle Here," *New York Times*, December 18, 1900, 8.
18. T. Allston Brown, *A History of the New York Stage from the First Performance in 1732 to 1901* (New York: Dodd Mead and Co., 1903), 606.
19. "May Yohe Here Again," *New York Times*, December 25, 1900, 7.
20. "Theaters in Manhattan: The New York," *Brooklyn Eagle*, December 26, 1900, 15.
21. "Drama and Music: The Greatest Thing in the World," *Boston Daily Globe*, March 19, 1901, 8.
22. Gates, *Hope Diamond*, 219–220.
23. "Lord Francis Hope's Mistake," *Auckland Star*, May 3, 1902, 5.
24. "Lord Leaves His Lady," *Los Angeles Times*, March 30, 1901, 2.
25. "Lord Leaves His Lady," 2.
26. *Chicago Daily Tribune*, April 22, 1901.

27. "Yohe Faints on Stage," *Chicago Daily Tribune*, April 23, 1901, 1.
28. "Yohe Faints on Stage."
29. "Yohe Faints on Stage."
30. "Yohe Faints on Stage."

Additional references for this chapter include:
"Lady Francis Hope Sued," *New York Times,* October 11, 1900, 5.
"Plays and Players: News of the Drama in the Great Metropolis," *Los Angeles Times,* April 2, 1901, C3.
"Says May Yohe That Was," *Brooklyn Eagle,* April 1, 1901, 8.

Playbill:
The Giddy Throng, New York Theatre, New York, December 31, 1900.

CHAPTER NINE: Exotic Romance

1. Wyndham, *Chorus to Coronet.*
2. "Escaped Tale that Shocks Two Cities," *Los Angeles Times,* July 13, 1901, 2.
3. "Romance in New York," *Los Angeles Times,* July 13, 1901, 2.
4. "Romance in New York," 2.
5. "War Department inclines to be Lenient with Strong," *San Francisco Call,* July 14, 1901.
6. "Officer in a Scrape," *Washington Post,* July 14, 1901, 2.
7. "A Tangled Web Growing More Complicated," *The Atlanta Constitution*, July 25, 1901, 6.
8. Wyndham, *Chorus to Coronet*. Also, variations such as "At first there was Hope. After that there was a Strong chance of misery." *El Paso Herald*, January 5, 1912.
9. Gates, *Hope Diamond*, 223.
10. "Putnam Bradlee Strong's Denial," *New York Times,* December 4, 1901, 2; "Hope-Strong Alliance," *Los Angeles Times,* December 4, 1901, 10.
11. Gates, *Hope Diamond*, 224.
12. Gates, *Hope Diamond*, 224.
13. Gates, *Hope Diamond*, 225.
14. Gates, *Hope Diamond*, 226.
15. Gates, *Hope Diamond*, 219–27.
16. "May Yohe in New York," *Boston Daily Globe,* April 29, 1902, 4.
17. Gates, *Hope Diamond*, 227.
18. *The Evening World*, Night Edition, July 19, 1902, 3.
19. "Tales of the Town. Cut by his Old Friends: Putnam Bradlee Strong Had a Bad Day at the Races," *Washington Post,* July 27, 1902, 15.

Additional references for this chapter include:
'Hope v. Hope and Strong," Probate, Divorce, and Admiralty Division, *The Times*, March 22, 1902, 6.
"May Yohe Divorced," *Boston Daily Globe*, March 22, 1902, 14.

CHAPTER TEN: Betrayed, Again

1. Gates, *Hope Diamond*, 230.
2. "Major Strong Is Missing," *New York Times*, July 20, 1902, 1; "May Yohe Now Mourning For Jewels and Strong," *Atlanta Constitution*, July 20, 1902, 3; "May Yohe's Lover Breaks Away from Her," *Los Angeles Times*, July 20, 1902, 5.
3. Yohe, "Hope Diamond Mystery," chap. 10.
4. "Major Strong is Missing."
5. "Strong Missing: Yohe Deserted," *Chicago Daily Tribune*, July 20, 1902, 5.
6. "May Yohe on His Trail," *Washington Post*, July 22, 1902, 3.
7. "Major Strong is Missing," 1.
8. "Miss Yohe Threatens Arrest of Major Strong," *New York Times*, July 21, 1902, 1.
9. "Strong Missing: Yohe Deserted," 1.
10. "Major Strong Accused of Grand Larceny," *New York Times*, July 22, 1902, 2.
11. "Miss Yohe Threatens Arrest," 1.
12. "May Yohe Relates Strong Tale of Woe," *Atlanta Constitution*, July 24, 1902, 6.
13. "Major Strong Accused," 2.
14. "Miss Yohe Threatens Arrest," 1; "Can't Find Him," *Boston Daily Globe*, July 21, 1902, 7.
15. "Strong Missing; Yohe Deserted."
16. "May Yohe Jealous," *Los Angeles Times*, July 21, 1902, 3.
17. "May Yohe Relates Strong Tale of Woe," 6.
18. "Yohe May Cause Strong's Arrest," *Chicago Daily Tribune*, July 21, 1902, 4.
19. "May Yohe Orders Strong's Arrest," 1.
20. "Unhappy May," *Boston Daily Globe*, July 22, 1902, 2.
21. List published in "Major Strong Accused," 2.
22. "May Yohe Relates Strong Tale of Woe," 6.
23. "May Yohe Orders Strong's Arrest," 1.
24. "Major Strong Accused of Grand Larceny," 2.
25. "May Yohe's Claim Paid," *Chicago Daily Tribune*, July 23, 1902, 3. Also quoted in "May Yohe to Sail for Japan," *Brooklyn Eagle*, July 23, 1902, 6. Also quoted in "Out of Pawn," *Boston Daily Globe*, July 23, 1902, 3.

26. "Strong and Miss Yohe en Route to Japan," *New York Times*, July 23, 1902, 1.

27. "New York's Latest," *Atlanta Constitution*, July 24, 1902, 6.

28. "Strong Arrives in London," *Chicago Daily Tribune*, July 25, 1902, 3; "Strong Denies Robbing May," *Atlanta Constitution*, July 25, 1902, 2.

29. "May Yohe Sails Also," *Boston Daily Globe*, July 25, 1902, 7.

30. "Says Strong Tells Lies," *Los Angeles Times*, August, 1, 1902, 3; "Batch of Lies," *Boston Daily Globe*, August 1, 1902, 2.

31. "Says Strong Tells Lies," 3; "Batch of Lies," *Boston Daily Globe*, 2; "Article 1-No Title," *New York Times*, August 1, 1902, 5; "Talks of Forgiving Him," *Los Angeles Times,* August 1, 1902, 3; "May Yohe Blames Strong," *Washington Post*, August 1, 1902, 1.

32. "Says Strong Tells Lies," 3; "Batch of Lies," 2; "May Yohe in England," *New York Times*, August 1, 1902, 5; "May Yohe Lets Drive at Her Flitting Lover," *Atlanta Constitution*, August 1, 1902, 3; "May Yohe Blames Strong," 1.

33. "May and Puttee to Get Together," *Atlanta Constitution*, August 2, 1902, 1; "May Yohe Forgives All; Asks Strong to Come Back," *Chicago Daily Tribune*, August 2, 1902, 1.

34. "Hysterical May Yohe Wants her Bradlee," *Los Angeles Times*, August 2, 1902, 2; "Yohe Sighs for Strong," *Washington Post*, August 2, 1902, 1; "Miss Yohe and Strong Likely to Be Reconciled," *New York Times,* August 2, 1902, 3; "Yohe in London," *Boston Daily Globe*, August 2, 1902, 3; "May Yohe Forgives All; Asks Strong to Come Back," 1.

35. "May and Puttee To Get Together," 1.

36. "Yohe Flies to Lisbon to Join Her Bradlee." *Atlanta Constitution*, August 14, 1902, 1; "Strong and May Yohe are Together Again," *New York Times*, August 14, 1902, 1.

37. "Yohe Flies to Lisbon to Join Her Bradlee," 1.

38. "Yohe Flies to Lisbon to Join Her Bradlee," 1.

39. Yohe, "Hope Diamond Mystery", chap. 11.

40. Gates, *Hope Diamond*, 235–236.

41. Gates, *Hope Diamond*, 237.

42. "May and Putty Wedded at Last," *Atlanta Constitution*, October 5, 1902, A11; "Points of Interest," *Washington Post*, October 5, 1902, 11; "Strong and May Yohe Married," *Boston Daily Globe*, October 5, 1902, 28.

43. "Letter of Marquise de Fontenoy," *Chicago Daily Tribune*, October 6, 1902, 12.

44. "May Yohe in England," *New York Times*, August 1, 1902, 5; "May Yohe Lets Drive at her Flitting Lover," 3; "May Yohe Blames Strong," 1.

45. "May Yohe Back to the 'Halls'," *Washington Post*, April 24, 1904, B2.

46. "Quips and Cues," *Los Angeles Times*, October 9, 1904, E1.

47. "The Drama—Players, Playhouses, Music and Musicians," *Los Angeles Times*, December 25, 1904, D1.
48. "Down in the Subway," words by William Jerome, music by Jean Schwartz, 1904.
49. "The Drama—Players, Playhouses, Music and Musicians," *Los Angeles Times*, July 2, 1905, VI1.
50. Franklin Flyes, "New York Summer Attractions," *Washington Post*, June 11, 1905, TP6.
51. "Other 3—No title," *Washington Post*, May 19, 1907, E4.
52. Yohe, "The Hope Diamond Mystery," chap. 17.
53. "Other 1—No title," *Washington Post*, June 16, 1906, 6.

Additional references for this chapter include:
"Divorced Hubby Pays May Yohe," *Atlanta Constitution*, January 2, 1903, 1.
"May Yohe Abuses Strong," *Chicago Daily*, August 1, 1902, 5.
"May Yohe is in Paris but Strong is Not," *Atlanta Constitution*, August 4, 1902, 1.
"'Merely May Yohe' Talks to Scribe," *Easton Free Press,* February 23, 1905, 1.
"Not Too Late As A Warning," *Washington Post*, July 22, 1902, 6.
"P. B. Strong Dunned by Deputy Marshals," *New York Times*, June 3, 1905, 2.
William R. Taylor, *Inventing Times Square* (Johns Hopkins University Press, 1996).
"The Romance of Capt. Putnam Bradlee Strong and May Yohe," *Washington Times*, July 27, 1902, 10.
James Traub, *The Devil's Playground* (New York: Random House, 2004).

CHAPTER ELEVEN: Independent Woman

1. "Why May Yohe Longed for the Footlights Again," *Washington Post*, August 28, 1910, M8.
2. "Music and the Stage," *Los Angeles Times*, November 30, 1907, 115.
3. "May Yohe, Who Has Been in Retirement Near Portland, Says She Needs the Money," *Los Angeles Times*, July 29, 1910, 13.
4. "Back to Stage for May Yohe," *Los Angeles Times*, April 23, 1910, 13.
5. "Yohe, the Hopeless, Happy and Hopeful," *Los Angeles Times*, January 8, 1908, 11; "May Yohe Who Might Have been a Duchess," *Penny Illustrated*, February 1, 1908, 67.
6. "Yohe, the Hopeless," 11.
7. *Vanity Fair*, August 31, 1906.
8. *New York Telegraph*, clipping, April 26, 1907.
9. "May Yohe May Wed," *New York Times*, April 26, 1907, 9.
10. "Personal and Otherwise," *New York Times*, April 28, 1907, X4.

11. "Gossip of Society," *Washington Post*, January 9, 1908, 9.
12. "All That Glitters is Not Gold," *Los Angeles Times*, January 17, 1908, II4.
13. "Remarkable Jewel a Hoodoo," *Washington Post*, January 19, 1908, M4.
14. "Remarkable Jewel," M4.
15. "Remarkable Jewel," M4.
16. "Sale of the Hope Diamond," *The Times*, June 25, 1909, 5.
17. "Sale of the Hope Diamond," 5.
18. *Toledo Blade*, August 6, 1910.
19. Unidentified Memphis newspaper clipping, September 18, 1910.
20. Evalyn Walsh McLean with Boyden Sparkes, *Father Struck It Rich* (Boston: Little, Brown and Co., 1936).
21. McLean, *Father*, 172.
22. McLean, *Father*, 174–75.
23. The contract memorandum is included in "Jewelers Who Sold Hope Diamond Bring Suit to Recover Purchase Price," *Jewelers' Circular Weekly*, March 15, 1911, 71; Gates, *Hope Diamond*, 203.
24. Gates, *Hope Diamond*, 175.
25. "May Yohe says Hope Diamond Terrified and Injured Her," *Marion Daily Mirror*, February 2, 1911, 4.
26. Gates, *Hope Diamond*, 66–67.
27. "Why I've Become an Uplifter."
28. Unidentified newspaper clipping, April, 1911.
29. "Still in the Ring," *Boston Daily Globe*, September 4, 1911, 9; *Philadelphia Inquirer*, clipping, September 5, 1911.
30. "Former Mistress of Hope Diamond Dies as $16.50-a-Week WPA Clerk," *Atlanta Constitution*, August 29, 1938, 16; "May Yohe's Death Ends Varied Career," *Philadelphia Inquirer*, August 29, 1938.
31. *Boston Herald* clipping, July 1912.
32. "Why May Yohe Longed for the Footlights Again.," M8.
33. *Toledo Blade* clipping, 1912.
34. *National Telegraph*, June 19, 1912.
35. "Why May Yohe Longed for the Footlights Again," M8.
36. "Against Woman Suffrage," *Boston Daily Globe*, August 23, 1909, 10.
37. "What Is Life Without Hope," *Boston Daily Globe*, April 4, 1912, 15.

Additional references for this chapter include:
Lynn E. Bragg, *Myths and Mysteries of Washington* (Guilford, Connecticut and Helena Montana: Globe Pequot Press, 2005.)
"Diamond Dealer Fails for $150,000," *New York Times*, January 8, 1908.
"Diamond Not Unlucky," *Metropolitan*, vol. 35, no. 6 (April 1912) , 30.

Abel Green and Joe Laurie Jr., *Showbiz from Vaude to Video* (New York and London: Garland Publishing, Inc., 1985).

"Hope Diamond Not Worn," *New York Times*, February 5, 1911.

"Is Weary of Notoriety," *Los Angeles Times*, March 10, 1910, 13.

"J. R. M'Lean's Son Buys Hope Diamond," *New York Times*, January 29, 1911, 1.

Kurin, *Hope Diamond.*

"May Yohe Dispossessed," *The Globe*, August 5, 1907, 12.

"May Yohe Far From Suicide," *Boston Daily Globe*, June 12, 1912, 4.

"May Yohe is in Limelight," *Los Angeles Times*, March 9, 1910, 13.

"May Yohe Not His Bride," *Washington Post*, December 21, 1910, 1.

"May Yohe's Strange Career," *Washington Post*, April 23, 1911, SM3.

"May Yohe's Third Venture," *Washington Post*, May 11, 1909, 5.

"May Yohe to Wed Again," *Boston Daily Globe*, October 25, 1908, 11.

"May Yohe Weds Again," *Washington Post*, December 14, 1910, 10.

"Oft-Married Actress Becomes Mother," *Los Angeles Times*, May 10, 1909, 12.

Strong v. Strong, Finding of Fact and Conclusion of Law, Circuit Court of the State of Oregon for Clackamus County, April 26, 1910.

"Wife Cause of Shooting," *Los Angeles Times*, November 5, 1908, 17.

Wilson, T. Edgar, "The Hope Diamond," letter to the editor, *New York Times*, November 9, 1911.

"Yohe Entices New Angel," *Los Angeles Times*, January 19, 1908, VII.

Documents:

National Archives and Records Administration (NARA); Washington, DC; Index to Naturalization Petitions and Records of the U.S. District Court, 1906–1966, and the U.S. circuit court, 1906–1911, for the District of Massachusetts; Microfilm Serial: *M1545*; Microfilm Roll: *103*

Papers of Evalyn Walsh McLean, Manuscript Division, Library of Congress, Washington, DC.

Robinson Locke Collection, Billy Rose Theatre Division, New York Public Library

United States Census, Los Angeles, California, 1920.

United States Census, Mt. Vernon Ward 5, Westchester, New York, 1910.

CHAPTER TWELVE: War Bride

1. "Every Woman Can Come Back Once, Declares May Yohe Who's Trying Again," *Evening Telegram*, May 15, 1921.
2. "New Notes of the London Stage," John Ava Carpenter, *Chicago Daily Tribune*, July 13, 1913, B2.

3. "May Rewed May Yohe," *Washington Post*, August 14, 1913, 1.
4. "Will Not Rewed May Yohe," *New York Times*, August 16, 1913, 4.
5. "The Chorus Girl and The 'Nut': May Yohe to the Rescue," *The Advertiser* (Adelaide, Australia), September 18, 1913, 19
6. "May Yohe to the Rescue," 19.
7. "May Yohe to the Rescue," 19.
8. "The Stain of their Guilty Love Cleansed in War's Fierce Fire," *Washington Times*, August 18, 1918.
9. "Every Woman Can Come Back Once."
10. "Every Woman Can Come Back Once."
11. "Every Woman Can Come Back Once."
12. "Every Woman Can Come Back Once."
13. "Every Woman Can Come Back Once."
14. "Every Woman Can Come Back Once."
15. "Every Woman Can Come Back Once."
16. "Every Woman Can Come Back Once."
17. "Farmer May is Going Home," *Los Angeles Times*, September 13, 1920, II1.
18. "Public Notice Paragraphs," *The Straits Times*, March 12, 1918, 8.
19. "May Yohe's Concert," *The Straits Times*, March 21, 1918, 7.
20. Gates, *Hope Diamond*, 243.
21. Gates, *Hope Diamond*, 243–245.
22. Bragg, *Myths and Mysteries*.
23. "May Yohe, Janitress," *Atlanta Constitution*, January 19, 1919, B4.
24. Bragg, *Myths and Mysteries*.
25. "May Yohe, Janitress."
26. "Farmer May is Going Home."

Additional references for this chapter include:
"Blaze Consumes Blue Diamond Inn," *Boston Daily Globe*, November 6, 1924, 2.
"Famous Stage 'Queen' Happy Chicken Farmer," *Evening Herald*, November 30, 1918.
"May Yohe Back on the Stage," *Boston Daily Globe*, March 11, 1923, 60.
"May Yohe of Hope Diamond Fame to Become War Nurse," *Washington Times*, July 8, 1918, 9.
"May Yohe on Way to France," *Washington Post*, July 8, 1918, 3.
"May Yohe, Once Titled Beauty Back to B'Way," *Chicago Daily Tribune*, January 5, 1922.
Documents:
United States Federal Census, 1920, Los Angeles, California, Assembly District 71, Roll T625 111 p. 23B, Enumeration District 311, image 1023.

World War 1 Draft Registration Cards, King County, Washington, Roll 1991892, Draft Board 5.
California Passenger and Crew Lists, 1893–1957, M1410:108.

CHAPTER THIRTEEN: Cursed

1. "May Yohe, Toast of Stage in '90s, is Near Death," *Chicago Daily Tribune*, July 2, 1935, 7.
2. "M'Lean Heir Killed by an Automobile," *New York Times*, May 19, 1919.
3. *Hartford Herald*, April 5, 1911.
4. Patch, *Blue Mystery*, 35.
5. Yohe, "The Hope Diamond Mystery," chap. 1.
6. Gates, *Hope Diamond*, 253.
7. Gates, *Hope Diamond*, 252, 255.
8. *Washington Post*, August 18, 1986, C1.

Additional references for this chapter include:
Kurin, *Hope Diamond.*
The Hope Diamond Mystery, directed by Stuart Paton, written by May Yohe, screen adaptation by Charles Goddard and John B. Clymer, Kosmik Films, 1921.
"The Legendary Hope Diamond," *Life*, March 1, 1995.
"Who Will Next Own this $180,000 Death Jewel?" *Atlanta Constitution*, July 13, 1919, 24.
"Will Hope Diamond Work Harm to Latest Owner," *Tacoma Times*, January 30, 1911, 1.

CHAPTER FOURTEEN: Domestic Tranquility?

1. "May Yohe, of More Ups and Downs Than an Elevator, Stages a Comeback," *Chicago Daily Tribune*, December 2, 1922.
2. *Variety*, November 23, 1920.
3. "More Ups and Downs."
4. "More Ups and Downs."
5. Unknown source.
6. "More Ups and Downs."
7. "May Yohe in Unusual Number at Keith's: Songs of Days Gone By Put in a Jazz Setting," *Boston Daily Globe*, March 13, 1923, 8.
8. "Smuts Puzzles Police. Inquiry Into Shooting of May Yohe's Husband Goes On in Boston," *New York Times*, November 21, 1924, 3; "May Yohe's Husband Wounded by a Bullet, He Warns Police Not to Trouble Her," *New York Times*, November 20, 1924, 1.

9. "Smuts Puzzles Police."

10. "'Hope Diamond No Unlucky Gem' Says May Yohe," *Boston Herald*, August 1925.

11. "'I'm Coming Back!' May Yohe Dreams," *Cumberland Evening Times*, April 24, 1926, 2. Also see "Youth for May Yohe," *The Kokomo Daily Tribune*, March 13, 1926, 13.

12. Unknown newspaper article. Also see "With the Women of Today," *Sarasota Herald-Tribune*, August 7, 1926, 11. The rumor of May Yohe and Consuelo Vanderbilt going into the hotel business probably grew out of their association with the Hopes' Deepdene estate at Dorking, which, before it had been turned into a hotel, had been rented to the dowager duchess of Marlborough, the stepmother of Consuelo's former husband. There is no evidence of any business dealings between Yohe and Vanderbilt.

Additional references for this chapter include:

"Again Hope Diamond Blamed for Misfortune," *Atlanta Constitution*, December 21, 1924, F8.

"Capt Smuts, Husband of May Yohe, Expected to Recover from Wound," *Boston Daily Globe*, November 21, 1924, 19.

"May Yohe As Auctioneer," *New York Times*, November 12, 1921, 21.

"May Yohe Keeps Gay," *New York Times*, January 27, 1935, 27.

"May Yohe Lays Smuts Shooting to Hope Diamond," *Chicago Daily Tribune*, November 21, 1924, 16.

"May Yohe, Once Owner of the Hope Diamond is Ill," *Chicago Daily Tribune*, June 18, 1935, 1.

"May Yohe Sent to Nursing Home," *Los Angeles Times*, July 8, 1935, 1.

CHAPTER FIFTEEN: Mother?

1. "May Yohe to Fight Claim," *Los Angeles Times*, December 13, 1935, 5.

2. "May Yohe Surprised at Alleged Daughter," *Washington Post*, December 30, 1925, 3.

3. "Illinois Woman Thought to Be Yohe Daughter," *Washington Post*, July 11, 1935, 6.

4. "Seeks Recognition as May Yohe's Son," *New York Times*, December 11, 1935, 28.

5. "May Yohe's Husband Scouts Story of 'Son,'" *New York Times*, July 6, 1935, p. 16; "Seeks Recognition as May Yohe's Son," 28.

6. *Los Angeles Times*, July 9, 1909.

7. "26 Years a Stranger to Her 'Son' To Save Him from a 'Curse'?" *New York Sunday Mirror* Magazine Section, September 22, 1935.

8. "May Yohe's Ex-Mate Denies Actor's Claim," *New York Times*, December 4, 1936, 30.
9. "Suit by Self-Styled Son Scores May Yohe," *Los Angeles Times*, December 11, 1935, 3.
10. "May Yohe to Fight Claim."
11. "May Yohe to Fight Claim."
12. "May Yohe to Fight Claim;" "May Yohe's Ex-Mate Denies Claim."
13. Petition for Adoption in the County Court of the State of Oregon for Multnomah County, Petitioners E. R. Thomas and Rosa M. Thomas, Thomas exhibit 6, New York Supreme Court, Appellate Division, First Department, In the Matter of the Judicial Settlement of the Account of the Proceeding of Central Hanover Bank and Trust Company as Executor of, and as Trustee for Putnam Bradlee Strong under the Will of Mary Urbana Strong, deceased, Robert E. Thomas, appellant against Dorcas Aborn Hope, et al., Robert H. Aborn, et al., Samuel Koenig as Special Guardian, etc., Central Hanover Bank and Trust Company and Putnam Bradlee Strong, respondents.
14. Petition for Adoption.
15. Petition for Adoption, testimony of Dr. Harry Stanley Lamb, fols. 888–889, 912–913.
16. Petition for Adoption, fols. 341, 690, 894–906, 983.
17. Petition for Adoption, fols. 336–337.
18. Petition for Adoption, finding of judicial referee O'Connor, 23.
19. "May Yohe Held After Story of Gunplay on Bus," *Chicago Daily Tribune*, February 18, 1937, 7; "May Yohe is Stricken with Hallucinations," *New York Times*, February 18, 1937, 11.

Additional references for this chapter include:
"A Young Movie Actor's Claim to a Famous Mama—and a Huge Legacy," *Sunday Mirror Magazine Section*, February 21, 1937, 2.
"If He's May Yohe's Son—Then Who Was His Father?" unidentified newspaper magazine clipping, 1937, 11.

CHAPTER SIXTEEN: Poor, Ill, and Un-American

1. James T. Powers, *Twinkle Little Star: Laughter, Tears, Thrills: Sparkling Memories of Seventy Years*, (New York: G.P. Putnam's Sons, 1939), 247–248.
2. "Soon Forgotten," *Washington Post*, April 6, 1938, X9.
3. "Former Beauty has W.P.A. Job," *Los Angeles Times*, May 5, 1938, 3.
4. *Los Angeles Times*, May 5, 1938.
5. "Broadway Fails Dead May Yohe," *Daily News*, August 29, 1938.

6. "Cremation Rites Ordered for May Yohe," *Journal,* August 29, 1938.
7. Unpublished article for "My Say," by Evalyn Walsh McLean, 1938. Papers of Evalyn Walsh McLean.
8. "A Line O'Type or Two: A Myth Goes Glimmering," *Chicago Daily Tribune,* August 31, 1938, 8.

Additional references for this chapter include:
"May Yohe, Hope Blue Diamond are Known to World," *Bethlehem Globe Times,* June 24, 1942, 93.
"May Yohe Rites to Be in Boston on Wednesday," *Herald Tribune,* August 29, 1938.

Epilogue

1. "May Yohe's Death Ends Varied Career," *Philadelphia Inquirer,* August 29, 1938.
2. Ethel M. Wood, 37, and Smuts were reported to be married in Dorchester on December 2, 1938, cf. *New York Daily News,* June 15, 1939.
3. This information is according to a post to the Yohe Family Genealogy Forum at http://www.genforum.genealogy.com by Ray Barrell on January 3, 2002. It has not been substantiated. Barrell claims his maternal grandmother was Smuts' first wife and that none of his relatives knew what had happened to him until his father saw the 1938 *Life* magazine feature about May with photos of Smuts. Barrell claims his mother and her siblings then got in touch with Smuts, who by then, after May's death, had remarried.
4. "Bethlehem Hotel Embraces Ghost Stories with 'Room with a Boo,'" *USA Today,* March 12, 2007.
5. cf. Hotel Bethlehem website, "Room with a "Boo," The Friendly Ghosts of The Historic Hotel Bethlehem, Room 932," http://www.hotelbethlehem.com/hanuted.php.
6. "Room with a 'Boo.'"
7. Powers, *Twinkle Little Star,* 247–248.
8. "Wow! If May Yohe Should Write Book!" *San Francisco Call,* December 22, 1910.

Additional references for this chapter include:
"Bethlehem Woman Once Owned Hope Diamond," by Richmond Myers, *Sunday Call Chronicle,* May 30, 1965.
Brochure, *The Friendly Ghosts of The Historic Hotel Bethlehem.*
"Captain John Smuts, Veteran of 2 Wars, Husband of the Late May Yohe, One-Time Actress, Dies," *New York Times,* June 12, 1939, 21.

"Diamond's Legend Involves Late Bethlehem Woman," *The Morning Call*, December 3, 1971, 49. "Duke, Long Owner of Hope Diamond," *New York Times*, April 22, 1941, 21.

"Gem 'Ferhexed' Bethlehem Girl," *Sunday Call Chronicle*, November 9, 1958, 1.

"Putnam B. Strong, Son of Ex-Mayor, 70," *New York Times*, November 17, 1945, 17.

ILLUSTRATION CREDITS

Frontispiece. May Yohe's signature, On and Off, *1894, 45.*

p. viii. Sketch by R. Ponsonby Staples from The Westminster Budget, *March 1896, New York Public Library for the Performing Arts, MWEZtNCZO.3 60..*

p. 5. Painting by John Valentine Haidt. Smithsonian American Art Museum, gift of the American Art Forum 1987.32.

p. 8. Lithograph, c. 1874. Bethlehem Historical Society, Bethlehem Public Library.

p. 11. Illustration in "Portraits of Celebrities," The Strand Magazine, *vol. 10, 67, July-December, 1895, London, from a photograph by M. A. Kolchner, Bethlehem, Pennsylvania.*

p. 17. Illustration in "Portraits of Celebrities," from a photograph by Husted, Philadelphia, Pennsylvania.

p. 19. Illustration in "Portraits of Celebrities," from a photograph by W. Höffert, Dresden, Germany.

p. 21. Illustration in "Portraits of Celebrities," from a photograph by C. Allevy, Paris, France.

p. 26. Photograph used in packaging for "Old Judge" cigarettes. Collection of Carl Van Vechten, Billy Rose Theatre Collection, New York Public Library for the Performing Arts, T PHO A, 565537.

p. 27. Mid-Manhattan Picture Collection/New York City Theatres, New York Public Library, PC NEWYC-The.

p. 33. Engraved illustration, The New York Clipper, *August 22, 1874.*

p. 36. Photographic card by Baker, Columbus, Ohio. Billy Rose Theatre Collection, New York Public Library for the Performing Arts, T PHO A, 565538.

p. 39. Photograph in "Actresses who have become Peeresses," A. C. Wheeler, The Cosmopolitan, *vol. 20, no. 2, December 1895, 135.*

p. 40. Photograph by Max Platz, Chicago, Illinois. Billy Rose Theatre Collection, New York Public Library for the Performing Arts, T PHO A, 565539.

p. 48. Sketch after a photograph by Alfred Ellis, London, Chicago Daily Tribune, January 11, 1897, 3.

p. 49. Painting by William Beechey. © National Portrait Gallery, London, NPG 4574.

p. 51. Mezzotint by Thomas Goff Lupton after Charles-Marie Bouton, 1823. © National Portrait Gallery, London, D656.

p. 52. Sketch by Allyn Kurin, after an illustration by Edwin W. Streeter, Precious Stones and Gems, *London: Chapman and Hall, 3ʳᵈ edition, 1882.*

p. 53. Painting by Sir Thomas Lawrence, c. 1820. © National Gallery of Scotland, PG 139.

p. 54. Sketch of the Hope diamond set in a medallion, from Henry Philip Hope, A Catalogue of a Collection of Pearls and Precious Stones, *compiled by Bram Hertz, London, 1839.*

p. 55. Illustration from a photograph by John Jabez Edwin Paisley Mayall, Illustrated London News, April 3, 1858, 352.

p. 59. Engraved portrait by Rudolph Blind, printed by Phototype, Paris, France. Manuscripts & Special Collections, University of Nottingham, Ne 4 1/30.

p. 62. British Museum Library, Enthoven Collection.

p. 63. The Illustrated Sporting and Dramatic News, *January 28, 1893, 694. New York Public Library for the Performing Arts, MWEZ+NC 20, 360.*

p. 64. Penny Illustrated Paper, *January 28, 1893, issue 1652.*

p. 66. The Illustrated Sporting and Dramatic News, *May 27, 1893, 434. New York Public Library for the Performing Arts, MWEZ+NC 20, 360.*

p. 68. Photograph by Alfred Ellis, October 24, 1893, London. John Culme's Footlight Notes Collection.

p. 69. Penny Illustrated Paper, *June 6, 1896, issue 1828.*

p. 71. Photograph by Alfred Ellis, October 24, 1893. London, National Archives, United Kingdom, Kew, no. 14827-19, copy 1/414/302.

p. 72. Color lithograph after a photograph by Alfred Ellis, c. 1893, published by Hopwood & Crew, London. John Culme, Footlights Notes Collection.

p. 75. Image after a photograph by Alfred Ellis; case attributed to George Hunter, England, and sold by H. Lewis & Co. Courtesy Aspire Auctions, Inc.

p. 76. Lithograph by John Player & Sons. George Arents Collection, New York Public Library, 213486.

p. 81. Photograph by Alfred Ellis, London. National Archives, United Kingdom, Kew, copy 1/414/209.

p. 82. Photograph by Hayman Seleg Mendelssohn.

p. 84. Unattributed newspaper clipping. New York Public Library for the Performing Arts, MWEZ+NC 20, 360.

p. 85. Photomezzotype by London Stereoscopic Company, The Era Almanac, *London, 1894, 25.*

p. 88. Photograph by Alfred Ellis, London. Unattributed clipping, New York Public Library for the Performing Arts, MWEZ+NC 20, 360.

p. 89. Photograph by Alfred Ellis, London, "Gallery of Players," no. 7, Illustrated American, *1895.*

p. 90. Photograph from John Culme, Footlight Notes Collection.

p. 91. Photograph c. 1900, courtesy Matthew Beckett, England's Lost Country Houses, www.lostheritage.org.uk.

p. 95. Photograph by Alfred Ellis. London, Billy Rose Theatre Collection, New York Public Library for the Performing Arts, T PHO A, 565540.

p. 98. Unattributed newspaper clipping. Furness Theatrical Image Collection, Rare Book & Manuscript Library, University of Pennsylvania.

p. 100. Color lithograph published by Chappell & Co., London. John Culme, Footlights Notes Collection.

p. 101. © Francis Frith Collection, 29567.

p. 104. Drawing after a photograph by Alfred Ellis, Chicago Daily Tribune, *November 24, 1896, 3.*

p. 105. Photograph by Alfred Ellis, April 17, 1895, London. National Archives, United Kingdom, Kew, no. 18235-15, copy 1/420/127.

p. 106. Courtesy of Dr. Keith Blayney.

p. 107. George Grantham Bain Collection, Library of Congress, Prints and Photographs Division, ggbain 06278.

p. 111. Photograph by Lafayette, Ltd. © Victoria and Albert Museum, neg. no. 2098.

p. 114. Brown Brothers, BB-18416-J-72.

p. 120. New York Times, *November 24, 1895, 13.*

p. 121. Photograph from the Herald Tribune-Acme, *1901, included in the promotional booklet for the movie* The Hope Diamond Mystery. *George Kleine papers,*

Library of Congress, Manuscript Collection, box 31, Kosmik Films, Inc., file no. 2, 1919-1924.

p. 123. Composite photo-illustration circa 1901. Hastings-on-Hudson Historical Society.

p. 124. Brown Brothers, BB-175-3-72J.

p. 125. Hastings-on-Hudson Historical Society.

p. 133. Unattributed newspaper clipping. New York Public Library for the Performing Arts, MWEZ+NC 20, 360.

p. 135. Drawing published in the St. Louis Star, *March 9, (unattributed year). New York Public Library for the Performing Arts, folder Yohe, May, 2669.*

p. 136. Brown Brothers, BB-06231-D-72J.

p. 141. Brown Brothers, BB 06231-A-72J.

p. 154. Museum of the City of New York, no. 93.1.1.20361.

p. 156. 1905 photograph published in Time *magazine, May 18, 1938, 30.*

p. 165. Photograph by Gehrig. University of Washington Libraries, Special Collections, UW23871.

p. 168. May Yohe as a vaudeville actress, circa 1909, photograph by Gehrig. University of Washington Libraries, Special Collections, UW23871.

p. 169. Hastings-on-Hudson Historical Society.

p. 173. Sketch in the Elizabeth Times, *1911. New York Public Library, folder Yohe, May, 2669.*

p. 178. Brown Brothers, BB-17597-2-72J.

p. 185. George Kleine papers, Library of Congress, Manuscript Collection, box 31, Kosmik Films, Inc., file no. 2, 1919-1924.

p. 191. Evalyn Walsh McLean Collection, Library of Congress, Prints and Photographs Division, LC-USZ62-71459.

p. 192. Atlanta Constitution, *July 13, 1919, 24.*

p. 194. Syracuse Herald, *October 24, 1920, Sunday Magazine, 4.*

p. 194. George Kleine papers, Library of Congress, Manuscript Collection, box 31, Kosmik Films, Inc., file no. 2, 1919-1924.

p. 195. Brown Brothers BB-17597-172J.

p. 196. George Kleine papers, Library of Congress, Manuscript Collection, box 31, Kosmik Films, Inc., file no. 2, 1919-1924.

p. 197. The American Weekly, *March 30, 1947, 6. New York Public Library for the Performing Arts, MWEZ+NC 20, 360.*

p. 201. Washington Post, *January 7, 1922, and the* Granite Monthly New Hampshire State Magazine, *vol. 55, 1923.*

p. 203. Photograph by United Newspictures, Chicago Daily Tribune, *November 22, 1924, 28.*

p. 210. Associated Press Image, July 4, 1935, ref. 431558.

p. 221. Photograph from c. 1905 published in Life, *May 18, 1938, 30.*

p. 222. National Archives and Records Administration, Index to Naturalization Petitions and Records of the U.S. District Court, 1906–66, and the U.S. Circuit Court, 1906–11 for the District of Massachusetts, microfilm serial M1545, microfilm roll 103.

p. 223. Associated Press Image, 1938, ref. 431557.

p. 229. Courtesy of the Hotel Bethlehem.

INDEX

Page numbers in **boldface** type refer to photos and illustrations.